Mr D Cornick
36 Greenfields Avenue
ALTON
Hampshire
GU34 2EE

C000265484

Aldershot's Buses

1906-1992

Peter Holmes

Published by
Waterfront Publications
463 Ashley Road, Parkstone, Poole BH14 0AX

In Association With Nicholas Smith International Limited

Contents

Foreword 3

Preface 3
    Chapter One

Setting the Scene 4
    Chapter Two

The Motor Bus Arrives in Aldershot 6
    Chapter Three

Aldershot and District 10
    Chapter Four

Post-War Recovery and Expansion 20
    Chapter Five

The Bus Wars 28
    Chapter Six

A Period of Growth 33
    Chapter Seven

The "Tracco" at War Again 60
    Chapter Eight

Nationalisation by Instalments 67

    Chapter Nine

Alder Valley 102
    Chapter Ten

Deregulation and Privatisation 117
    Chapter Eleven

Garages and Other Premises 123

Route Map 137

List of Services Operated 138

Aldershot & District Fleet List 141

Alder Valley Fleet List 149

Liveries 151

Summary of Operators 154

Tickets 156

Printed Matter 159

Accidents 162

List of Officers 165

Statistics 166

Acknowledgements and Bibliography 168

© P. Holmes & Waterfront Publications
1992
ISBN 0 946184 70 4
Typeset by PageMerger, Southampton
Printed in England

Foreword

by Richard Soper, Managing Director, Alder Valley Ltd

I am very pleased to be asked to provide a foreword for this history of Aldershot's buses. During the first half of this century the rapid growth of motor bus services played a significant role in changing patterns of travel to work, school and places of entertainment, which has sometimes been ignored by writers of books on local history. At the same time, the introduction of the charabanc, and later the luxury coach, presented new opportunities for leisure travel for every class of society.

The motor bus services around Aldershot were among the earliest to be started by private entrepreneurs, and present day bus people, beset as they have been with unforeseen problems, will learn from this book that their predecessors did not always have an easy ride. Unsympath-etic local authorities, oppressive taxation, financial crises and labour problems all appear in these pages: all too often the remedies have come too late to reverse their predictable adverse effects. For more than six decades, up to the time when it came into national ownership, the old 'Tracco' generated strong local loyalties among both staff and customers. Now, in the era of privatisation, we have an opportunity to reassert the benefits of local control of our affairs.

I hope that the book will be received as a valuable contribution to the written history of the area over the past 86 years, and that it will be of interest to bus people, transport enthusiasts and the general reader alike.

Preface

This book is the result of a suggestion, some thirteen years ago, that I should write a history of the Aldershot & District Traction Co, to be illustrated largely from Eric Nixon's very extensive collection of photographs. Although a manuscript was prepared and typed, the potential market was covered by the publications connected with the company's 75th anniversary in 1981, and it was decided to shelve the project. It is only recently that, with the previous books long out of print, the scope for a new book has become apparent. With the Marketing Department of the Alder Valley company already geared to the needs of the enthusiast industry, the opportunity has now arisen to resurrect the manuscript and bring it up to date.

During the intervening period, many changes have been imposed on the bus industry both by the politicians and by the whims of the travelling public. Nationally, these have included the breakup and privatisation of the National Bus Company, and the removal (indeed the reversal) of all of the restraints on competition first introduced by the 1930 Road Traffic Act. Locally, there have been three moves of the company's head office, two changes of ownership, complete closure of three of A&D's five garages and a return of the bus livery from red to green. On the technical side, driver-only operation has become universal, and the small-capacity bus, for many years considered to be an unacceptable complication in fleets standardised on buses carrying fifty or more passengers, has made a dramatic return, to constitute a third of Alder Valley's fleet.

A detailed account of all these recent changes would make a sizeable book in its own right, but in order to preserve a balance with the previous history of the area's buses, I have limited my coverage to those aspects which best illustrate the impact of the changes on the general public during the Alder Valley era, rather than chronicling all the underlying national, local and NBC politics.

Despite the decline of the bus industry over recent years, I remain convinced that there *is* a future for it. As in many other fields, a prerequisite for stability would be the removal of public transport from the political arena, which would require a universal recognition that the 'efficiency' of public services should not always be judged from their financial balance sheets alone. The 1980 Market Analysis Project was a brave attempt to reconcile the needs of the travelling public with the requirement to cut operating costs: it is not the fault of the man or woman in the driver's seat or the scheduling office if the industry still suffers from frequent crises.

Peter Holmes
Sandhurst
September 1992

The acknowledgements section explains how these premises could claim to have been the birthplace of this book. The enquiry office at 101 East Street, Farnham, seen shortly before its closure for redevelopment in 1967. The A&D bus shelter stands beside it, also soon to become redundant with the road alterations which made this a one-way street. *Alder Valley*

Chapter One
Setting the Scene

At the start of the twentieth century, public transport in the area in which the Aldershot and District Traction Company eventually operated was provided mainly by the London and South Western Railway Co. Its main line from London ran through Woking, Farnborough, Fleet, Basingstoke and Winchester, while at Woking the line to Portsmouth diverged to run through Guildford, Godalming, Haslemere and Petersfield. At Pirbright Junction a line to Aldershot, Farnham, Alton and Winchester turned off the main line, while cutting across all these was the South Eastern Railway's Reading line, passing through Farnborough, Guildford and Dorking. With various other secondary routes, the area was well served by rail, and it is hardly surprising that the first appearance of motor buses should have been a railway-sponsored feeder service.

In the autumn of 1904, the LSWR negotiated with the motor manufacturers John I. Thornycroft & Co. Ltd., of Basingstoke, for the latter to operate a bus service over the twelve miles from Farnham to Haslemere, via Hindhead. This was to run for one year, with all the revenue going to the LSWR, which in turn guaranteed 10d per vehicle mile to Thornycroft. After some experimental runs in November, a service was started with a 20 h.p. bus

AA 2186 was one of three Thornycroft buses employed on the London and South Western Railway's Farnham–Haslemere service. It is shown in Farnham station yard. Note the steps to the rear entrance platform, and the chain drive to the rear wheels. *P.C. Harrod*

(AA 768) at the end of January 1905, but was withdrawn before the end of February, as the vehicle was underpowered. A service of two journeys per day recommenced on 6 September 1905, this time using a dark green Thornycroft Type B4, registered AA 2044. This was a 24 h.p. 16-seat single-deck bus with its entrance in the rear end of the body. The inside seats faced inwards along the sides and front bulkhead, and there was also an outside bench seat beside the driver. A 4-cylinder petrol engine with accumulator (rather than the usual magneto) ignition was fitted, driving the rear axle through chain transmission. C.E. Lee's booklet quoted Mr C.J. Searle, the original driver provided by Thornycroft's, who recorded that a spare set of accumulators was carried, with a changeover switch, while useful accessories carried included a length of rope for use in emergencies and to give a friendly tow to horse-drawn vehicles up the many steep hills along the route. It was necessary to carry tools, and a can of water as lubricant, for hammering back into the wooden rear wheels any segments of the two three-inch wide rubber tyre strips which worked loose or fell off along the road.

At the end of the year's contract on 5 September 1906,

receipts had exceeded the guaranteed 10d/mile by about £115, and the LSWR exercised its option to buy the bus and run the service itself. Initially two journeys were run every weekday, starting from Farnham, Bush Hotel, passing Farnham Station and arriving at Haslemere station exactly 1½ hours after setting out. The single fare for the full journey was 2/- and the minimum fare was 3d. The original route had run via Churt on the southbound journey and returned on the opposite side of Frensham Pond, past the hotel, but from 30 October 1905 both directions took the Churt route.

The LSWR obtained an 18-seater charabanc body to fit AA 2044 for summer use, and in May 1907 it was superseded in regular service by two improved 16-seat Thornycroft vehicles AA 2186/7, in the LSWR's oak brown livery. AA 2139 followed in 1908 after use elsewhere. These all had a lower chassis frame and smaller front wheels than the earlier model, and a staircase led from the rear platform to the flat roof for luggage (and for a few more adventurous passengers!) A summer service of three journeys each way was operated: in June 1912 these left Farnham at 8.30am, 10.30am and 2.38pm and returned from Haslemere at 10.20am, 12.55pm and 4.28pm. The vehicles were based at Farnham.

The widespread Army installations in the Aldershot area gave rise to a need for off-duty travel for the troops and journeys for their families, and for civilian staff of the various organisations set up to serve the demands of the large garrison. In addition to facilities at Aldershot (formerly South Camp) itself, there were barracks and quarters stretching out to North Camp, near Farnborough, and numerous training grounds from the ranges at Bisley and Ash to the ballooning ground at Laffan's Plain, Farnborough – later to grow into the Royal Aircraft Establishment.

Although a three-mile walk to work or to the nearest railway station was a normal feature of life in those days, enterprising transport pioneers saw scope for an expanding trade in easing the lot of the traveller. Horse buses ran, over a long period, between Aldershot station and Farnborough Queen's Hotel, via Queen's Avenue and North Camp. Even before that station opened in 1870 a bus had run from the centre of Aldershot to meet the trains at Tongham station. In 1881, a horse tramway operator, the Aldershot and Farnborough Tramways Co., laid a track from Farnborough (LSWR) Station alongside the present A 325 Farnborough Road to the Queen's Hotel, Farnborough, where it turned off to run to North Camp (SER) Station. Operation was, however, very spasmodic, with long periods of inactivity during the 25 years of its existence, up to 1906.

The horse bus service was provided by a succession of operators, but in the early years of the twentieth century there were two regularly on the route, William North and Alfred Young with his four sons. Both provided a service from Aldershot terminating at the Queen's Hotel in Farnborough. Three-horse double-deck buses were used, and each operator ran at a half-hourly frequency, at a fare of 3d for the full distance. Any competitors stood little chance against the entrenched operators, and on the eve of the motor bus era, North bought out G. Blackeby's Aldershot Omnibus Company in May 1906.

The Aldershot and Farnborough Light Railway Co. was set up in 1906 to revive, electrify and extend the moribund horse tramway. Its initial scheme came to nothing, as indeed did a subsequent attempt a few years later – only some 350 yards of heavier track were ever laid, at the Farnborough end. This left the way clear for a service of motor buses.

ALDERSHOT AND FARNBOROUGH

Motor Omnibus Co.,

LIMITED.

OPENING

OF THE NEW

Service of Motor Buses

BETWEEN ALDERSHOT TOWN STATION & FARNBOROUGH.

This Service is provisional only, and subject to Amendment

The Company do not in any way guarantee their Buses running at the times named, but will use every endeavour to observe the same.

WEEK DAY SERVICE:

Motor Buses will leave the Aldershot Town Station for Farnborough every half-hour from 8 a.m. till 9 p.m.

The Queen's Hotel, Farnborough, for Aldershot Town Station every Half hour from 8.30 a.m to 9.30 p.m.

Buses will leave the Aldershot Theatre every evening after the performance to the North Camp Hotel, Farnborough, returning to Aldershot.

SUNDAY SERVICE:

Buses will leave Aldershot Town Station for Farnborough (L. & S.W.R.) Station at 3, 5, and 7 p.m., leaving Farnborough at 3-30, 5-30, 7-30 p.m. for Aldershot

Buses will leave Aldershot Town Station at 9 for Queen's Hotel, Farnborough; returning to Aldershot at 9.30.

FARES:

TO AND FROM

Aldershot and Queen's Hotel, Farnborough	-	-	3d.
Aldershot to Headquarters	-	-	2d.
Headquarters and Queen's Hotel	-	2d.
(Soldiers in Uniform)	-	1d.
Queen's Hotel and Farnborough Station		3d.

Notice is hereby further given—

The Aldershot and Farnborough Motor Omnibus Company, Limited, are the only Company authorised to run their Motor Buses between Aldershot Town Station and Farnborough, through the Military Camp, and are in no way connected with the Hampshire Motor Bus Company, Limited.

By order of the Directors,

B. C. KEITH SNAGG,

Aldershot, June 1st, 1906.   Secretary.

Chapter Two
The Motor Bus Arrives in Aldershot

After an Aldershot solicitor, Mr William Edward Foster, had obtained permission from the garrison commander, General Sir John French, to run a motor bus service through the military area, a meeting was convened under the chairmanship of Alderman J. May, JP, on 30 March 1906. It was decided to register a company to operate the buses, which was done on 11 May 1906. It was named the Aldershot and Farnborough Motor Omnibus Co. Ltd., and had an authorised capital of £3,000. In addition to Alderman May, the directors were Captain Batchelor, Mr R.H. Lloyd, Mr R. Johnstone Sterling and Mr T.M. Foster. Mr B.C. Keith Snagg was appointed secretary.

Thomas Matheson Foster, then aged 26, was the son of William Foster, and the remainder of his life was devoted

Sir William Foster: from a magazine article at the time of his knighthood in 1918.

*Author's collection
courtesy Lady Foster*

Tom Foster, photographed in the early days of the Aldershot and Farnborough company. His shoulders betray the malformation of the spine which resulted in his being barely five feet tall.

Author's collection courtesy Lady Foster

to the service of the company. Of a quiet disposition, perhaps associated with his obvious physical handicap, he was a keen amateur engineer, and used his flair for motor vehicle adjustment and maintenance to good effect during the early years of the company's operations.

To operate its service, the company bought two 1904 vintage 20hp 28-seat Milnes-Daimler double-deck buses for £450 each. They were registered DY 116 and DY 118, and came from the Hastings and St Leonards Omnibus Co. Ltd., which had recently become a subsidiary of the London and Westminster Motor Omnibus Co., which operated its London buses under the 'Ensign' fleet name. Bus services in Hastings had been abandoned after electric trams had been introduced, so the vehicles, carrying the legend 'To and from Memorial' on their sides, were now up for sale.

After trial runs for the shareholders on 31 May, the service from Aldershot Station to Farnborough, Queen's Hotel, commenced on 1 June 1906. In exchange for the concession of running along the military-owned Queen's Avenue through the centre of the barracks area, which no other motor bus operator apart from A & F's direct descendant, Aldershot and District, received, soldiers in uniform were allowed to travel at a special fare of 1d between Command Headquarters and the Queen's Hotel, the normal fare being 2d. Over the full distance the single fare was 3d. Buses left the termini every half hour from 8am to 9pm towards Farnborough and from 8.30am to 9.30pm towards Aldershot. In addition, buses waited every evening for the end of the performance at Aldershot Theatre to run to the North Camp Hotel. On Sundays a different pattern was operated: the service was extended from Queen's Hotel to Farnborough LSWR Station, with journeys leaving Aldershot at 3, 5 and 7pm and one at 9pm to Queen's Hotel only, each setting out on its return journey half an hour later. The fare for the section Queen's Hotel – Farnborough Station was 3d.

It was considered prudent to print, at the bottom of the opening announcement, a statement disclaiming any connection with the Hampshire Motor Bus Company, which had published its ambitious prospectus during the same week. Based on Mr G.C. Waterfield's motor and cycle works at Lynchford Road, North Camp, the first of three routes proposed by this company was a circular journey from North Camp, along Farnborough Road, to Aldershot Station, and thence via Ash Wharf Bridge to Ash Vale and North Camp. The other routes were to be via Frimley Green to Blackdown Barracks, and via Aldershot to Farnham, but the venture never materialised.

The operation of the Aldershot & Farnborough company's first service required the use of both vehicles, and the staff at the outset numbered eight. The Registered Office was established at 126 Victoria Road, Aldershot, which was the office of William Foster's firm of Foster and Wells, solicitors. The operating office was a small hut on wheels, in which the daily takings were secreted overnight in the waste paper basket, in the absence of a proper safe. By the end of the first week of operation, the *Aldershot News* had published a reader's letter on the excessive speed of the motor buses. Since 1906 was the first year in which such vehicles were seen in any numbers in Britain, and roads were in a poor state, these doubts about their desirability were understandable.

Telegraphic Address: FOSTERING, ALDERSHOT.

TELEPHONE Nº 58.

FOSTER & WELLS,
SOLICITORS.
W E FOSTER.
S C WELLS.

ALDERSHOT 29th March 1906
(AND AT FARNBOROUGH: HANTS.)

Dear Sir,

The Aldershot & Farnborough Light Railway promoters having abandoned their scheme for an electric railway between Aldershot & Farnboro' leave the way open for the establishment of a service of motor Omnibuses between these places.

But Mr Foster has obtained the right from the Military Authorities of running a service through the Camp which right is limited in point of time.

We shall be glad therefore if you will attend a meeting to be held at this office tomorrow Friday at 5 pm

to meet other gentlemen who are interested in the matter

Yours truly,
Foster Wells

Similar letters to

C E Mills Esq — Dickson L
R Johnstone Stirling Esq The Chace Crockham
Capt Batchelot Campamento Farnboro'
J May Esq Cargate
Pullock Messrs Jobmasters Guildford
R H Lloyd Esq Aldershot
H Wells Esq Jr "
J Salter Esq "
Wilson Hughes Esq Frimley
H Hollings Esq J P D L Watchetts Frimley
R E Mills Esq

Draft of the letter from Foster & Wells, solicitors, inviting interested parties to a meeting to discuss starting a motor bus service.

Alder Valley

A third bus was purchased from Hastings shortly after the opening day. This was a 28hp 36-seat Leyland-Crossley, LC 4446, but it proved unsatisfactory and was very soon part-exchanged for two more of the Hastings Milnes-Daimlers, DY 35 (a 36-seater) and DY 106. The fleet of four buses was housed in a large garage – Lawes' Motor Works – near the centre of Aldershot, for the first three years of operation.

Although the horse bus crews had many laughs at the expense of their former colleagues who crewed the first motor buses and coped with their frequent breakdowns, the advantage soon passed to the Milnes-Daimlers. The Young family ceased to run, and in April 1907 Mr North sold his two vehicles*, harness and permits to the bus company for £50. His two conductors also transferred to the A & F company, and the motor buses were thereafter unchallenged.

From 26 December 1906, the Farnborough terminus was changed to the Town Hall, which was approached via Alexandra Road, though Guildford, Osborn and Lynchford Roads were used for the return journey until April 1907.

For a few years the activities of the company were hampered by strife among the directors. On many issues, Tom Foster was to be found as a lone voice against the rest of the Board, but he gained support and in January 1907 he and a new director, Mr C.J. Harland, were appointed Joint Managing Directors. A year later, he became sole Managing Director and also took on the duties of secretary, which put him into a powerful position, such that a threat of resignation usually made his colleagues see his point.

James May resigned in April 1908 and the new Chairman was Dr David Donald. He was to find his medical talents of value to his company in the following year when on 13 June, 1909, DY 35 left the road and hit a telegraph pole. Several passengers were detained in Connaught Hospital, and the worthy doctor both ministered to them and settled their claims for compensation!

An innovation in June 1908 was the opening of a parcels service between Aldershot and North Camp, using the buses for the main journey, at a price of 2d per item, and offering delivery by hand within a one-mile radius of the termini, at a cost of a further penny.

A new service to Ash started about June 1908, but was suspended in November in favour of one to Deepcut, via Ash Vale (LSWR) station and North Camp (SECR) station. To the south-west of Aldershot, Farnham saw its first

---

*   The remains of one of these buses still survived in a yard in Reading Road, Farnborough almost fifty years later!

Two of the A&F Milnes-Daimlers, DY 116 and 106, standing outside their Aldershot base at Lawes' Motor Works in 1906. They both carry their new fleetnames, but DY 106, on the right, still retains the original owner's 'To and From' with the destination painted out. On the extreme left is Bill Shepherd, the Chief Conductor who later became A&D's Chief Inspector, while Conductor Herbert Essam, later Depot Inspector at Guildford, lays a proprietary hand on DY 106. This photo is half of a panorama which showed all four buses and all of the staff: the full picture is now only known as a small snapshot, taken at the same time.

Alder Valley

In February 1911, Commer charabanc LN 3124 joined the A&F fleet. (It bore the name 'Emily' beside the driver's feet.) It is seen in Halimote Road, outside the Co-operative store, which many years later became the A&D canteen. Note the entrance to Vick's garage in the left background. The occasion seems to be a wedding, judging from the buttonholes and bunting.

Alder Valley

ALDERSHOT AND FARNBOROUGH MOTOR OMNIBUS COMPANY, LIMITED.

Motor Char-a-Banc Excursions

Will be run (weather permitting, and providing there are a sufficient number of passengers) as follows:—

SUNDAY, June 18th, to

HAMPTON COURT,
Return Fare 3/6.

Leaving Imperial Hotel, Aldershot, at 2.0 p.m.
Returning from Hampton Court at 7.30 p.m.

THURSDAY, June 22nd, to

HENLEY-on-THAMES
Return Fare 4/-.

Leaving Imperial Hotel, Aldershot, at 11 a.m.
Returning from Henley at 8 p.m.

FRIDAY, June 23rd, to

HINDHEAD, RETURN FARE 2/6.

Leaving the Imperial Hotel, Aldershot, at 3 p.m.
Returning from Hindhead at 7.30 p.m.

SATURDAY, June 24th, to GOSPORT for the

ROYAL NAVAL REVIEW
Return Fare 7/6.

Leaving Imperial Hotel, Aldershot, at 6.30 a.m.
Returning from Gosport about 10.30 p.m.

N.B.—THIS TRIP WILL NOT BE RUN UNLESS SUFFICIENT SEATS ARE BOOKED BY 21st JUNE.

SUNDAY, June 25th, to

WINDSOR, RETURN FARE 3/6.

Leaving Imperial Hotel, Aldershot, at 2.30 p.m.
Returning from Windsor at 7.30 p.m.

Seats may be booked at the Company's Office, Halimote Road, Aldershot, in advance, and must be paid for at the time of booking. Seats will be allotted in order of application, and will only be booked up to the day before that on which the Excursion is advertised to run. Should the Excursion not take place the money paid for the seats will be refunded. Any seats not booked will be filled at the Imperial Hotel.

The Company will make every effort to maintain the service, but they give no guarantee that the same shall be performed, and the Company shall not be liable for any loss or damage that any passenger may sustain for any failure to maintain the same, or for want of punctuality in the service, or for any delay caused through any mechanical breakdown.

BY ORDER.
13th June. 1911.

H. C. Smith, Printer, Wellington Street, Aldershot. (3257)
Aldershot. (3257)

A & F buses in July 1908, though the first service, via Weybourne, was primarily aimed at the leisure market and consisted of two return journeys on Sunday afternoons only. The fare was 6d, and return tickets were available at 9d.

The company was in need of premises of its own, to replace its rented garage space, and in the spring of 1908, Messrs Alderton and Sumpster, coal and general merchants, sold a corner of their site with a 50-foot frontage onto Halimote Road. A brick garage to hold four buses was opened in 1909. In addition to the bus operations, facilities to serve the general motorist were established. The firm became an agency for numerous motoring requisites, as well as providing a car hire service, and the Halimote Road Garage was appointed an Official Repairer to the Royal Automobile Club at the end of 1909. The company also obtained a contract from the Junior Army and Navy Stores to operate and maintain its two Halley vans. A branch known as the Halimote Garage was also opened in Fleet, in the Market Place, some time before buses started to run between Fleet and Aldershot.

Dr Donald resigned in September 1910, as he planned to emigrate, and Mr William Foster took over as Chairman. The family was now firmly in control of the company.

In February 1911 the company acquired a Commercial Cars Ltd (Commer) charabanc, LN 3124, with about 20 seats, which was to be used for private hire work and for excursions: all local sports clubs, regimental messes, etc. were circularised. Although it was provided with a roof, the open sides of this vehicle must have made it very uncomfortable in bad weather. With journeys to coastal resorts taking upwards of three hours at the statutory 12 m.p.h. it is not surprising that excursions were advertised as 'weather permitting'.

On 14 April 1911 the Farnham service was increased to operate on Monday, Wednesday and Sunday afternoons, though it reverted to Sundays only for the next winter. The Deepcut service, by now cut back to the North Camp stations, was suspended on 24 February 1912, but in the previous month a Saturdays-only service of two journeys plus a late theatre bus from Aldershot to Deepcut had been inaugurated.

Chapter Three

Aldershot and District

Despite its pioneering of several new routes, the Aldershot and Farnborough company was still a small enterprise, and six years after its foundation still had no more than its four original second-hand buses, plus the Commer charabanc. New capital was needed for re-equipment and expansion, and approaches were made in appropriate circles.

The British Electric Traction group had been established in 1896, to promote schemes for electric tramways. In 1905 it set up a subsidiary, the British Automobile Development Co. Ltd., originally to manufacture motor buses, but later to finance and enter into partnership with emergent motor bus operators. This company (renamed the British Automobile Traction Co. Ltd. in 1912) made an offer to purchase the Aldershot and Farnborough company in opposition to one from the New Central Omnibus Co. Ltd. The A & F board favoured the BAT offer, worth £3 10s 0d per share, and an agreement was reached which inaugurated the Aldershot and District Traction Company Limited on 24 July 1912. The issued capital was £9,742 out of an authorised £15,000 and the directors were Mr William Foster (Chairman), Mr Tom Foster (Managing Director) and two members of BAT, Mr Sidney Garcke, the son of BAT's founder, and Mr W.S. Wreathall.

The Memorandum of Association stated the aims of the company as 'To carry on business as motor car, omnibus, van and cab proprietors, and carriers of passengers and goods, whether by mechanical or other motive power,

in and between the towns and districts of Aldershot, Farnborough, Fleet, Ewshot, Guildford, Ash, Farnham, Frimley and Camberley, or any other towns, districts and places in the United Kingdom and to manufacture, construct, purchase, equip, maintain, work and deal in motor cars, omnibuses, vans, carriages and other vehicles, or means of conveyance of every description (including aeroplanes) appropriate for the carriage of transport and goods, and to manufacture and deal in cycles, trucks, locomotives, accumulators, dynamos and other chattels and effects and conveniences required for making, equipping and working motor cars, omnibuses and other vehicles, and to carry on any other trade or business whatsoever which can, in the opinion of the board, be advantageously carried on by the company in connection with or as auxiliary to the general business of the company'. With Colonel Cody's early flying at Farnborough having achieved considerable fame during the preceding few years, the inclusion of the normally routine mention of aeroplanes must have held a real significance for the local directors, perhaps conjuring up visions of green aeroplanes filling the Hampshire and Surrey skies!

To launch the new company, the board entertained a number of prominent citizens to luncheon and took them on a trip to Camberley and Blackwater, where they had tea before returning to Aldershot.

With the financial support of BAT, the new company soon embarked on a period of expansion. Within a year,

The fleet of seven Leyland double-deckers acquired by A&D in 1912-13 is seen on parade, with Percy Rivitt in charge. Note the height at which the headlamps are mounted, and the unusually high radiator of this Leyland model.   *Alder Valley*

Right: In the summer of 1914, the staff of A&D, with wives and families, were taken on a firm's outing to Southsea. The outing was naturally spread over two days, and one of the Daimler CC buses, AA 5165, was used on each occasion. The stunted figure of Tom Foster is on the right, and at far left are Secretary Albert Webster (later to become General Manager of Hants & Dorset) and Chief Inspector Shepherd. *Alder Valley*

Below: Ben Chandler's Commer, P3769, stands outside the Royal Huts Hotel at Hindhead, on its journey between Haslemere and Grayshott. It was common practice at that time to paint the principal destination in permanent form in the position where the fleetname would have been sited in later years. This was another rear-platform bus. Chandler was keen on publicity, and at least ten views of this vehicle are known, as well as six of his Dennis charabanc, DB 285. The grandly-titled Royal Huts is now much rebuilt and carries the name of the Happy Eater restaurant chain! *Author's collection*

Hindhead, Royal Huts Hotel.

seven new Leyland double-deckers had been acquired, to replace the Milnes-Daimlers and to enable new routes to be opened. The livery chosen for the company's buses by BAT was similar to the A & F's dark green, with white above the waistline and light green for the upper parts of the double-deckers. The main dark green panels were lined-out in white, and the fleet name Aldershot & District Traction Co. Ltd. appeared in white along the full length of the panel beneath the windows. Registration numbers were AA 5040-3, 5076, 5162-3.

The first new service to be inaugurated was from Aldershot, via Crookham Cross Roads, to Fleet (Railway Hotel). This had four daily journeys, plus a late theatre bus on Wednesdays and Saturdays, and started just in time for Christmas 1912.

Early in 1913, the LSWR introduced a Bill into Parliament which contained clauses permitting the railway to run more passenger and goods motor vehicles and to increase the charges made to other operators using their station yards and forecourts. Strong opposition from local and county councils caused these clauses to be dropped, with the result that A&D was now able to negotiate for its buses to use the station approaches at Aldershot, Farnborough and Fleet, and it could also plan for its next new service – to Camberley – to terminate outside the station from the outset. Five journeys on the Farnborough route were accordingly extended to Camberley, through Frimley and Yorktown, on 19 June 1913. A more far-reaching effect of the agreement with the LSWR was that A&D took over the railway's Farnham-Haslemere service, from 12 June. A later journey in each direction was immediately added for the summer season, departing at 4.34 from Farnham and 6.12 from Haslemere. The working agreement with the LSWR provided, as these timings show, for connection with specific trains at Farnham and Haslemere. A&D at once ordered four powerful new 34-seat Daimler CC single-deck buses, AA 5164-7, for this route, where considerable quantities of baggage had to be conveyed up the hills to hotels and restaurants. These started work on 30 August, after a trial trip had been run for the interest of local councillors, including tea at the Huts Hotel at Hindhead.

Two more Daimler CD buses were ordered at the same time for Aldershot area services, and on 16 August one of the three ex-LSWR buses was used to start a service from Farnham to Shortheath, at a fare of 2d and a frequency of five journeys per day. From 17 September these were increased to eight, and all but one were extended from Farnham to Aldershot (Queen Hotel). The fact that the first departure from Shortheath was changed from 8.40 to 9.25am emphasises that the working population of the area still preferred to walk or cycle. The Farnham–Haslemere service was similarly extended on the same day, and three additional short workings to Frensham were provided, while fares were also reduced.

Following the acquisition of the LSWR buses, the company consolidated its position in the Hindhead and Haslemere area by purchasing the buses of Mr Ben Chandler. He was proprietor of the Royal Huts Hotel and livery stables at Hindhead. After a period in which a horse bus service, started by a Mr Dowsett in May 1905, had been operated between his hotel and Haslemere, he acquired a 28-seat Commer bus in 1912. This vehicle, P 3769, was fitted with a Bayley's body which was entered via a rear platform in the style of double-deckers of the period. Known as the Red Bus, it was used to provide a regular service from Haslemere (White Horse Hotel) via Hindhead, to Grayshott, and it also served Hindhead Golf Club. A second vehicle, a Dennis (DB 285) with a charabanc body, was also in use on these services and on private hire. Both of these vehicles were acquired by A&D when they took over the bus service on 29 October 1913, and Chandler's six hire cars and taxis probably formed part of the deal.

Towards the end of 1913, a number of new services were tried, all of which were destined to be short-lived. On 1 October an hourly service from Aldershot, via Ash ('Greyhound' and Shawfields Road) to the Bridge House Hotel, Ash Vale was started. This was reduced in frequency after two months and was withdrawn on 16 March 1914. On 1 December 1913 the buses released from the Ash Vale service were used to open another local route, this time turning right at the 'Greyhound' to Tongham. This was withdrawn on 6 February 1914. The next route explored was to Wellington College (now called Crowthorne)

station, which was provided with two services. One was a modification of the Camberley service from Aldershot, branching off at Yorktown (or on some journeys making a connection at Yorktown or Farnborough) to run via Sandhurst and Crowthorne village to the terminus at the station. The other ran from the 'Jolly Farmer' on the Bagshot road, to Camberley, Yorktown and Wellington College station. Both were started on 18 December and withdrawn after only seven weeks on 5 February 1914. In each of these four cases, the notice of withdrawal used the phrase 'owing to it not being sufficiently patronised by the public to warrant its continuance at this time of year'. However, the company never again ventured on this road north of Yorktown at any time of year.

Early in 1914, A&D was among four applicants to the Town Council for licences to start running motor buses in Guildford, which had not hitherto had many regular services. However, to ensure that it had the advantage of being first in the field, it started a service on 31 January from Aldershot via Ash, Pirbright (Fox Inn), Worplesdon and Stoughton to Guildford, and extended thence to Godalming. Over the latter section it filled the gap left by the withdrawal, for the winter, of the Guildford–Godalming–Haslemere service commenced in the previous year by Mr J. Flint's Haslemere Car Hirers Ltd. Based at Homeleigh Works, Shottermill, Mr Flint had a number of Daimler waggonettes, seating ten or more, and on 27 April 1913 he had started running a regular service from Haslemere to Midhurst Station. He also tried other routes later in the year: in November he ran the Guildford–Godalming–Haslemere route for a month, after which his licence was not renewed. A Guildford–Stoughton–Bagshot route was applied for in the following February, but no licence was issued. Eventually, after Mr and Mrs Flint's desperate efforts to maintain their original Midhurst service without assistance, the business collapsed into bankruptcy in April 1914.

Not having been licensed in Guildford and Godalming, A&D was only allowed to pick up passengers in those areas if they had booked in advance, the agent being Miss Lane, stationer, of 21 Farnham Road, Guildford. Initially, three journeys daily and one on Sundays were planned, but at the last minute one extra journey out from Aldershot in the morning and one return journey from Guildford in the evening were added to enable a vehicle to work to Guildford for another service, this time via Chilworth to Dorking and Leatherhead, on weekdays only. This started on Monday 2 February, and was at first run in conjunction with a local service to Merrow. The bus arriving from Aldershot thus ran first out to Merrow and then embarked on a through Merrow–Guildford–Leatherhead journey. The complete service consisted of two full-distance return journeys, two short workings Merrow–Guildford–Shalford Green and the morning and evening runs to and from Merrow*. Again Miss Lane acted as ticket agent in Guildford.

The Leatherhead route took A&D into competition with the East Surrey Traction Co., which immediately countered by starting up a short route westwards from Dorking along the Guildford road to Westcott. After threats by A&D to open further routes in the Dorking area, this East Surrey service was withdrawn in May, and an agree-

---

* Mileage returns show that one journey to Dorking and back ran on 31 January. The full local service, Guildford–Merrow, started on 31 January, Guildford–Dorking ran in full on 2 February and Dorking–Leatherhead appears to have begun on 3 February.

In 1914, A&D bought its first Dennis buses for service in Guildford. The body design, with space behind the driver, was characteristic of Bayley's. After the war, one of these bodies, with the space now incorporated into the saloon, reappeared on a Daimler chassis, while one of the original chassis was in use as a lorry. *Alder Valley*

ment was reached which gave A&D the monopoly of the Guildford road in return for its undertaking to make no more incursions into East Surrey's area.

Apart from A&D, the three other applicants for licenses in Guildford in January were M. Puttock & Son, the Guildford jobmasters (i.e. hirers of horses and carriages), who had operated a Dennis charabanc since 1911, the vehicle manufacturers Dennis Bros. Ltd. themselves, based at Guildford, and Mr Walter Flexman French, of Balham, who had already founded the Maidstone and District Motor Services. By the time the Watch Committee had considered the applications on 23 January, the four had paired off. Between them, A&D and Puttock applied for 14 licences, on the understanding that if they were granted Puttock would become the company's Guildford area manager. Mr French lent his support to Dennis Bros., which aimed to set up a company named Guildford and District Motor Services, and which would naturally use Dennis buses exclusively. William Foster gave an interview to the local press, in which he emphasised the difficulties due to A&D's not yet having a licence to operate in Guildford. He claimed that the Aldershot–Guildford route was already being operated by Dennis vehicles, and expressed his willingness to operate every one of its anticipated Guildford services with the local manufacturer's products.

After six weeks of manoeuverings, the Watch Committee recommended the council to grant twelve licences to each group for one year, and the awards were confirmed in the last week of February. On 12 March, Guildford and District Motor Services Ltd was formed, its first bus chassis having already been supplied by the Dennis works. Imme-

diate plans were to operate to Merrow and Ripley, with other local services to Shalford and Bramley and to Stoughton. Longer runs to Witley, via Farncombe and Godalming and to Dorking, via Albury and Shere were to be started when more buses became available. G & D actually obtained a licence from the Dorking council, but never operated that far as an independent concern. Other proposals included routes to Ash and to Woking: the latter reached the stage of a licence application.

However, within three months, A&D had acquired a large proportion of the G & D shares, and appointed three of its own directors to the board. G & D thus became the operating agents for the Guildford-based routes of the larger company, i.e. those from Guildford to Godalming, Merrow and Leatherhead. This arrangement continued until December, when the traffic on these routes reappeared in the A&D's monthly returns, and G & D had become a wholly-owned subsidiary of its larger neighbour, Tom Foster and William Wreathall being directors of both companies. G & D nevertheless retained its identity for some years thereafter, and its buses, in their separate livery, were to be seen operating on all of A&D's Guildford-based services.

A&D acquired an operating base for its services in the Haslemere area by the purchase of the Haslemere Motor Co. Ltd. in April 1914. This had a garage on Clay Hill, near the railway bridge, and as at Aldershot, the company continued to provide facilities for the ordinary motorist, under the name The Motor House. These were continued until 1919. The motorists' garage at Fleet had, however, been sold to Mr H. Watmore in January 1914 as the Atlas

Above: In front of the village stores at Chiddingfold, Guildford & District Dennis LH9026 waits to start its return journey to Guildford. The route started in December 1914, when G&DMS was already a wholly-owned subsidiary of A&D, but it continued to use its separate livery for several years more.
Author's collection

Right: A relatively rare photograph of an A&D Foden steam wagon actually at work, carrying a load of hay for the Army. *Author's collection*

Motor and Cycle Works. The Aldershot car business was sold later to Vick Bros for £3,650, on 1 August 1917. The new owners continued to use the Halimote Road premises for many years, with a right of way over A&D's roadways.

A number of parcels vans were obtained for the inauguration of an Express Delivery Parcels Service towards the end of 1913. Agents were appointed in most of the towns and villages then served, though when the Guildford area opened up in 1914 it was not at first included in the scheme, except for the company's office in the centre of Guildford. Parcels were received by these agents for consignment by bus or van to other receiving offices or to railway stations for onward transit by rail. Most agents, as well as the company's own offices, would deliver parcels to addresses up to one mile away, A&D employing boys with hard-carts painted in its familiar green livery. By 1916, the service had been augmented by enabling conductors on five routes to accept parcels for delivery, and after suspension during the latter part of the war, this facility was gradually reintroduced

and expanded from 1918 onwards.

Passengers' luggage was at first conveyed at a charge of 2d per item, or 4d for large or bulky articles. Bicycles, perambulators and mail carts (the precursors of the push-chair) were charged at 6d if the accommodation on the bus was suitable. In 1916 new rates were set for heavy trunks and dress baskets (6d each), mail carts (6d), bicycles (6d up to 20 miles, 1s 0d over that distance) and perambulators (1s 0d if accommodation permits).

The very first Aldershot & Farnborough service in 1906 (and indeed its horse-drawn predecessors) had included an untimed late journey from Aldershot to North Camp after the end of the performance at the theatre, and this practice continued for many years, to an increasing number of local destinations. The Aldershot Hippodrome and the Theatre Royal both provided variety programmes, with other attractions at intervals, and the late buses served the nearby Palace Cinema as well. On other routes, the last bus of the regular service was shown as waiting for the end of the

To all Military & Police Authorities.

No.

Permit the Driver of

Fill in for
one vehicle
only, two
must be
struck out.

Lorry No.............. Foden No.............. Car No..........

belonging to the Aldershot and District Traction Coy.,

Limited, to travel within your area with Moderate

Lights, on urgent Military Service.

(By Order.)

S. H. LYNN, Colonel,

A.D. of S. & T. Aldershot Command.

Head Quarters,

Aldershot,

29th January, 1915.

NOTICE TO DRIVERS.

All drivers must be careful to see they have the permit for the particular vehicle they are driving, and in all cases where the driver changes vehicles, he is to hand in the permit and obtain the correct one before taking out the new vehicle.

second performance, some time after 10 p.m. Guildford also had late buses from the Theatre Royal on certain days soon after services first began there.

During the spring and summer of 1914, various services were increased, but it was not until 1 August that further new ground was broken, when the Grayshott route was extended to Headley and a service from Aldershot to Rowledge was opened, as an extension of the existing Shortheath route, in response to a local petition.

At this point, the narrative must be interrupted by pointing out a difficulty facing the researcher into A&D history for this most interesting period: the company's minutes from June 1912 to April 1919 have disappeared. Coupled with the absence of the cash book for 1912-15 from the company archives (as well as the gap in Hampshire's motor vehicle records for registrations AA 4001-9999 and HO 1-6800), this means that the history has had to be reconstructed from press reports, photographs and timetables. The lack of documentation has hampered several researchers' attempts to trace the development of the company's passenger and goods fleets over the period of the 1914-18 war. The official fleet list volume was a post-war innovation!

The outbreak of war on 4 August 1914 found the company ideally situated to play an important role in serving the Army's needs in and around Aldershot – known as 'The Home of the British Army'. Tom Foster immediately placed the company's fleet of buses and other vehicles at the disposal of the War Office and on the following day all

services, with the exception of Aldershot–Farnborough Town Hall, were reduced to a skeleton level. Later in the week, buses with soldiers in charge were seen carrying meat and bread supplies from Aldershot to the garrison at Bordon. By removing windows for ease of access, single-deck buses could be used as ambulances for transporting casualties from railway stations to military hospitals. The first batches of wounded returning from the battle of Mons later in August were carried in this way, and later, German prisoners of war were carried to their camps in hired buses. The War Office naturally used its influence in ensuring that the company received adequate supplies of fuel, spares and other requirements to keep its vehicles on the road. Before long, the immediate effects of wartime dislocation were overcome, and the timetables for early 1915 showed few differences from those of a year earlier. The number of routes on which special reduced fares for soldiers in uniform were available multiplied during and after the war (these arrangements in fact continued through to the 1939-45 war). Reduced fares were also available to the large number of civilian workers at the Royal Aircraft Factory (later Royal Aircraft Establishment) where books of special tickets were sold at the main gate office and some morning and evening journeys were diverted past the gate.

The A&D goods services flourished on early wartime business. A contract was signed with the War Department for goods haulage for the Army, and a stock of steam and motor lorries was rapidly built up. The former were all of Foden manufacture, and both 3-ton and 5-ton over-type wagons were represented among the 20 acquired. The motor lorries were mostly 3-tonners built by Belsize of Manchester, whose products were among the few not automatically earmarked for military service. Forty lorries were purchased during this period, and in a few cases, at least, lorry bodies were temporarily mounted on bus chassis. Understandably, there are also reported instances of goods vehicles being used as rough-and-ready transport for troops, prisoners of war and munitions workers.

When military camps were built at Bramshott and Witley, an A&D van collection and delivery service was provided for passengers' heavy luggage between Haslemere station and the camps and other addresses in the Hindhead and Haslemere area. To avoid having to carry weighing equipment on the vans, to weigh goods accepted en route, regular customers were recommended to open deposit accounts, from which the charges were deducted after weighing at the offices at Haslemere or the two camps.

Once the immediate military transport emergency was past, A&D was once more able to contemplate development of its public services, and in November 1914 it started running on a route from Haslemere to Midhurst Station, previously operated by the defunct Haslemere Car Hirers, Ltd.

A&D's Rowledge service was withdrawn in November 1914 and did not reappear for almost ten years, and a service from Guildford to Walton via Woking and Chertsey, opened in December 1914 by Guildford & District, closed three months later, never to reappear. However, with this exception, 1915 saw a general expansion of passenger facilities. Very few vehicle manufacturers were by this time allowed to continue production for civilian customers, so A&D was unable to buy more Daimlers or Leylands to run its new and increased services. Fortunately, in September 1914, it had been possible to hire thirteen Daimler CC buses from another BAT company, the Northern General Transport Co. of Gateshead, Co. Durham. These stayed

Within two months of the outbreak of war in 1914, several journals published this official photograph of Daimler CC AA 5368, carrying several German prisoners on top of a load of logs destined for their camp at Frimley. The chassis was owned by A&D, and photographs taken at other times show it with both single- and double-deck bus bodies.

Author's collection

The Belsize 3-ton chassis, with a 28 hp engine, was first obtained for A&D's goods fleet, but was later used for passenger vehicles. AA5659 appears on this postcard published by a firm in Bramshot Camp, where the view was taken. The body, to a design by Brush, seems a trifle too long for the wheelbase of the chassis, but, because of the small rear wheels, no adaptation was necessary. *Author's collection*

for just a year, though some of their double-deck bodies were retained by A&D for service on other chassis.

In March 1915, the Guildford Watch Committee received a letter from A&D concerning the plight of the Guildford and District company. Since the latter had had some of its vehicles commandeered for military service, it was proposed that the parent company should take over the remaining three buses and their licences for the time being. The Town Council approved this move on 30 March, thus legalising the de facto position, and allowing the two companies to be operated as one in the Guildford area, with Tom Foster as Managing Director of both. In charge at Guildford was Inspector Herbert Essam, who had

been the conductor on the very first journey of the Aldershot and Farnborough company in 1906. He had his home above the company's office, inherited from G & D, at 198 High Street. With a Guildford base at Puttock's garage, beside the nearby White Horse Hotel, it was no longer necessary to work A&D buses out from Aldershot; in fact on 17 April 1915 the Aldershot–Guildford–Godalming service was reduced to Sundays only, though extended to Witley (White Hart).

The G & D company remained officially in existence, though dormant, until it was wound up on 26 October 1926. In the March of each of the intervening years, A&D paid over a sum of money to its subsidiary, and formally

Five of the A&D Foden steam wagons are posed with their crews and a trophy which they had won in their later years of service, when business was slack and participation in carnivals, etc, was a frequent event. The location is the junction of St. Michael's and St. George's Roads in Aldershot.

P. Smith

received most of it back as dividend a few days later. Mr French's connections with A&D continued for some years, although he moved his pioneering efforts to Bournemouth, where he founded the Bournemouth & District Motor Services Ltd in 1916. During 1918-19, when new vehicles were in short supply, he arranged an extended loan of two A&D Daimler buses, to open up new routes, and upon the formation of the Hants and Dorset Motor Omnibus Co. Ltd. in 1920, he became its first chairman.

The next move by A&D was the opening of services on the Guildford–Haslemere route. On 27 August 1915 the Aldershot–Guildford service was restored to daily operation, though now running along a route between Normandy and Guildford instead of via Fox Inn and Worplesdon. From Guildford, the route was extended beyond Godalming and Witley to Haslemere. Earlier in the year, a separate service had started from Guildford to Chiddingfold over the same roads, as far as Witley, and from 1 November the long journey from Aldershot was split at Guildford. The section to Haslemere was combined with the Chiddingfold service to give two alternative routes between Guildford and Haslemere, diverging at Witley to run either via Chiddingfold and Fisher Street or via Witley Camp and Grayswood.

During the first year of the war, the Army Service Corps had built up its own fleet of vehicles, and had no further need for a large haulage contract with A&D. To soften the blow, the War Department agreed to place a reduced contract to last from August 1915 until March 1916. Over this period, the monthly WD mileage, which had been around 30,000 for the 'petrol lorries' and 10,000 for the steam wagons, declined steadily. Alternative employment had to be found for the fleet, and private hire was resumed from August 1915. In December, the lorries started a London parcels service, and from the following March, two regular timetabled goods services to London were operated: one from Haslemere and Hindhead and one from Bramshott and Witley Camps. Later in that year an Aldershot–Farnborough–London goods service was also advertised.

When WD work finally ceased, six of the steam wagons were sold to Mr Walter Webb of Southampton, whose offer to give jobs to their crews was taken up by several of the men. Business for the remaining goods fleet was improved by accepting sub-contract work from Commercial Car Hirers Ltd., an organisation originally set up in 1909 to operate surplus vehicles for its parent Commer company, and greatly expanded on the freight haulage side during the war. Other contract hire took A&D's Fodens long distances from their home base; records survive of them being based at Birmingham and Mildenhall. Their drivers were responsible for buying their fuel and supplies locally, and accounting to head office at Aldershot on a weekly basis.

A Commercial Motor Hire department was set up to manage goods fleets based on Aldershot and Haslemere in June 1916. The normal allocation was 7 steam and 12 petrol vehicles at Aldershot and five of each at Haslemere. Records exist of runs from Aldershot to Petworth and to Arborfield, and from October to December 1916, haulage of wood for Gridley's of Haslemere provided a busy time for the Fodens.

Many of the 28hp Belsize lorry chassis made redundant by the ending of the WD contract were adapted for passenger duties. A variety of bodies were acquired second-hand from other bus companies, and others were taken from old A&D stock, since bodies and chassis were frequently separated and interchanged in those early days. Most of the Belsizes were given single-deck bodies, though a few carried double-deck bodies, and with these additions the fleet strength reached 49 in December 1916.

Throughout the war, no matter how serious the situation, military pageantry was still to be seen in Aldershot, and attracted sightseers in their hundreds, as in the peaceful years before and after. Royal occasions – massed reviews of the Army, or investitures – justified the laying on of special buses to the parade ground, from Aldershot Station, and sometimes from nearby towns as well.

New territory was penetrated by routes from Aldershot to Basingstoke, on 1 December 1915, from Aldershot to Reading, on 1 March 1916, and from Guildford to Knaphill in January 1916. The latter was cut back to Brookwood after a few weeks (on 1 March) but was extended again, to Woking, on 5 August. A route from Guildford to Ripley opened in June 1916, while a local route from Aldershot to Upper Hale Road also started on 1 December 1915. From 5 August 1916 the existing Aldershot–Haslemere service was paralleled over the section from Haslemere to Hindhead Golf Club by a First Class service, timed to connect with the same trains at Haslemere, and operated by a Belsize bus, AA 5527, equipped with curtains, comfortable seats and other luxury fittings. The minimum fare was 3d and the full journey cost 1/6d compared with 1d and 8d on the normal buses. In mid-1916 this vehicle was in full-time use on this route, but it appears that it was also employed on the Haslemere–Grayshott route at some time after it was extended to Bramshott Camp in November 1914. As no separate timetable has been located, it presumably ran in parallel with normal buses on this route.

The rapid expansion of goods and passenger traffic at Aldershot necessitated a large increase in garage space, which was provided by taking over the site of a brickworks adjacent to the Halimote Road premises in 1915. A new two-level building was erected, with workshops on the upper floor, at the level of the road outside (the Top Shop) and a bus garage below, where the ground had been excavated by the previous owners. The old garage was initially retained as additional workshop space. A roadway at the lower level served both the new garage and a shed for the steam wagons, which was built with a sufficiently high roof to accommodate double-deck buses if necessary in the future. Beyond the steam shed was the 'petrol garage' where the motor lorries were maintained, and another building opposite housed the remainder of the bus fleet, of which up to 40 were now able to have covered accommodation. An interesting feature of the whole new development was the design of the drainage system to feed a sump where rainwater could be collected for use in the steam wagons. The new premises were in full use by the autumn of 1916.

At the end of May 1916, the railway and general carrier business of M. Larbey of Haslemere was taken over, together with a Dennis van (DB 534) which had been used to serve the Haslemere, Hindhead and Grayshott area from its base in Wey Hill. This carrier service was destined to continue for many years after the rest of A&D's goods traffic ceased.

Manpower problems were now becoming serious. Although in October 1915 conductresses ('lady conductors') began to be recruited, the Army's demands made heavy in roads into the numbers of available staff, especially fitters. The Traffic Manager, Mr E.G. Hawkins, made numerous appearances before tribunals to claim exemption for his men, but to little avail. By June 1916 only two

Above: In the old-timers' interview mentioned in the preface, it was stated that there were three Belsize double-deckers, but only one photograph, of AA 5643, has come to light. From November 1909, Park and Sparkhall had an arrangement that they could issue vouchers, exchangeable for A&D bus tickets. The privilege was open to other tradesmen, but it was agreed that no other *drapers* could participate. *E. Nixon collection*

Right: With A&D already providing much of the goods transport around the Haslemere area, it was a logical move to buy Larbey's railway and general carrier business in 1916. His 1912 Dennis van, DB 534, had been registered, like many other vehicles built by Dennis Bros, in Stockport, to obtain the 'DB' prefix. It was repainted with A&D colours and fleetname, with 'General Carrier' on the van sides, and lasted till 1919.

Author's collection courtesy G. Hall

experienced fitters, plus young apprentices, were left to service a stock of 86 vehicles – 42 buses, 22 petrol lorries, 12 steam wagons, 6 parcels vans and 4 motor cars. This, combined with restrictions on fuel and other supplies, made it increasingly difficult to maintain ordinary passenger services, and on 8 December 1916 a notice announced that within the next three weeks no fewer than eight services would be temporarily and indefinitely suspended. These were Aldershot–Reading, Haslemere–Midhurst, Guildford–Merrow, Guildford–Ripley, Guildford–Woking, Guildford–Dorking–Leatherhead, Guildford–Haslemere and Aldershot–Basingstoke. On 2 April 1917 Aldershot–Upper Hale, Aldershot–Deepcut (Saturdays only) and

Aldershot–Blackdown also ceased. The latter was reinstated for a time on 21 July, running via North Camp instead of Ash, but after its second demise, only seven services remained until the war was over: Aldershot–Farnborough–Camberley, Aldershot–Farnham–Shortheath, Aldershot–Haslemere, Haslemere–Grayshott–Liphook, Aldershot–Ash–Guildford and Guildford–Godalming–Witley Camp.

These cutbacks took place at a time when Tom Foster had succumbed to the stresses of running the company, combined with physical overwork in helping to keep the fleet on the road. He suffered a serious breakdown during 1916, and was away from work for many months. BET arranged for A&D to have the temporary services of a

Right: 'Lady conductors' of the First World War are assembled at the bottom of Foden Road for this photograph. Chief Inspector Shepherd is in the centre, with Jack Robart seated in front of him. (Being a foreign national, he was exempt from military service, which was a source of irritation to many.) Behind Mr. Shepherd is the Lady Inspector, Mrs. Matthews, and others identified are Emily Stone (right of back row) and Gert Pharo and Elsie Ridgers, to the left and right respectively of Mr. Shepherd. *Author's collection*

manager who had several years' experience in running tramway concerns, Mr George Cardwell. After helping A&D through its most difficult period, he left to join the Army in 1917. He later achieved considerable eminence in the bus industry, with the Thames Valley Traction Co., the North Western Road Car Co., and in the headquarters of Thomas Tilling Ltd. In 1949 he reached the top of his profession as Chairman of the Road Passenger Executive for the British Transport Commission.

The effect of the enforced cutbacks at the end of 1916, combined with the ending of War Department contract work earlier in the year, was to bring the company's finances into a very parlous state. Up to 1914, a 10% dividend had been declared. In 1914-15, receipts trebled and operating profits rose from £4,667 to £22,551. A 40% dividend was distributed in 1915, and £2,000 was shared among the staff

as a bonus. The year 1915-16 was not quite so profitable, perhaps because about one-third of the 2½ million passengers carried were soldiers at reduced rates. Even so, a 10% dividend was easily covered. In 1917, however, the dividend was passed, in view of the poor results and absence of any reserve. A rapid recovery over the following year restored receipts to almost their 1916 level, and the customary 10% dividend was once again declared for 1918.

Manpower problems persisted: the company was allowed to retain three drivers for every two buses in service, but early in 1918 there were only 36 to run 26 buses, and William Foster argued forcefully with the Tribunal that their insistence that exempted men should join the volunteers was unreasonable. Their military training obligations and liability for call-up in emergencies were incompatible with running a reliable bus service.

1915 produced such handsome profits that the company decided to pay a bonus to every member of its staff. They are shown here, outside the cottages at the bottom of Halimote Road which served as the company's office, awaiting their share. In addition to the well-known figures of Messrs Rivitt and Shepherd (one in front of each doorway), the crowd includes members of every department, from junior office girl to the Foden driver on the extreme left, complete with goggles. *Alder Valley*

Chapter Four

Post-War Recovery and Expansion

After the end of the war on 11 November 1918, the return of staff from the armed forces permitted the gradual restoration of the services which had been cut back or suspended. Some form of commemoration was called for by several returning ex-servicemen, and a meeting of company employees on 28 April 1919 resolved that an Athletic Club should be formed. Tom Foster was unanimously elected President, and the committee started looking for a suitable ground. A year's lease of a level field near the foot of Eggar's Hill, off the Weybourne road, was

Daimler Y HO 2332, a bus on a government surplus chassis, is shown here with its Brush 32-seat body and an AEC radiator from one of the company's three B-type buses. The latter were officially described as Daimlers, since that company sold the well-known London model to the wider market.

E. Nixon collection

Post-war re-equipment involved the purchase of several Dennis Subsidy chassis from government surplus stocks. HO 2339 is posed in Foden Road, carrying a 34-seat body which originated with the Birmingham and Midland Motor Omnibus Co. The oil sidelamps and carbide headlamp are clearly visible. An official warning had to be issued in January 1920 telling crews not to dispose of spent carbide in gutters and over garden walls, because of the stench! The driver is Tom Clancy, and the conductress is Elsie Ridgers, who later married his brother Edward: eventually nine Clancys, of two generations, worked for A&D. *E. Nixon collection*

obtained, and a further meeting agreed unanimously that all employees would pay 2d per week to cover the costs. At the end of the year, negotiations for purchase of the ground were successful. £200 was raised by loans from members and the balance of the purchase price was obtained through a mortgage.

The company's operations in Guildford had been shut down at the beginning of 1917 except for the service to Witley Camp, which required only two buses, and the Aldershot–Guildford service, which was operated from Aldershot depot. Restoration of full services was a high local priority, to the extent that, pending delivery of new buses, the local licensing authorities gave permission for the new services to be started with a lorry fitted with transverse seating. To provide accommodation for an adequate fleet of buses, A&D purchased, in May 1919, the site of an uncompleted dance hall in Onslow Street (not far from the original Dennis works). Their new garage was completed there about the end of the year, whereupon the garaging arrangements with Puttock's were terminated.

In May 1919, the company became embroiled in six months of expensive litigation against Farnborough Urban District Council. The issue was one of local fares within the council's area. As part of a general revision of fare tables, some increases had been made which the council considered unjustified (e.g. Farnborough Town Hall to LSWR Station raised from 2d to 3d). A&D were refused renewal of licenses, so from midnight on Friday 23 May, no passengers could be picked up in the area, other than those travelling under special arrangements with the Army, the LSWR or the Ministry of Munitions (Royal Aircraft Establishment). In June, the company applied to the High Court for an order of mandamus against the council: in October the latter was served with a rule nisi to show reason why a writ of mandamus to re-hear the licence application should not be issued. The dispute was then settled rapidly, and normal service was resumed on 1 November. As a parting shot, the council exercised its right to demand a fee of £50 to permit buses to run a new route to Cove along Victoria Road: this issue was not resolved until almost two years later.

HO 2461 was one of three single-deckers built on Dennis Subsidy chassis in 1919. Their construction differed from contemporary double-deckers on Subsidy chassis, in that the radiator and bonnet were set much lower, giving a much more modern appearance. *E. Nixon collection*

Right: In 1921, the Fleet Primitive Methodist Sunday School outing to Southsea was carried by a Dennis charabanc, seen here on Portsdown Hill, with the track of the Portsdown and Horndean Light Railway in the background. The Subsidy chassis HO 2343 carried a 28-seat body which had seen previous service on a wartime Belsize chassis, when it was known, because of its unique livery, as the 'Silver Queen'. *Author's collection courtesy E. Roe*

In the immediate post-war period, a considerable number of second-hand chassis were purchased by A&D for reconditioning and the fitting of new or second-hand bodies. These chassis had been built by Daimler (pre-war CC and wartime Y models) and by Dennis, whose 30hp 'subsidy' lorry chassis was introduced in 1913. Under the Subvention or 'Subsidy' scheme of 1912, certain types of 3-ton chassis had been approved by the War Department for military use. Civilian users were given a £50 purchase premium and a £20 annual maintenance premium for vehicles kept in good order. In return the WD was entitled to purchase them at 72 hours' notice at times of national emergency, which it did on the outbreak of war in August 1914. Now, after demobilisation, large numbers of these and other ex-service vehicles were available for civilian customers. A&D's were bought from the large military disposal depot at Slough.

Bodies for these reconditioned chassis, Dennis HO2320/ 34-44, 2460-71, Daimler Y HO2325-33 and Daimler CC HO 2478, 2956) came from a variety of sources including earlier A&D buses. Second-hand double-deck bodies originated from the London General Omnibus Co., Northern General Transport, Thomas Tilling Ltd., Birch Bros. and the Immisch Launch Co., a boat-building subsidiary of BET. Some of the single-deck bodies had originated from Bayley's and Brush, but a number were built in A&D's own workshops in 1919-21. These included seven 28-seat charabanc bodies, which were mounted on Dennis HO 2464 and Daimlers HO 2472-7. The A&D bodies were allocated the lowest numbers in a series of body numbers which continued throughout the whole subsequent existence of the company. These were painted on the offside of the body, about floor level, below the first window aft of the driver's cab.

An opportunity for the company to explore the traffic potential of a number of hitherto untapped areas came at the beginning of October 1919, when a short rail strike, regarded by many in that uneasy post-war period as a 'German plot', caused considerable disruption. A once-per-day charabanc service from Farnham and Aldershot to Hyde Park Corner had only just begun on 29 September. Now additional services were provided for London-bound passengers from Aldershot to Hounslow tram terminus (1 to 8 October). Other services were provided from Aldershot

HO 2477, one of the seven Daimler Y charabancs with bodies built by A&D's own body shop, is seen on an excursion to the Surrey beauty spot of Waggoner's Wells. *E. Nixon collection*

AA 5368, a pre-war Daimler CC, is pictured here with a double-deck body, at the head of a line of special buses outside Aldershot station during the rail strike of October 1919. (The bus behind is destined for Hounslow). In the early days, bodies were frequently exchanged between chassis, and photographs exist of AA 5368 as a lorry in 1914, a double-decker in 1919 and finally as a single-decker in the early 'twenties.

E. Nixon collection

to Whitehill (4-8 October), Aldershot to Rafborough (the RAF quarters at Cove: 3-8 October), Haslemere–Chichester (4-8 October) and Guildford–Cranleigh, via Bramley (1-14(?) October). To operate these services, makeshift bodies were mounted on some of the company's motor lorries: the revenue earned by them was about £500. The goods fleet was also involved in its own right in the emergency arrangements. Those vehicles which were based in their home area were commandeered by the Army, while those working at a distance – at Monmouth, Cheltenham and Chatham – were ordered to report to the local Food Control Centres.

The opening of new bus routes was still restricted in some areas by inability to reach agreement with local authorities on charges for the wear and tear of the roads. In May 1916 the Local Government (Emergency Provisions) Act had enabled councils to levy a mileage charge for the use of any road not already part of a bus route. A few months later this problem had prevented A&D from starting services from Guildford to Wonersh and to Horsham, and after the war the same difficulty delayed the opening of the aforementioned regular service to Cove until October 1921. The Road Fund licence scheme was introduced in that year to replace these local arrangements for financing road maintenance.

Places of public entertainment had multiplied during the war years. In 1912, seven 'picture palaces' were listed in the original A&D area. By 1919, 17 were listed in the company's much-expanded domain. Special late services from Aldershot had continued throughout the war, and about the end of the war the Bramshott Garrison Theatre was also given the same facility. Over the next few years, there was a steady increase in the number of cinemas provided with late buses, either scheduled or special.

By the end of 1919, all of the services suspended 'for the duration' had been restored. In June of that year the existing services were allocated letters in the public time-table, replacing the route numbers, allocated in order of introduction, which had been used for internal purposes for some years*. B to L went to the services which had run throughout the war, plus those already restored, M, N and O were suspended services which were restored in June 1919 and so on. T to W were completely new services opened in late 1919 and early 1920. 'A' was used later for a new Aldershot–Alton service, starting in June 1920.

The scope of the parcels service was widened to include general goods, although special arrangements had to be made for items weighing more than 56 lbs. When a bus service from Haslemere to Guildford was reintroduced in September 1919, it was advertised that 'This service will provide accommodation for carrying milk churns and farm produce'. In later years the use of vans and the local delivery elements of the parcels service were abolished, and customers had to collect their own parcels from the agent or office.

The Guildford–Dorking service (Service S) was resumed in September 1919, with four journeys on weekdays and two on Sundays from Guildford station to the 'White Horse' in Dorking High Street. However, since Dorking had been agreed with the London General Omnibus Company as a boundary town, the operation of services onward to Leatherhead now became the province of that company. Nevertheless, on 1 August 1920 an increased A&D service of six journeys on weekdays only was extended to the LBSCR station (Dorking North). The service expanded rapidly: on 18 June 1922, two of the journeys in each direction were extended to Aldershot station, and in the following year the frequency was stepped up to hourly and most journeys ran through between Dorking and Aldershot.

For a time after the end of the war, the goods services continued both for private hire and on scheduled runs, and in the spring of 1919 another route from Aldershot to Basingstoke via Farnham, Crondall and Odiham was advertised. However, during 1920 the wartime camps at Bramshott and Witley were run down and the company's offices closed. The related contracts and the Haslemere carrier business naturally diminished, and in April 1920 17 3-ton motor lorries, 10 5-ton Fodens and two 3-ton Fodens – the surviving half of the original goods fleet – were advertised for sale, although still in service at the time. In fact, no offers were received, and the under-employed goods fleet soldiered on. A record exists of timber haulage in Gloucestershire and Monmouthshire during this period, and of transport of hops from the Crondall area to the Hop Exchange in London.

In February 1920, the company ventured into a new area, when an attempt was made to establish local services around Basingstoke. Up to that time, three journeys each way had been operated daily from Aldershot to Basingstoke via Church Crookham as service L. Now a vehicle was outstationed at Basingstoke to work the first of four runs to Aldershot, and each one arriving from Aldershot ran two or more short trips to Cliddesden (service W) or Old Basing (service V) before embarking on its return journey. An office was opened in London Street and it appeared as though A&D had come to stay. Yet by the end of the year the local services had ended and by the spring of 1921 the office and the services (passenger and goods) to Aldershot were also abandoned. It was almost two years before the green buses reappeared in Basingstoke, on a new route from Aldershot via Farnham (service 7).

This rapid reversal of policy was the result of a serious cash flow situation having arisen towards the end of 1920. A new issue of shares was raised, for sale as quickly as possible, and in February 1921 an Emergency Committee was set up to report to the Board on possible economies. Four weeks later, a variety of proposals were accepted for urgent implementation. These included the closure of the Basingstoke activities, the not unexpected closure of the Foden Department, a reduction of office and depot staff, small reductions in bus crews (including all 'lady conductors'), the closure of the body-building shop, and the elimination as soon as feasible of all types of bus other than Daimler Y and Dennis, with consequent elimination of spares stocks for those types no longer used.

The majority of the remaining goods business had been run down at the end of 1920, and the steam wagons and most of the surviving Belsize and other motor lorries were disposed of early in 1921, apart from those retained for the Haslemere carrier service.

The company's body-building shop, which had built the series of seven charabanc bodies, had built a single-deck

---

* In A&D parlance, 'route' was a term used to describe the roads on which a scheduled 'service' ran.

bus body (No. 2), in 1919, which was mounted on Dennis chassis HO 2334. This had unusual vertically-hinged windows, opening like the pages of a book. At the time of the closure of the department, the skeleton of a second body, No. 9, was in hand, and it was arranged to transfer it to the Farnham firm of Arnold and Comben for completion. It was mounted on Daimler Y chassis HO 8855 and entered service in May 1922. Arnold and Comben subsequently built eleven more bodies to the same basic design: their 34 seats were reduced to 26 in later life.

By December 1920 it had become obvious that the introduction of new services would very soon use up the remaining letters of the alphabet, so a change was made to numbers. The system used was initially very logical. All Aldershot-based services were covered by numbers 1 to 16, Haslemere services became 17 to 19 and Guildford services 20 to 30. Regular short workings of the longer routes, previously included under the same letter, now had separate consecutive numbers, so that 3 was a short working of 2, which was itself a short working of 1, 9 was a short of 8, 11 of 10 and so on. However, since this left no vacant numbers, new short workings or variants of the original routes had to be distinguished by suffix letters instead at an early stage, the first being 3a in October 1921. New services were allocated the lowest vacant number, if any. Otherwise higher numbers from 31 upwards were used, in order. When routes were extended, the full-distance service took the original number, while short workings to the former termini took the 'a' suffix, e.g. 14, to Alton, became 14a when the service was extended to Winchester. (The reverse process happened many years later, when in 1970 service 21a was promoted to plain 21 after the longer route

An Arnold & Comben publicity photo shows Daimler Y HO 8855. The body had in fact been started in A&D's body-building department, but was unfinished when that enterprise was abandoned, and early in 1922 the shell was transported for completion by the Farnham firm, thus becoming the prototype for eleven more generally similar bodies for A&D. The design, first used for the one bus body actually completed by A&D, had windows which opened like a page of a book, on vertical hinges.
E. Nixon collection

21 was curtailed).

Early in 1920, it had become obvious that the Chairman, William Foster, who had been knighted in 1918, and whose health had been a problem for many years, was no

A broadside view of a Daimler Y fitted with a body built slightly later by Arnold and Comben, but developed from the design handed over in 1922 by the A&D body-building team. Many of the features, such as the characteristic windows, were retained in A&C's version.
E. Nixon collection

23

Seen on a Bramshott choir outing, Daimler Y charabanc HO 6173, of 1923 vintage, shows the A&D fleetname on its side, and the bonnet number Y64, thus breaking the anonymity which was characteristic of the company's charabancs in the first half of the 'twenties. The body, which shows its number 21 in the bottom right-hand corner, had 32 seats and was of the less common type with a central gangway rather than a separate door for each row of seats. Two of these bodies were built for A&D by the East Kent Road Car Co. Originally on solid tyres, this vehicle received pneumatic tyres after two years' service.
P. Smith

Dennis built this one-off charabanc, PE 6859, for A&D in 1925. It seated 30, and had pneumatic tyres. Photographs of charabancs with the hood erected are relatively rare.
E. Nixon collection

longer able to carry out his normal duties. Board meetings had to be held at his residence, and arrangements were made in anticipation of his eventual resignation. Tom Foster was to be appointed Deputy Chairman, and a suitable person was to be sought to become Assistant Manager, to supervise the day-to-day activities. Mr G.C. Campbell Taylor was appointed in June 1920.

Sir William, active in mind but crippled in body, officially retired in April 1921, and he died three months later, on 7 July. He was given a funeral befitting the company's first Chairman. After a service at his Aldershot residence, Lindum House, "the coffin was reverently carried to a single-decker motor-bus, in which a special platform had been fitted, and in one of the vehicles of which he was so proud the last sad journey was commenced. At the head of the procession from Lindum House were the employees of the Traction Company, followed by the Police, the latter marching on either side of the vehicle, and behind walked Mr Hugh M. Foster, deceased's second son, representatives of public bodies and traders. Passing the Traction Company garage the employees lined up along the footpath. At the top of Halimote Road the drivers and conductors and Police halted and, facing inward, formed a pathway through which the motor-bus slowly passed to proceed, with a final salute, on its lonely journey to Lincolnshire.

The interment at the family seat at Moulton was attended by Jack Robart, Secretary (representing BET), Percy Rivitt, Chief Engineer, and William Shepherd, Chief Inspector."

As a precaution on this long journey through unknown rural country, the space below the coffin was packed with cans of petrol!

The company's new chairman was a 'caretaker' appointment, Mr Clarence Shirreff Bayard Hilton, from the Board of BAT, who had incidentally acted as chairman of the Guildford & District company since it was absorbed by A&D in 1914. He took up his duties on 1 April 1921, and on the same day, Mr Campbell Taylor resigned as the company's first General Manager, Major Harold Darby, was appointed. Tom Foster was duly appointed Resident Deputy Chairman, a post which he held till his death. However, he remained in daily contact with operations, and in consequence received a larger director's remuneration than his part-time fellow board members. His younger

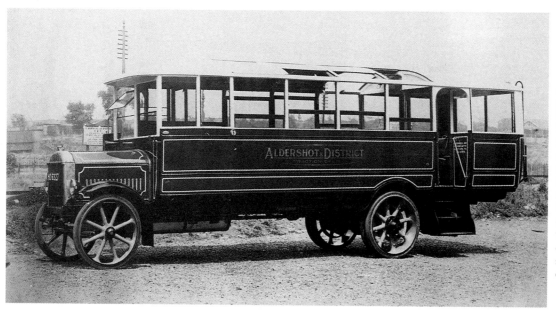

An official photograph, taken in Strachan and Brown's works yard, beside North Acton station, shows Dennis HO 6327 when brand new in July 1924. Some of the panels of the patent roll-top body have been opened to demonstrate the mode of operation.
Alder Valley

brother, Hugh Matheson Foster, became the senior partner in his father's firm of solicitors, which naturally dealt with many of the company's legal interests. After a distinguished career, which included the offices of Mayor of Aldershot and President of the Law Society, he eventually followed his father in receiving a knighthood.

New routes were opened to a number of distant outposts in the early 1920s. Of the routes from Aldershot, service 1 commenced running to Sunningdale late in 1920 and was extended to Egham in the summer of 1921: In June 1921 service 6 opened to Whitehill and some six months later three out of eight journeys were extended to Petersfield. In June 1920 service A had reached Alton, and, as 14, the route was continued to Winchester on 17 July 1922. Service J, which had run from Haslemere to Midhurst since 1913 was extended, as 19, to Chichester in the summer of 1921, and another outpost, Horsham, was reached by a new service 33 from Guildford in the spring of 1923. These towns, together with Basingstoke, Dorking and Reading, first included in A&D timetables some years earlier, thus marked out the full extent of the company's operating area at a very early stage. These boundaries with neighbouring operators were eventually consolidated by the signing of formal area agreements.

By July 1921, the company owned 55 passenger vehicles, though A&D, in subsequent years' accounts of its rapid growth, perpetuated the incorrect figure of 40 buses and 7 charabancs: this appears to have been the average number *in service* during 1921, as the number *owned* in any month was never less than 54.

Mr Hilton's time as Chairman ended on 17 January 1922, when Mr Leo Mielziner Myers took over. He had lived for many years in New Zealand, where he had achieved fame in 1903 by driving the first motor car from Wellington to Auckland. On returning to England, in 1920, he had joined the boards of several BET companies.

In March 1923, two Daimler chassis, HO 6172/3, received 32-seat centre-gangway charabanc bodies built by the East Kent Road Car Co., another BAT company. In the summer of 1922 three bus bodies had been hired from the same source and ran in their red livery on Service 6, again on Y-type chassis.

The era of Dennis domination of the fleet started in 1923 with a series of new vehicles with registration numbers scattered in the ranges HO 6221-38 and 6403-12, plus a few with Surrey (PE) registrations, presumably obtained for customers by the Dennis company. These deliveries included the 4 ton double-deck model with 32.8hp engine, the 3/4 ton and 2½ ton single-deck versions, again with the 32.8hp engine. Dennis were by now building their own engines, as they had in 1919 bought out their principal suppliers, White and Poppe, of Coventry, and had transferred production to Guildford. They also built six single-deck bodies and supplied one complete charabanc, PE 6859, in this period, but the majority of Dennis buses up to the end of 1925 had double-deck or single-deck bodies by Strachan and Brown.

This firm introduced its special roll-top single-deck body in 1922, and a proportion of the bodies delivered to A&D up to 1927 were of this type. The idea was to combine the benefits of the charabanc for fine weather with a means of rapidly protecting the passengers from bad weather, without the need to stop and erect the hood. A central spine along the roof contained rollers on to which the roof panels on either side could be wound independently.

A close connection was soon to grow up between A&D and Dennis Bros., Ltd., to the extent that all but a small proportion of the fleet from the mid-1920s until the mid-1950s came from this one factory and A&D became their prime customer. Dennis were often able to turn to A&D for evaluation of prototypes and design modifications under normal service conditions, with the advantage of their engineers being almost on the spot for any repairs and modifications which were found to be necessary.

1923 therefore saw the last batch of the reconditioned wartime Daimler Y type chassis entering service. These continued the series which had appeared in the previous year with Hampshire heavy goods registration numbers scattered between HO 6088 and 6219. Some carried single-deck bodies by Strachan and Brown (32 or 34 seats) while other bodies of similar capacity were built by Arnold and Comben.

The most important annual event in the company's calendar throughout the 1920s and '30s was the Aldershot

HO 6155, a 1922 Daimler Y with the first Strachan and Brown roll-top body bought by A&D, pauses beside Churt Post Office before starting the long climb up to Hindhead, on its long journey to Bognor on service 19.

E. Nixon collection

Tattoo, when the Army displayed its skills, equipment and pageantry to the public for a week of nightly performances in June, in Rushmoor Arena. Many school children also had the benefit of the full-dress daylight rehearsal. The arena was opened in 1922, a mile west of Aldershot, and the Tattoo moved there in 1923 from its previous venue on Cove Common. The company provided a shuttle service of buses to the Tattoo from nearby public railway stations, as well as from the Government Siding, where the special trains arrived in the late afternoon and early evening, and the buses returned the spectators to these points after the performance ended. Special combined road-rail tickets simplified the task of the bus conductors.

Military regulations did not permit buses with outward-opening doors on Army premises, so those which did not have folding, recessed or sliding doors had to queue up every evening outside the body shop to have their doors removed and chains fitted, and the reverse process happened in the early hours of the morning after the show in time for the next day's normal duty.

Another annual event in the Army's calendar was the summer camps, when each regiment migrated from its regular quarters to spend a fortnight under canvas, enabling them to take part in training exercises on unfamiliar ground. Permanent sites were laid out in the vicinity of the main garrison towns, and there were several within a few miles of Aldershot. West of Aldershot, Rushmoor, Bourley and Tweseldown camps were not near any of the regular bus routes, and from 1915 onwards these camps were provided each summer with a special service into Aldershot for off-duty travel. (In 1931 the number 57 was allocated to this service.)

Special services were naturally provided to Arena for the other major events held there, namely the Aldershot Show, a major equestrian occasion, and royal reviews of the Army. Further afield lay Tweseldown racecourse, and a frequent service was provided from Aldershot and Fleet stations during the period of the annual race meetings. Unlike the other events, these survived after the Second World War and the company continued to provide special

buses from Aldershot to Tweseldown for the rest of its existence.

The 1923 Commercial Motor Show at Olympia, London, included a Dennis double-decker, PD 8344, with a 48-seat open-top body built by Hickman. This was in A&D livery, but in addition to having more elaborate lining than usual, it carried a new style of fleet name, 'Aldershot & District' surrounded by an oval loop. This style was employed in various forms by a number of operators, but the exact similarity to the contemporary trade mark of the local coachbuilders Arnold & Comben of Farnham is noteworthy. (The unrelated Amersham & District company not only used the same sized oval, but its contemporary Dennis buses also bore an identical livery to A&D's!) The Hickman-bodied bus was the first known appearance of an A&D vehicle at the Show, but it remained unique in the fleet, as Strachan and Brown (later Strachan (Successors) Ltd.) of North Acton, London, W3 were to become the regular body builders to the Company over a number of years thereafter.

From 1923 onwards, the most prominent fleet identification number was the bonnet number, based on vehicle type, and painted near the upper edge of the bonnet side panels. Each chassis also had a number, but this was not always readily visible, especially when in later years body panels started to cover the chassis frames. With all this wealth of numbers, it is surprising to find that the registration number was, until the 1950s, used for all everyday purposes as the means of identification – a photo of the Chief Engineer's office in 1938 shows his wall chart to have used these numbers only.

A&D's neighbouring BAT company to the south, Southdown Motor Services, proposed in November 1923 that they should share in the acquisition of the business of Mr W.G. Dowle, of Chilgrove, who had established a service between Chichester, Singleton and East Dean under the name of Summersdale Motor Services. A&D decided that it did not wish to take a share in Dowle's vehicles or premises, but agreed to contribute £200 towards purchase of the goodwill. By this means, it consolidated its existing

Hickman's were the builders of this unique 48-seat body on Dennis chassis PD 8344 for the 1923 Commercial Motor Show. It was painted in A&D colours (although the corners of the lining-out were distinctly non-standard!) on the understanding that the company would buy it (and its Dennis-owned chassis) after the show. It was also given the new oval fleetname which was introduced in the same month. Although it served its full life with A&D, the coachbuilder received no further orders from the company. *Alder Valley*

In January 1925, this little 14-seat Morris charabanc OR6049 was introduced. Its chassis and capacity (and its OR registration) remained unique in the A&D fleet, and it was sold after only three years' service. Its bonnet number M2 does not imply the existence of another Morris: it means that the number 2, previously used by a Daimler CC, was now vacant. Although, in this period, bonnet numbers were as prominent as those on London buses, they were never used as a means of identification in official documents or day-to-day operations.

E. Nixon collection

The Dennis company, keen to retain the loyalty of the many purchasers of ex-service Subsidy chassis, offered a conversion to long wheelbase, at less than £300 per chassis, and in the autumn of 1924 A&D took advantage of the scheme for its 17 double-deckers of this make. New 48-seat bodies were obtained for the rebuilds – 11 from Strachan and Brown and six from Dennis – thus prolonging their lives until around 1930. HO 2320 is shown here, after receiving its new Strachan and Brown body. Note that it retained oil side lamps, although the headlamps were electric. Between 1924 and 1926 the company bought 15 new Dennis 4-ton chassis and fitted them with similar 48-seat Strachan & Brown bodies. These proved to be its last open-top double-deckers. Mr. Lansdown, the one-armed timekeeper, is the man in the suit, while George Rapley stands at the back.

Author's collection courtesy E. Clancy

territorial rights on the Midhurst–Chichester road, and obtained Southdown's agreement to the extension of service 19 beyond Chichester to Bognor. This started on 1 April 1924, when the route was also extended at the other end by taking in the long-established service 16 from Aldershot to Haslemere. Thus 19 became A&D's longest route, and remained so for many years. The Chichester–Bognor section was the first of the company's routes to offer return tickets, from 1 June 1925.

In addition to buying new buses from Dennis, the company took advantage of their scheme for improving the 'Subsidy' chassis to the standard of the post-war long wheelbase Dennis chassis. During 1924-5, all those 17 which had carried second-hand double-deck bodies were lengthened and provided with new 48-seat bodies built by Dennis or Strachan and Brown, thus prolonging their lives till the end of the 1920s.

Comfort for passengers on special services and excursions was improved from the summer of 1925 when pneumatic tyres were fitted to some of the company's charabancs. Six 30-seat Dennis buses were also delivered during the year with pneumatic tyres, and another vehicle with this feature was acquired later in the year when the

Progressive Bus Service, owned by Mr Thomas Spragg of Bracknell, was taken over by A&D's neighbouring company, Thames Valley. His almost-new Dennis, MO 6184, fitted with a 30-seat Dennis body was immediately re-sold to A&D. The purchase price included a contribution towards removal of competition along the Camberley–Yorktown road from Spragg's Reading–Camberley service, though by allowing Thames Valley into Camberley A&D had effectively relinquished any rights over the Camberley–Crowthorne route which had been briefly pioneered in 1914.

The company was seriously embarrassed on 30 June 1925, when its Secretary, Mr Jack Robart, who was of Dutch parentage and had been on the staff since before the war, was summoned to the General Manager's office to provide an explanation of an item in the cash book. On being sent to find documents to support the dubious entry, he left the building and promptly disappeared abroad. A subsequent audit unearthed other unauthorised transactions, and extradition proceedings were started. However, they were unsuccessful, and the shareholders were advised that a suspense account of £1,000 would be necessary to cover the anticipated discrepancies in the accounts.

When rival companies started to compete by providing more comfortable vehicles, A&D decided to order six 30-seat buses, on pneumatic tyres, from Dennis. They appeared in March 1925, and were based on the light 2½-ton chassis. Unusually, they had detachable-rim wheels. Being all-Dennis vehicles, they were registered in Surrey, but the precise identity of the vehicle photographed in the Dennis works is unknown.

E. Nixon collection

Chapter Five
The Bus Wars

The history of route developments over the second half of the 1920s was dominated for A&D, as for all major operators, by the financially disastrous 'bus wars'. Numerous small operators, often one-man concerns, obtained buses and in addition to pioneering new routes, frequently attempted to compete among themselves and with the major operators over existing routes. The local authorities found themselves, as licensing authorities, in the unhappy position of acting as adjudicators in situations where sympathy with the enterprising ex-Serviceman who had staked all his savings was at variance with the need to ensure public safety by preventing buses overtaking or crossing on narrow roads, being grossly overloaded, or causing obstruction by standing at bus stops until just before a competitor's bus was due to pick up passengers.

For this reason, the story of A&D's routes must now be told on an area-by-area basis, up to the time when the situation was restored to relative normality by the 1930 Road Traffic Act.

Early in 1924, Mr H.H. Wolstenholme of Hillside, Wrecclesham started running a small bus from Farnham to Rowledge. As he later complained, A&D, which had abandoned that route in November 1914, and since shown no interest, heard of his plans and hurriedly started a service a few days before his 'Blue Bus', bearing the number 10a. By taking liberties with the official timetable, A&D later ran 'chasers' to poach Blue Bus passengers waiting along the route, a few minutes ahead of Wolstenholme's times, and also indulged in fare-cutting, particularly by issuing cheap return tickets (at one time cheaper than their own single fare) to ensure that their own passengers would not choose to return by Blue Bus. Nevertheless, Wolstenholme retaliated and survived in business, using a new 14-seater Chevrolet, registered PF 1107. On 25 August 1927, however, a new company, Farnham Coaches Ltd. was registered by Mr C.W.S. Temple, with its head office at his London office, 9/10 Pancras Lane, Queen Street, EC4. He already had interests in Farnham, as the same office was also the registered office of Phoenix Coachworks Ltd., which employed Arnold and Comben, and later E.D. Abbott Ltd., to construct bus and coach bodies marketed under the Phoenix brand-name. The other director of Farnham Coaches was Mr J.R.S. Whiting, of Frensham, and the new company immediately bought out

Farnham Coaches pioneered a London express service late in 1927 with this coach, a 20-seat Gilford with a body built by Arnold & Comben. When A&D acquired Farnham Coaches on 23rd January 1928, it ordered more Gilfords to start its own express services, and later in the year it had four similar bodies, with 25 seats, built by Arnold & Comben. PH 4233 (apparently in a very light green version of the A&D livery) advertises the coachbuilder's commercial success in a carnival procession.
Author's collection courtesy M. Comben

Mr Wolstenholme and operated his Rowledge route at increased frequency in competition with A&D. More ambitious moves followed – competition with A&D's service 10 from Shortheath to Aldershot, as well as an express Farnham–London service. On 9 December, their Aldershot service (also carrying the number 10) commenced, using five old 40hp Daimler double-deckers (LP 8090, 8094, 8357, 8361 and 8363) originally built for member companies of the BAT group in 1913, and garaged at Victoria Road, Farnham. A sixth bus, LP 8364, was never licensed and was presumably obtained for spares. Aldershot Council refused to license these antiquated vehicles, so they could only pick up holders of return tickets within the borough boundaries. Farnham, with visions of having its own bus company, was not so squeamish. Fares were the same as A&D's. However, on the following day, A&D cut its return fares drastically. Farnham–Aldershot and Farnham–Shortheath became 2d return and Farnham–Rowledge (previously 6d) became 3d. Farnham Coaches immediately followed suit, later in the day. A&D then put on two 'chasers' for each rival bus, one ahead and one behind, leapfrogging at successive stops.

Without waiting for a formal licence, Farnham Coaches put on a service in mid-December from Farnham to The Bourne and Frensham. They also bought a new Gilford coach, with which they commenced their express service to London. Early in January, the unauthorised service was regularised, but within a week the bus war was over. The double-deckers came off the Aldershot route, and only the small bus on the Rowledge and Frensham routes remained. On 23 January, A&D bought out Farnham Coaches, with their nine vehicles, which, with the exception of the Gilford, PH 4233, were immediately re-sold. PF 1107 was sold back to Mr Wolstenholme, who had been acting as the local manager for the London owners, and now moved away to start again as Andover and District Motor Services. Before long the victorious A&D was able to restore fares and frequencies on the disputed routes to economic levels.

A contemporary takeover in the Farnham area was that of Mr William Avann's service from Farnham to Tilford (Avann's home village) and Churt ('Pride of the Valley'). On 23 February this was replaced by a new A&D service 16c, which was extended to Hindhead and Grayshott. For several years only small buses were permitted by the District Council on this route.

Another route won without a war was that from Farnham to Elstead and Godalming. Early in 1927 A&D let it be known that they were interested in this route, and on 1 January 1928 they took over the stage services operated by Mr D. May, of Cock Hill, Elstead, together with three small red liveried vehicles: a Fiat, a Guy and a Dennis 30 cwt. The routes became A&D's 45 (Farnham–Elstead–Milford–Godalming), 45a (Cock Hill–Milford–Godalming) and 46 (Elstead–Shackleford–Godalming). Buses continued for many years to be outstationed at May's garage, which is still in business as a service station today.

To the south and east of Guildford, Mr George Readings had started the Surrey Hills Motor Services in 1921 and pioneered several routes. However, the LGOC and its subsidiary East Surrey Traction Co. wished to consolidate in the area, and entered into a series of discussions with A&D about the possible takeover of Surrey Hills. Agreement was eventually reached for A&D to purchase the business on 16 January 1926, including the stock of five Lancia buses and a small garage at Ewhurst. The routes absorbed were Ewhurst–Cranleigh–Guildford and Guildford–Newlands Corner–Gomshall to Ewhurst and Holmwood alternately. An agreed period of five months elapsed before A&D started to integrate these routes into its own system, and during this period a Cranleigh–Horsham service was started. The route via Newlands Corner was discontinued from 15 July, as that road was claimed as East Surrey's territory. The Gomshall–Ewhurst service was consequently re-routed as A&D's 25b (Guildford–Albury–Peaslake–Ewhurst), although an existing independent concern, Messrs Trice and Smith's Tillingbourne Valley bus company continued to serve the Newlands Corner route, and another independent, A.R. Rudall's Magnet Omnibus Service, promptly opened up on the same road. Cranleigh–Horsham was given the number 38, but closed almost immediately; Guildford–Ewhurst via Run Common became 23b and the alternative route via the 'Leathern Bottle' became 23c. Having sold out, Mr Readings moved to Cheltenham, where he founded the well-known Black and White Motorways Company.

After further negotiations, a boundary agreement between A&D, LGOC and East Surrey was completed on 27 September 1927. This defined their respective rights in the area bounded by Dorking, Guildford and Horsham. In addition, the LGOC paid £2,500 towards the Surrey Hills purchase price and took over two of the five buses, which it probably never used. The agreement provided for joint working by A&D and East Surrey on the Guildford–Dorking route, whereby from 29 February 1928 the journeys of a half-hourly service were operated alternately by the two companies, both using the existing A&D service number 25. The A&D journeys ran through from Aldershot (service 20) while the East Surrey journeys made advertised connections at Guildford with the alternate workings of 20. At the same time a new joint service (numbered 44 by both companies) was opened over the Newlands Corner route from Guildford to Peaslake and Ewhurst, and A&D withdrew its 25b which, as already explained, had previously served these two villages via the Shalford route. Despite the established presence of A&D and East Surrey on the main road to Dorking eastward from Gomshall, Tillingbourne Valley attempted a competing service in August 1929, but the two major companies put 'chasers' on the road, and the interloper withdrew three months later. On 24 February

1930, A&D, East Surrey, Tillingbourne Valley and A.T. Brady introduced a co-ordinated timetable over the Guildford–Shalford–Albury road, and on 1 December the three former concerns and Magnet concluded a similar timetable and fares agreement for the Newlands Corner route, which was now carrying heavy day-tripper traffic to the beauty-spots of the Surrey hills.

North-west of Guildford was the rapidly-growing area of Stoughton, on A&D's main route to Woking (service 28). Although an unsuccessful West Surrey Light Railway Co. Ltd. had been authorised to build a tramway to Stoughton in 1905, no local service was actually provided until A&D commenced short workings on 1 March 1920. In 1925, A&D started to build up the frequency of service 28a in order to compete with Yellow Bus Services of Stoughton. This concern had been started by Messrs Frank Hutchins and Sydney Hayter in January 1921, to run from Guildford to Stoughton via Manor Road; A&D's 28 and 28a used the main Worplesdon Road route. To poach intermediate traffic, A&D transferred some of its workings to Manor Road, and on 11 March 1927 started no less than 36 journeys each way by this route. In addition, they started cutting fares to uneconomic levels. The Guildford Watch Committee, whose permission for the change of route had not been sought, requested better co-ordination of timetables, but the war went on for another two years, a return fare of 1d being charged over the whole distance in April 1929! However, YBS survived the competition, and in December 1929 the two operators signed an agreement on fares and frequencies, which enabled them to work these services more or less in harmony for the next 29 years.

Close to Stoughton lay the large new estate being built off the Aldershot Road, an area which became known as Westborough. Mr Arthur B. Newman, who had run his first bus in 1924, obtained a licence late in September 1927 to start a service from North Street, Guildford, to the Aldershot Road Housing Estate, via Weston Road and Beckingham Road, under the fleet name of 'Safeguard Coaches'. A&D retaliated by putting on a frequent service (20c) from 6 October, but Safeguard survived the competition. On 21 April 1929 A&D struck what should have been a mortal blow – their return fare over the full distance was cut without notice from 5d to 1d, and the headway was reduced from 20 minutes to 10 minutes. Safeguard, with only 14-seater Chevrolets against A&D's full-sized buses, could only respond with a 3d return fare. However, a sympathetic Watch Committee allowed them to extend from Westborough through Guildford Park to Onslow Village, thus attacking the termini of A&D's 27, 27a and 30. Finally, in December, agreement was reached: Safeguard was to cut back from Onslow to Guildford Park, and A&D would withdraw from Westborough as from the 18th of the month. Fares were then restored to about 1d per mile. Guildford Park continued to be served by both operators, the route being extended to Dennisville in 1936 and to Guildford Cathedral in 1963. 40 years after the agreement, Safeguard journeys on the joint route were shown for the first time in A&D's timetable for Service 27!

A bus war in the Fleet area was initiated in June 1927 when Mr Alfred J. Warren, of Atbara Road, Church Crookham, first applied for licences for Bramshott Golf Club–Fleet Station–King's Road–Aldershot and for Fleet–Bramshott–Cove–Aldershot. The application for the former was deferred, and that for the second route was refused. However, Fleet Council eventually permitted the King's Road route, though as Aldershot would not grant a license,

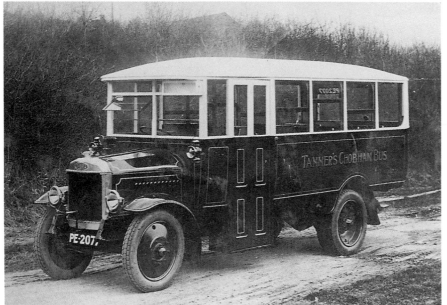

Above: Competition appeared in 1927 from A.J. Warren's buses, operating from Fleet. After a period of cut-throat conflict, a co-ordination agreement was reached at the end of 1929, which lasted until Warren's Fleet Coaching Co was taken over in 1936. RO 7188, a Guy BB, was the earliest vehicle of his white and red liveried fleet. In July and August 1933 it carried a military band 2046 miles on a tour of southern and midland counties, only three weeks after covering 1626 miles on a similar tour of the north. *R. Peskett*

Left: This pneumatic-tyred 2½-ton Dennis, PE 2077, with 20 seats, was an acquisition in October 1928, when the small fleet of Stanley Tanner, of Chobham, was taken over. It served A&D for another four years. *E. Nixon collection*

Warren had to start it with permission to issue tickets only to passengers starting at the Fleet end. Warren, who traded as the Fleet Coaching Company, appealed to the Ministry of Transport over the Aldershot council's refusal, which had enabled A&D to pioneer the route with its service 8a, opened on 17 June, just ahead of the Fleet company's intended starting date.

A&D put on two chasers for each Warren bus, and started cutting fares. A&D's initial full-distance return fare had been 1/3d, cut to 1/- when Warren opened up with a 10d fare, and before long again reduced to 3d, to the distress of Fleet's tradesmen, who were losing their customers to the shops of Aldershot. The war went on until the end of 1929, when the larger company agreed to run no more chasers, which were an expensive measure over a long period. In January 1930 co-ordinated timetables from Fleet Station to Aldershot were introduced, with a 1/- return fare. It was agreed that the service operated by A&D along the Cove Road was to cease, and there were to be connections at Crookham Cross Roads into Fleet off the Fleet company's service from Aldershot to Ewshott Camp. This

regularised the situation at that focal point, where the larger concern had for some time complained of passengers waiting in its own shelter for Warren's white buses.

The market town of Alton had been served by A&D from Aldershot in 1920 and from Haslemere in 1924, and an outstation had been established for the former service in the old fire station. As the centre for a number of agricultural villages, Alton gave scope for an operator of small buses which could pick up the sparse traffic along narrow country lanes. In 1925, Mr C.A. Clifford, of Chawton, started running his 'Ruby Queen' buses, named after the colour of his first vehicle, a Crossley. Over the next five years he experimented at one time or another with services to almost all of the nearby villages. In 1928 A&D decided to establish Alton as a centre of operations, and three new services were started on 2 May (52 to Petersfield, 54 to Medstead and Bentworth and 56 to East Tisted).

Faced with such powerful opposition, Mr Clifford immediately offered to sell his business, but A&D responded with a derisory offer of a job as a driver plus £100 for goodwill. However, as the company now controlled the most promising routes, it was content to leave Ruby Queen to operate others, albeit under the watchful eye of its inspectors, for a further seventeen years. Only one of Clifford's routes, that to Odiham, ever came into the hands of A&D, and that was only because it had been abandoned by Ruby Queen soon after the outbreak of war in 1939.

In 1931-2 a new garage was built at Alton to replace the makeshift sheds which had previously been used on the same site. A feature of Alton garage for many years was its allocation of a number of small one-man buses for these and subsequent rural services.

A&D made another attempt in 1928 to establish itself as the major operator in the Basingstoke area. Although area agreements were in force with neighbouring major operators, the area west of Basingstoke was unoccupied territory. With the backing of the locally based vehicle manufacturer, Thornycroft, a new concern, Venture Ltd. had started operations from Basingstoke in May 1926, so A&D, with only service 7 from Aldershot, had to build up rapidly. On 2 February 1928, service 52, eastwards along the London road to Hartley Row opened, and on 2 May it was extended all the way to Egham. On that day, 7 was also extended westwards to Andover, via Whitchurch, in competition with Venture Ltd. A Basingstoke outstation was established, on which two buses for 7 and one for 52 were based. Within a few months, however, Venture's new Thornycrofts triumphed, and the A&D Andover extension was abandoned, while Venture Ltd. agreed to give up its Basingstoke–Hartley Row service, henceforth to be covered by A&D's 52, cut back to this relatively short original section of the route to Egham. Thus Basingstoke became established as the boundary town between the two companies' areas, and the pattern of agreements with neighbours was complete. The A&D area was now defined within the limits Basingstoke–Camberley–Bagshot–Egham–Chertsey–Woking–Dorking–Horsham–Midhurst–Petersfield–Winchester–Basingstoke. Two routes extended, by agreement, beyond this area: services 12 to Reading and 19 to Bognor.

Following the agreement with Venture Ltd., A&D held exploratory talks about a merger, but the larger company was unable to accept that a small competitor should be rewarded with a seat for Mr Tom Thornycroft on the Board, and as other difficulties were unresolved, the talks were inconclusive. Venture tried again in 1933 to sell their goodwill for £40,000 but A&D had by then decided that it would be a poor business proposition.

Although only once subjected to the fury of a full-scale bus war, Woking's council found the management of its local operators' rivalries a time-consuming activity over a number of years. Literally every council meeting heard a report on some bus matter such as new route applications, overcrowding, unsafe vehicles and poor timekeeping. Large operators were slow to move into the area. A&D had first reached Woking in December 1914, with the short-lived Walton service operated by its Guildford subsidiary. It reappeared there in August 1916, with its route from Guildford via Brookwood and Knaphill (later service 28), and subsequently another route from Guildford, via Stoke, was extended beyond Woking to augment the service over the section to Knaphill. Thames Valley had entered Woking on 1 May 1922 with its service 3 from Ascot, which only survived for a year. There was scope for enterprising small operators to serve the growing villages and estates around the town, and throughout the latter half of the 'twenties and early 'thirties there were always a number operating.

Some were content with one owner-driven vehicle on a single route. Others, and one in particular, were more ambitious.

A&D's consolidation in the area really started in the summer of 1926, when it bought out the service run by Arthur G. Smith, of Highclere, Knaphill. This followed the route Woking–Knaphill–Brookwood–Deepcut–Blackdown and became A&D's 28b on 9 June (later 4a). The small garage at Knaphill was also purchased, and was used as a base by the new owners for the three buses taken over – two Republics and one Overland – and subsequent additions.

The next acquisition in the area occurred by accident. The bus which Mr S. Spooner of St. John's had been running from Woking, via Horsell, to Lower Knaphill was destroyed by fire. Mr J. Hampton, one of the four operators on the main Woking–St. John's–Knaphill route, provided a temporary substitute, but the goodwill of the business was sold to A&D, service 41 starting on 15 December 1926.

In 1928, which was the peak year of A&D's expansion throughout its area, one of the first businesses it purchased was that of Mr C. Ross, of Orchard Garage, Maybury. He had been running for some years on the route Woking–Ottershaw–Chertsey Church. A&D immediately extended this service to Chertsey Bridge and numbered it 48. At the same time Ross's local service from Woking to Maybury became 47. Two of his buses were taken over – a 20 seat Republic, PE 7147, and a Morris, PE 9181, which was fitted with a second-hand charabanc body.

A further takeover took effect during 1928, on 8 October, when the three small Dennis buses run by Mr Stanley Tanner, of High Street, Chobham, joined the A&D fleet. Mr Tanner had been running buses, bearing the explicit fleetname 'Tanner's Chobham Bus', for some five years, and in 1926 started a service Woking–Chobham–Windlesham (Sun Inn)–Bagshot–Windlesham (Windmill Inn). This formed the basis for A&D's 55a, though omitting Bagshot, while the shorter Woking–Chobham–Burrow Hill service became 55.

On 25 March 1929, Mr J.F. Hampton of Woking sold his service from Woking to Knaphill, which augmented A&D's service over the same road. His three small Ford buses and one Caledon charabanc were included in the deal, but were immediately sold without being given A&D stock numbers.

We must now look back a few years to trace the origins of the last major takeover of this era. On 1 April 1921, Mr James R. Fox had started operating a small Ford Model T bus between Woking and St. John's. Later, trading as J.R. Fox and Sons, he ran his maroon buses under the fleet name 'District', and later 'Woking and District'. Over the next ten years he built up a network of routes in the area bounded by Woking, Chertsey, Windsor, Bagshot and Camberley, and became the largest independent operator in the area. He had several acrimonious disputes with A&D, and built on the fears of councils at Woking and elsewhere that the larger company was becoming too powerful. The result was that A&D routes were often subjected at short notice to enterprising competition, and on several occasions the councils had to step in to regulate services in the best interests of the public. On 25 February 1926, Woking District Council, which had just printed its own area bus timetable, was incensed to find that A&D had rendered it useless by altering its timings on service 34 (Guildford–Woking–Knaphill–Bagshot) in the course of extending the service, on a hourly basis, to Camberley and Yorktown. A reprimand was issued, but worse was to follow, as Fox immediately abandoned his published timings between Woking and Bagshot, in order to run his vehicles a few minutes ahead of his rival's. Eventually the two operators were persuaded to provide an evenly-spaced half-hourly service over this section, but trouble broke out again late in 1927, when Fox started attacking the Woking–West End route by running his buses ten minutes ahead of A&D's. The latter retaliated by applying the same tactics between Woking and Bagshot. An uneasy truce was finally agreed in February 1929, and the Council's bus inspector was reported as saying he had never had such a happy time!

One useful outcome of this era resulted from A&D's observation to Woking Council that it was unreasonable to attempt to control operators in its own area in isolation, as many routes ran into neighbouring councils' areas. As a result a Through Omnibus Services Joint Advisory Committee was set up to co-ordinate the consideration of licence applications and timetable changes affecting more than one council area.

Early in 1928, A&D had planned for an expansion of its area northwards to Windsor. Two services were proposed, to start on 23 March, namely the 50 from Aldershot and 51 from Guildford, their routes converging at Ascot, where they would enter the area of the Thames Valley company. At frequencies of 8 and 7 journeys per day respectively, this involved the outstationing of two buses at Windsor. Although handbills were actually printed, a last-minute hitch occurred. Mr Sidney Garcke, who in addition to being a director of A&D, was chairman of Thames Valley, advised that the latter would vigorously oppose licensing of these services, and demanded a general discussion of territorial arrangements between the companies. Although negotiations continued, a further complication arose when, in July 1929, Fox applied for a Guildford–Windsor route, this time via Woking, and Woking Council was disposed to approve his application, even though the Joint Committee had turned it down. At the same time, the Council refused A&D permission to open a new route from Woking to Chertsey, via Six Cross Roads, which the Joint Committee had supported. Mr Fox attended the council meeting, as did A&D's top management, led by Tom Foster. The A&D team threatened to 'flood the streets of Woking with buses' and to put one ahead of every Woking & District bus on every route. This resulted in their parking buses directly outside the council offices, ready to move off just before W & D buses were due. Without the approval of the Joint Committee, A&D revised their times on the routes to Camberley and Sunningdale so as to run just ahead of W & D, and on 16 August started a completely unauthorised service 48b from Woking to Chertsey, again just ahead of Fox's times. The council told A&D to discontinue it forthwith, or else face the prospect of losing all licences when they were next due for renewal, in October. The company, they said, would have to be shown that the council, and not a large bus operator, ruled Woking. The threat succeeded, and A&D signed an agreement, withdrawing the unauthorised service.

Fox's activities in the Windsor and Weybridge area had alerted the mighty LGOC to the need to consolidate its boundary region, and a takeover of W & D offered the prospect of a significant entry into Woking. Following an initiative by A&D, an agreement was reached on 13 January 1931 between A&D, LGOC and East Surrey to buy out Woking and District. A&D, nominally the purchaser of the whole business, paid 25.6% of the £25,000 purchase price and received five buses, Tilling-Stevens B10A2 32-seaters registered VB 1272, 4060, PG 9382-4, out of the fleet of 20. The remainder, as well as the garage at St. John's, were passed over immediately to LGOC and East Surrey. Two routes, Woking–Knaphill and Woking–Camberley, went to A&D as well as the option to purchase the goodwill of the Woking–Chertsey section of Fox's Woking–Windsor route. The Woking–Camberley service became A&D's 34c and was subsequently incorporated as an extension of the existing 48a from Weybridge to Woking.

With this acquisition, A&D became the major operator in the Woking area. Over a period of six years the businesses of Smith, Spooner, Ross, Tanner, Hampton and Fox had been absorbed. A new centre of operations was now required, as the premises at Knaphill were no longer adequate, and buses were also being operated from Tanner's former base at Chobham. A temporary garage was leased in Walton Road, near the centre of Woking, in 1929, and on 1 June 1931 a new garage was opened in Goldsworth Road, capable of housing all of the area's allocation of vehicles, including the double-deckers recently supplied. Because of some low railway bridges, A&D could only make limited use of such vehicles in the Woking area.

This well-known photograph of PG 9384 is the only one known depicting one of the Woking & District Tilling-Stevens B10A2 buses taken over by A&D when the fleet was shared with the LGOC and East Surrey in January 1931. With bonnet number TS25, it served its new owners for a further six years. *Author's collection*

Chapter Six
A Period of Growth

We can now return to the more general aspects of the company's development in the second half of the 1920s.

The rapid growth of the company since the war had increased the total staff to 585 by the beginning of 1926. They were based on the main garage and workshop at Aldershot and the other garages at Guildford and Haslemere, as well as a number of outstations.

The number of vehicles owned in March 1926 was 120, all of the most recent additions being on Dennis chassis registered in Hampshire (HO and OT) or Surrey (PE and PF). These all had 'normal control' (i.e. the driver's seat was behind the engine) and most carried Strachan and Brown bodywork (48-seat double deck and 36 or 30-seat single-deck) though a few had bodies built by Dennis. New ground was broken with the delivery of a small number of low-capacity buses, commencing early in 1926 with PE 7879. These had 18-seat Strachan and

Right: To open up new rural routes, and to contain the numerous rival operators which were springing up, A&D invested in a number of 18-seat Dennis G buses in 1928. This one, OT 8598, is passing Guildford fire station, in North Street, on service 44, which was jointly operated with East Surrey on the Newlands Corner route to Peaslake. Note the guard rails under the body: these were soon to become obligatory.
E. Nixon collection

Below: PF 1793, a 2½-ton Dennis with 30-seat Strachan & Brown body, was one of six ordered early in 1926: it had pneumatic tyres from the start. It is seen during a layover at Fleet station. *E. Nixon collection*

Brown bodies on the 27.3hp Dennis 30 cwt chassis, and were to be used on rural services. In the event, they found another role as chasers during the bus wars.

The General Strike early in May 1926 had little effect on A & D, as all employees remained at work and normal services were run. However, charabanc excursions were all cancelled, and special services to London (Trafalgar Square) were operated for the benefit of those who would normally have travelled by rail. On 5 May, and for the duration of the strike, one journey was run from Haslemere, Hindhead, Thursley, Godalming and Guildford and back, and two journeys up from Farnham, Aldershot, Camberley and Sunningdale with one down journey.

1925 had seen the introduction of return tickets on the section of service 19 from Chichester to Bognor which ran

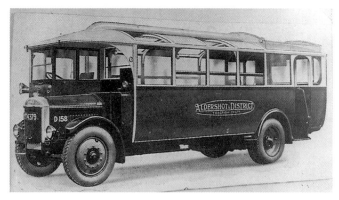

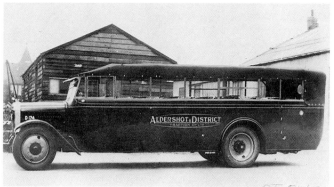

In April 1927, the Dennis E, introduced in the previous year, reached the A&D's fleet. With a dropped frame, permitting a lower floor level than previous models, it had a 5.7 litre 4-cylinder engine, and could carry up to 35 seats. The unusual location of the fuel tank, on the front bulkhead, is noticeable. OT 4379, one of A&D's first examples of the type, had a Strachan & Brown roll-top body. *E. Nixon collection*

The normal-control version of the Dennis E was the Dennis F, and was primarily used as a coach chassis. The term 'charabanc' was dropped in favour of 'all-weather coach' for these vehicles with 28-seat Strachan & Brown bodies, which appeared in the summer of 1927. OT 5410 is shown. *E. Nixon collection*

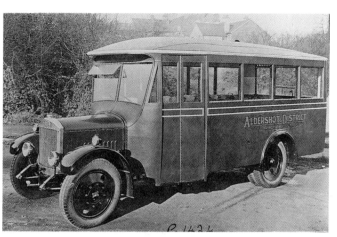

OT 6136 was one of a pair of Dennis E's placed in service in September 1927 with a new style of Dennis 35-seat body. The bonnet numbers of A&D buses were reduced in size around this time, and, naturally, were only displayed on the near side of forward-control vehicles. *E. Nixon collection*

OT 6861/2 were 20-seat dropped-frame Dennis G buses introduced at the end of 1927. Their bodies were built by Hoyal, and were A&D's only examples of the fabric-on-plywood construction commonly used in the motor car industry.

E. Nixon collection

over a road served by the neighbouring Southdown company, with interavailability of tickets. From September 1926, cheap day returns were offered over certain sections of a number of A & D routes. Many more became available in the latter part of 1927, and those costing over 2/6d were made valid for one month. In the spring of 1928 all returns were given the same longer validity.

From 1927 onwards, a through ticket arrangement was made with the Southdown company to facilitate travel to Worthing, Brighton, Bognor and Southsea by normal stage services. Advertised connections were made at Horsham for Worthing and Brighton (off Service 33), at Hindhead and Haslemere for Bognor (off 21 or 24) and at Petersfield for Southsea (off 6 and 24). By 1930 a similar arrangement was made with Hants & Dorset, to enable passengers off Service 14 to change at Winchester for Southampton.

A tragic accident gave A & D a new route when, in February 1927, Mr Frederick Pullen, the owner-driver of the "Brownie" bus from Guildford to Compton and Puttenham via Peasmarsh was fatally injured in a collision in fog with a contractor's lorry. A replacement service provided by A & D was included within its existing service 31a (over a different route) but was eventually given its own number, 31b, in 1929.

In March 1927, the company launched TEDS – the Traction Excursion Deposit Scheme. This was designed to enable prospective users of the summer excursions to pay by instalments. Cards with spaces for forty 6d gummed stamps were provided. These stamps were cancelled when the excursion was booked and a special exchange ticket issued for the journey.

In 1927, pneumatic tyres became obligatory on all new buses, together with four-wheel brakes. A & D's new intake for the previous year had included six pneumatic-tyred Dennis 2½-ton vehicles, but the ten larger newcomers were still on solid tyres. In November 1926, the decision was taken to start re-equipping the existing fleet, and by April of the following year, instructions covering all remaining single-deckers had been given. The first double-deckers were converted in November 1927, and by the end of March 1928 all 220 buses were on pneumatic tyres. The shareholders were proudly informed that theirs was the first double-deck fleet in the whole country to be thus equipped. From 1 October 1928, the speed limit for pneumatic-tyred buses was raised to 20 mph.

Most of A & D's new vehicles for 1927 were based on the Dennis E and F chassis, which had a dropped frame, allowing the floor level to be lower than on earlier models. The F model had normal control, and six delivered in 1927 had 28-seat Strachan & Brown coach bodies fitted with folding canvas roofs. Six more appeared in 1928. The Dennis E had forward control, with the driver sitting beside the engine, and all A & D's examples were fitted with bus bodies. The first batch delivered, OT 4377-9, went into service on the Winchester route (14) in April 1927. The Fs only lasted for four years as coaches, as in 1931-2 new chassis frames were obtained to convert them to Es and new Strachan bus bodies were fitted. A third new chassis introduced in 1927 was the Dennis G, which succeeded the 30cwt model as the basis for small buses of 18-20 seat capacity. These large purchases of 1926-27 expanded the fleet to a total of 158, including 18 coaches and charabancs, by the summer of 1927.

A new garage was built at Guildford in 1927 in Woodbridge Road to replace the old building close to the town centre in Onslow Street. Meanwhile a series of extensions had been carried out at Aldershot; new offices were opened in 1922-4, followed by a body and paint shop in 1927 and additional garage space in 1926 and 1929. These provided the central services necessary for the expanding fleet. Only minor engineering work was carried out at the other garages.

On 3 January 1928, the *London Gazette* listed the Aldershot & District Traction Co. Ltd. as recipients of 'a Warrant of Appointment to His Majesty King George V in the Royal Mews Department, with Authority to use the Royal Arms'. The company was described in the award as 'Road Transport Contractors', although the interpretation which it used in its publicity material became 'Public Service Vehicle Operators'. The application was in respect of the conveyance of members of the Royal Household from Windsor Castle to the Royal Ascot race meetings. (Incidentally Dennis Bros received Warrants in 1925 for the supply of a 30cwt van to the Royal Household and in 1928 as suppliers of motor mowers to Windsor Castle).

1928 was the peak year for expansion of the company, by opening new routes and by acquisitions. One of the most significant innovations was the commencement of express services to London. Although a daily charabanc to Hyde Park Corner had been tried in September, 1919, A&D took no further interest until other operators started limited stop services from Farnham and Aldershot towards the end of 1927. On 26 September South London Coaches (E. Burningham & Co. Ltd., Head Office 137 Elephant Road, London SE17, and depot at nearby Avonmouth Street, SE1) inaugurated a service of four coaches per day by providing three days of free travel. Their route was Farnham–Aldershot–Farnborough–Charing Cross (Embankment). As mentioned in the previous chapter, in the middle of December Farnham Coaches had bought a new vehicle, a 20-seat Gilford, with a body built by Arnold & Comben, and started running Farnham–London. This demonstrated the market potential, and when it took over the firm, A&D started its own express service on 28 January

With a large number of ex-servicemen on the staff, the company's sports teams were very active. Their most successful football season was 1927-8, when they won the Surrey Senior League Charity Cup, the Surrey Senior League Championship and the National Tramway Shield. Surrounding these three trophies are: (back row) Percy Rivitt, O. Evans, 'Rip' Coyne, B. Williamson, E. Varney, H. Wadsworth, G. Thompson, C. Clarke, Major H. Darby; (front row) B. Evans, H. Crossley, J. Bicknell, 'Punch' Applegate.

Author's collection

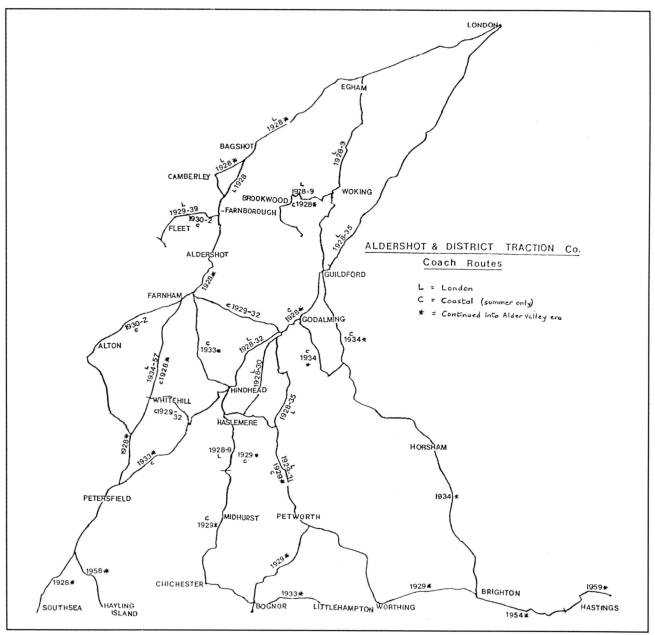

Map labels (Aldershot & District Traction Co. Coach Routes):

LONDON
EGHAM
L 1928 *
BAGSHOT
1928-9
L 1928 *
CAMBERLEY
L 1928
WOKING
L 1928-9 c 1928 *
BROOKWOOD
L 1929-39
-FARNBOROUGH
1930-2 c
FLEET
ALDERSHOT
L 1928-35
GUILDFORD
1928 *
FARNHAM
c 1929-32
1928 *
GODALMING
c 1934 *
1930-2 c
ALTON
c 1933
1928-32
c 1934
L 1934-57 c 1928 *
WHITEHILL
c 1929-32
L 1928-30
HINDHEAD
HASLEMERE
1928-35 L
1928
1933 *
c
1928-9 L
1929 *
c
1929-31 L c *
HORSHAM
PETERSFIELD
c 1929 *
MIDHURST
PETWORTH
1934 *
1929 *
1958 *
1928 *
CHICHESTER
1933 *
BOGNOR
LITTLEHAMPTON
WORTHING
1929 *
BRIGHTON
1959 *
SOUTHSEA
HAYLING ISLAND
1954 *
HASTINGS

ALDERSHOT & DISTRICT TRACTION Co.
Coach Routes
L = London
C = Coastal (summer only)
* = Continued into Alder Valley era

1928 over a route Bordon–Farnham–Aldershot–Farnborough–Bagshot–London. On 13 February a Camberley–London express service started, and on 25 April these two services were combined into a single Farnham–Aldershot–Farnborough–Camberley–Bagshot–London service, initially at a frequency of four journeys per day.

In A&D's other main area of operations, 'Cheap Day Excursions' by saloon motor coach were advertised for Wednesdays and Thursdays only from Haslemere, Godalming and Guildford to London, in January 1928. A special feature of the winter coach operations was the provision of rugs for each passenger! On 14 March, these excursions were expanded into regular express services, each running once daily. One ran from Grayshott via Hindhead, Thursley, Milford, Godalming and Guildford, and the other was from Haslemere via Ramsnest, Chiddingfold, Wormley, Witley, Milford, Godalming and Guildford, to Trafalgar Square. On 1 April, London Coastal Coaches Ltd. opened a coach terminal at Lupus Street, Pimlico, and soon afterwards the A&D coaches were diverted to it.

The new express services were marketed with the slogan 'Travel first-class at less than third-class fare', and to start them, the company ordered six new normal-control 6-cylinder Gilford coaches, fitted with luxurious 20-seat bodies from Strachan and Brown (OT 7917/20/1, 8375-7). Two months later, four more were ordered for use on coastal services, but this time the bodies were from the local coachbuilder, Arnold and Comben. These were 25-seaters (OT 9150/2, 9351/2), and were virtually identical to PH 4233, which had been taken over from Farnham Coaches. A special livery was devised for these coaches – cream, with a green relief at the waistband. The Haslemere area express services employed Dennis F coaches.

In an effort to balance the loading of these services, which was primarily up to London in the mornings and return in the afternoons and evenings, special 'rambler' tickets were made available for travellers in the opposite direction. For 2/6d more than the normal day return fare, they could have total freedom of all of the company's stage routes for the day. This was a spectacularly unsuccessful venture, and was withdrawn after 18 months, during which precisely three tickets were issued.

For the introduction of A&D's express services to London in 1928, Strachan and Brown built six luxurious 20-seat coach bodies on Gilford chassis. They had doors at both front and rear, and had curtains to their windows. This unidentified example was photographed in the coachbuilder's yard at Acton. Success was their downfall: just two years later they were replaced by larger coaches and were sold to the East Kent company. (In the process, the General Manager was reprimanded for pre-empting a board-room decision!) *E. Nixon collection*

To provide cheap travel for day trippers to the south coast, a once-daily express service was inaugurated for the 1928 summer season, starting on 21 July, from Camberley, Aldershot and Farnham to Portsmouth and Southsea. This was in addition to the normal programme of coach tours, which went to various coastal resorts in Hampshire and Sussex two or three times a week.

On more than one occasion during the rapid expansion in the 1920s, suggestions were made that 'Aldershot and

Three months after the Strachan and Brown coaches arrived, four more coaches appeared with Arnold and Comben bodies, also on Gilford chassis. These, however, had 25 seats, and introduced a new coach livery of cream with green reliefs, which was not perpetuated. OT 9351 is shown at Aldershot garage. *E. Nixon collection*

District' was becoming out of date as the company's title. In January 1928 the Registrar of Joint Stock Companies received a formal proposal to rename the firm 'The Southern District Traction Company Ltd'. After making the usual enquiries, the Registrar refused the application, and the familiar name therefore survived.

On 19 November 1928 a new Farnham Coaches com-

OT 7923, a Dennis G with 18-seat Strachan & Brown coach bodywork, arrived in time for the summer of 1928. However, it and its two sisters only lasted for four years with A&D.
T. Childerhouse

For many years, the 'White Swan' at Aldershot ran a summer outing. On 10 June 1928, this line-up, headed by 36-seat Dennis OT 4380, extended beyond the right-hand edge of the picture.
E. Nixon collection

In 1929 the Dennis E model was updated as the EV, with a new design of bonnet and radiator shell. OU 1117 was one of four with 32-seat Dennis bodywork, shown here at the Dennis works.
E. Nixon collection

pany, started by Mr L.G. Hillier of 482 Harrow Road, Paddington, and having no connection with the earlier company of the same name, put on four coaches per day on A&D's London route, but omitting Camberley. In the following May this became six journeys daily via Camberley, with the first inward and the last outward journey extended to Bordon. By then, the word 'Blue' had crept in, in small print, between 'Farnham' and 'Coaches', to help overcome any prejudice. By April 1930 the 'Blue' was in large print and from the 12th of the month a co-ordinated timetable was introduced by the two companies, A&D's service having been recently increased when South London Coaches had withdrawn from the route. Thereafter alter-

BY APPOINTMENT

NATIONAL SOCIETY FOR DISABLED MEN

ALDERSHOT & DISTRICT
TRACTION Cº LTᴰ
(IN ASSOCIATION WITH THE SOUTHERN RAILWAY COMPANY)

EXPRESS
DAILY SERVICE
by
LUXURY COACHES
between

Haslemere, Grayshott, Beacon Hill, Hindhead, Thursley, Milford, Godalming, Guildford, Ripley

and

LONDON

Summer Time Table

Commencing WEDNESDAY, MAY 14ᴛʜ
1930

For Booking Offices and Agents, and particulars of Through Bookings by Coach and Omnibus, see back page.

NOTE.—This service provides a direct and cheap means of travel for persons wishing to visit the County Sanatorium at Milford, The Holy Cross Sanatorium at Haslemere, and the Royal Horticultural Society's Gardens at Wisley.

Left: Strachan's also produced a body design for the Dennis EV in 1929, with 32 seats. This is a works photograph of OU 1119.
Alan B. Cross

Below: On 27 October 1934, Farnham Blue Coaches finally came into A&D's possession after several years of co-ordinated operation on the Farnham–London express service. The majority of the fleet consisted of Gilford 168OT coaches, with 28 or 30 seat bodies built by the local works of E.D. Abbott, using the Phoenix trademark. GF 5203, GK 8611 and GX 1240 are paraded in the coachbuilder's yard, half a mile from the Farnham Blue garage at Wrecclesham. The Gruss air springs either side of the radiator were characteristic of this model.
E. Nixon collection

nate journeys of a half-hourly service were worked by A&D and Farnham Blue, with the latter's office, formerly shared with South London Coaches at Town Hall Buildings, Farnham, as the starting point for both. The Farnham Blue terminus in London was Bush House (Aldwych).

The London destination of many of A&D's coaches was changed to Great Scotland Yard from 1 May 1929, though in 1930 restrictions were imposed on coaches in central London and the terminus reverted to Lupus Street. From 10 May 1929 the service from Guildford was augmented to an hourly frequency, to match a competing service which Mr Charles Dobbs' Skylark Motor Coach Company had started on 14 December 1928. However, there was not sufficient traffic for both hourly services, and A&D's frequencies were cut back as part of their economy measures later in the year. Over the years 1928-30 a variety of other express service routes and starting points were tried: Fernhurst and Camelsdale (29 October 1928); Worplesdon, Pirbright, Brookwood and Woking (11 June 1928); Petworth, Chiddingfold, Witley, Milford, Godalming, Guildford and Ripley (11 May 1929); Church Crookham (Wyvern), Fleet, Cove, Farnborough, Frimley and Bagshot (8 July 1929) and Crookham Village (12 April 1930). All these routes had only one or two coaches each

way per day. The Woking district's service was unable to compete with the fast rail service from Woking, and did not last long. During the summers of 1930 to 1932 more journeys appeared on the Haslemere route, but thereafter all but the Farnham services were trimmed down, and the Petworth service ceased in September 1931.

To cover these expansions of the express network, more coaches of higher capacity, on Dennis chassis, were obtained from Arnold and Comben. Early in 1929, six 30-seat bodies were built for Dennis E's OU 1096-1101. They had to be modified before entering service, as it was discovered that their interior headroom was less than the latest regulations demanded. This also applied to the five Gilfords already in use, which were 5ft 4in instead of the new minimum of 5ft 10in in height. Later in the year, six more coaches on Dennis EV chassis (OU 1120-5) went into service. These had various seating capacities (27, 31 or 32) and were equipped with lavatories – a feature which was not, however, perpetuated on subsequent coaches built for the company. All of these coaches supplied in 1929 appeared in the familiar dark green and white livery.

In the Budget of 1928, a petrol tax of 4d per gallon was imposed, to the distress of all public service operators. The immediate reaction of a number of companies, includ-

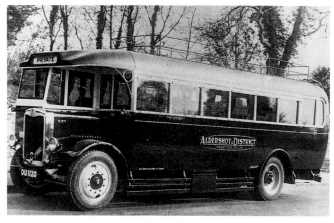

All of the 1929 Dennis EV's intended for coach use were bodied by Arnold and Comben. This one is OU 1120, with 32 seats and a rear entrance, but other versions had 31 or 27 seats, and some were provided, for a short time, with toilets. *E. Nixon collection*

In the summer of 1928, A&D broke new ground by introducing its first two covered-top double-deckers, OT 9062 and OT 9350. These had open-staircase 56-seat Strachan & Brown highbridge bodies on Dennis H chassis. Note the spare wheel stowed under the stairs! In its later guise, as a grey-painted treecutter, OT 9062 was familiar to everyone who used the roads in the A&D area, and its withdrawal in 1949 occasioned a memorial paragraph and cartoon in the 'Aldershot News'. *E. Nixon collection*

The Dennis E rapidly became the mainstay of A&D's single-deck fleet. OU 1091 had a 31-seat Dennis body, and was delivered in February 1929. The driver on this occasion was Billy Morey, and the photo was taken at the Bramshott terminus of a short working of service 24 (Guildford–Petersfield). This was one of the last 4-cylinder Dennis E's: from the following month onwards, deliveries were all of the 6-cylinder ES variant. *E. Nixon collection*

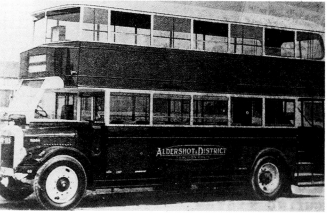

The next covered-top double-deck Dennis H's entered service in May 1929, and had 48-seat bodies built by Hall Lewis, of Park Royal. The 22 upper-deck seats were arranged in a herringbone fashion, and were described in the press release as 'comfortable armchairs'. The enclosed staircase gave the design a much more modern appearance. The photo shows OU1113: its companion OU 1112 did not have the V-front to the upper deck. All of the H's produced from 1929 onwards had 6-cylinder engines, and were designated HS. *Author's collection*

ing A&D, was to apply a surcharge to all fares until such time as they could be properly recalculated and approved by the authorities. Passengers had to obtain an additional ½d petrol tax ticket with every single fare below 1/-, and 1d extra was payable above this level. Returns were not affected. Mr Winston Churchill made a scathing attack on 'profiteering' bus companies, but it later emerged that he had mistakenly thought that these surcharges were levied on a per mile basis.

The Dennis H 30hp double-deck chassis was used for A&D's first covered-top double-decker in 1928. This vehicle, OT 9062, had a 56-seater open-staircase body by Strachan & Brown, which was unlike the A&D double-deckers of subsequent years, in that it had a full-height body. The company's routes were soon recognised as being more suited to the operation of 'lowbridge' vehicles, with about one foot less headroom. Ironically, OT 9062 was destined to spend at least half of its existence with an open top, as it was adapted for use as a treecutter in the late 1930s, and lasted in this form until 1949. Its highbridge sister, OT 9350, was withdrawn in the mid-30s.

At the height of the bus wars and after the period of most rapid expansion, Mr Darby resigned as General Manager, for undisclosed personal reasons, in November 1928. As a token of the Board's continuing goodwill, he was granted a full year's salary on leaving. With Tom Foster's past experience readily available the Board was in no hurry to make a new appointment, and it was not until October of the following year that it was announced that the new General Manager was to be Mr James Boothroyd Parker, previously the holder of the same post with the Tees-side Rail-less Traction Board.

Right: Another 1929 body design tried on the Dennis HS chassis was this rather old-fashioned looking product from Strachan, mounted on OU1110, and providing 48 seats.

E. Nixon collection

Below: The busiest time of the year for A&D was the week of the Aldershot Tattoo in June, when up to 70 buses were provided to shuttle spectators from railway stations to Rushmoor Arena. These seven buses lined up to meet a train at Government Siding are led by Dennis EV OU 1802, which entered service at the time of the 1929 Tattoo. It had a 32-seat Strachan body. *Aldershot Military Museum*

A small operator, Mr A. Payne of Ewshott, handed over his Ewshott-Farnham licence on 16 March, 1929, and his service became A&D 38. In May of that year, the next two covered-top double-deckers (Dennis H. OU 1112/3) appeared on the Guildford–Godalming road, with bodies built by Hall, Lewis & Co. of Park Royal, the forerunners of the better-known Park Royal Vehicles Ltd. These had a unique upper-deck seating arrangement with side gangways and 22 seats arranged in herringbone fashion, in pairs along the centre, to give passengers a more all-round view. There were 26 seats on the lower deck. In June the first of the lowbridge Dennis Hs from Strachan's coachworks, OU 1108-11, arrived, with more conventional seating but again with side gangways on the upper deck. The chassis were actually the HS model, with a larger 6-cylinder engine, whereas the first two Hs had four cylinders. Around this time the company sounded out each of the local authorities in its area to ascertain their views on the acceptability of longer double-deckers, either 30ft 6-wheelers or 27ft 6in 4-wheelers. A few councils such as Farnham offered no objection, but most did, and no such vehicles were ever purchased.

Following the success of the previous year's express service to Portsmouth and Southsea, a full range of daily coach services was inaugurated on 10 May 1929, to operate until the end of the holiday season. Other routes were served at weekends or Bank Holidays only. The principal towns of the A&D area fell into convenient groups, and most could be served by the two sets of services starting at Camberley (Frimley, Farnborough, Aldershot and Farnham) and Brookwood (Knaphill, Woking, Stoke, Guildford and Godalming). Grayshott, Hindhead, Haslemere and other picking-up points towards the south of the company's area were served by whichever of these suited the ultimate destination. Through fares were offered from those places not on any of the coach routes which had early connecting buses. The coastal towns involved were initially Brighton, Bognor, Portsmouth and Southsea. Littlehampton was added in the 1933 season, and in the same year the Camberley–Brighton coaches were re-routed via Haslemere and Petworth. This was to enable them to pick up and set down en route at Worthing, as Safeguard had established a prior claim to licences to Worthing from the Guildford and Godalming districts. From 1935 onwards, this service was extended to Eastbourne on Saturdays, Sundays and August Bank Holiday.

One group of towns and villages not provided for in the main scheme of things was Fleet, Crookham, Crondall

Left: Although A&D had long since given up its road haulage work, it embarked its most unusual load on 14th September 1929, when the Dennis chassis HO 6278 went to Calshot to collect the Supermarine S6 seaplane which had just won the Schneider Trophy. It was destined for the North East Coast Exhibition at Newcastle. The driver came through Aldershot at dead of night, to pick up his luggage, but on arrival at his destination he found his load to be highly controversial. It was installed in the pavilion of a local newspaper, the 'Evening World', and rival newspapers made much of the 'scandalous' charge imposed on those who wished to see the aircraft which, in their view, was already the property of the general taxpaying public. *Author's collection*

Below: In 1930, the small Gilford coaches used on the express services to London had to be replaced by larger vehicles, and a batch of seven was bought from TSM (as Tilling-Stevens Motors had just been redesignated). They had 30-seat dual-entrance bodies, and the high-backed coach seats are clearly visible. OU 6243 is standing in Castle Street, Farnham, and several of the seats can be seen to have the tartan rugs, supplied for passenger comfort before heaters were introduced, draped over them.

E. Nixon collection

and Alton, which from 1930 to 1932 had their own service to Portsmouth and Southsea. In 1933 this was replaced by a special feeder service linking Crookham and Fleet into the existing coaches calling at Aldershot (Queen Hotel). The 1935 season saw the introduction of a series of coaches starting from Hindhead, Grayshott and Haslemere to all destinations and from Guildford, Bramley and Horsham to Brighton only, to take the load off services starting further north. The resulting pattern continued to operate until the end of the 1939 season.

Vehicles used on these 'express services to the coast' were normally drawn from the ranks of the ordinary stage vehicles, which were always upholstered and trimmed to a very high standard. These were supplemented by the older coaches displaced from time to time by the arrival of new stock for the more exacting London services.

After a year of heated debate as to whether the railway companies should operate their own buses, the Southern Railway – successors to the LSWR – decided instead to acquire almost a one-third interest in A&D, exactly equal to the holding of BAT, which had amalgamated with its part-owner Thomas Tilling Ltd. in May 1928 to become Tilling and British Automobile Traction Ltd. The railway company paid 26/6d for each £1 share. Each of the principal shareholders now owned £62,112 out of the £200,000 issued ordinary capital. Two additional board members were appointed by the Southern Railway. The agreement took effect from 1 January 1930, when a Standing Joint Committee was inaugurated, with two members each from the SR and A&D. Early in 1931 this led to the introduction of combined road-rail tickets to popular destinations not served by rail – Hindhead, Frensham, Chobham, Knaphill, Hog's Back and Pirbright and Blackdown Camps. At the same time, interavailability of road and rail return and season tickets was arranged for certain routes which paralleled main railway lines: Aldershot–Farnham–Alton–Alresford–Winchester (excluding Aldershot–Farnham journeys) and Guildford–Godalming–Milford–Witley–Haslemere–Petersfield. A small supplementary fare was usually payable for return by rail, while for return by road (in those days invariably the cheaper form of public transport) an exchange ticket was issued for no extra charge or, in later years, for a small flat-rate fee.

It was with no little relief that the established p.s.v. operators welcomed the provisions of the 1930 Road Traffic Act, with regard to the licensing of routes, vehicles and crews, which had previously been subject to the individual local authorities and police forces, as we have seen. Until the passing of the new Act, differences in outlook between neighbouring councils had led to many anomalies. A&D's first entry into Guildford and Godalming in 1914 and Fleet Coaching Co's. difficulties in Aldershot in 1927, in both of which cases the operators were not allowed to issue tickets within the destination areas, were typical of the route licensing problems. Some authorities were also particularly vigilant over local vehicle licenses. In January 1928, A&D had been called to account by Farnham council for the use of unlicensed vehicles. Although 148 buses were licensed to run through Farnham, a report had been submitted that some unlicensed ones had been spotted. Having expressed due contrition, the company's spokesman pointed out the value of flexibility – surely it was preferable to transfer a vehicle from another area than to cancel a service altogether because the licensed bus was not available.

The Act set up Area Traffic Commissioners to take over all the licensing functions, and thereby permitted more coherent planning. Most of A&D's activities fell into the South Eastern Traffic Area or the short-lived Southern area except for those in Guildford and further east, which came under the Metropolitan Area. The index letters for the SE and Metropolitan areas, K and N respectively, became familiar to the public as the prefix to the license numbers worn by the company's bus crews.

Another welcome measure under the 1930 legislation was the raising of the speed limit for coaches from 20 to 30mph. This gave recognition to the improvements in brakes and suspension introduced with recent models.

By removing the freedom of any operator to alter routes, fares or frequencies at will, the Act ended the era of virtually uncontrolled 'bus war' competition. In the financial year 1928-29, the A&D accounts had shown a loss of £5,109 and no dividend was paid. This was largely attributable to the costs of combatting competition by use of chasers, uneconomically low fares and high service frequencies.

The reduction of these costs of competition, combined with economies such as the ending of the less promising express services and the imposition of a charge of 1d for timetable booklets, which had previously been free, enabled the accounts to show a small profit in 1929-30, although increased provision for depreciation on the expanding fleet meant that the dividend was missed for a second year.

By the summer of 1930, the company's fleet numbered 236 vehicles: 160 single-deckers, 21 covered-top double-deckers, 21 open-toppers, 19 coaches and 15 charabancs. With the withdrawal in the previous year of the last surviving Daimlers, the single and double deck fleet was now entirely of Dennis manufacture. Only among the coaches were any other types, mostly Gilfords, to be found, and in fact all of the Gilfords were sold to the East Kent Road Car Co. at the end of November. By then however, another new make had been introduced when the first batch of Tilling-Stevens B10A2 vehicles was delivered to replace the Gilfords on the London service. These were fitted with 30-seat Strachan coach bodies and were seven in number (OU 6241-7). They were followed in 1931 by twelve (OU 7944-55) with similar bodies fitted out as 31-seater buses.

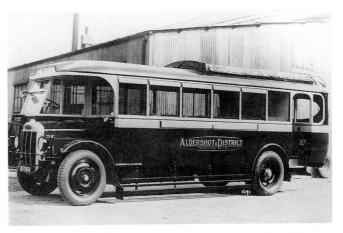

The stage carriage version of the Tilling-Stevens B10A2 was supplied to A&D in 1931: twelve of these 31-seaters were delivered, registered OU 7944-55. OU7954 is shown: its chassis number 562 is visible ahead of the front wheel, as well as its bonnet number TS18. This particular bus remained in use on workmen's services during the war, whereas most of its companions were consigned to open storage.   *Alan B. Cross*

After less than four years service, the Dennis F coaches of 1927-8 were all converted for use as buses. This involved alteration to forward control (i.e. to Dennis E specification) and the fitting of 30-seat Strachan bodies similar to those on the contemporary TSM buses. OT 4951, in its earlier guise, is illustrated in the 'Accidents' section of this book.   *E. Nixon collection*

The fleet of 20 was completed by the delivery in 1932 of CG 763 – a 32-seater bus, built for the Commercial Motor Show on the understanding that A&D would subsequently purchase it.

For some reason, the second major vehicle manufacturer in the A&D's area, Thornycroft, of Basingstoke, never succeeded in selling its products to the company. In 1931 a model BC demonstrator, with forward control and a 32-seat Strachan & Brown body, OU 4678, was painted in A&D livery, but Thornycroft's were told that although the company was prepared to try it, the likelihood of its being accepted was so small that it would be cheaper for it to be

Above: Two batches of Dennis HV double-deckers were acquired in 1930 and 1931 respectively, all having 48-seat Strachan bodies with enclosed stairs. OU 4322 is standing in Guildford station yard, which was used for layovers when the restricted kerbside site in nearby Park Street was used as a terminus. The driver's door has been removed for the summer. Dennis PH 1105 is in the background. *E. Nixon collection*

Left: A&D added to its fleet of TSM buses by the purchase in 1932 of CG 763. This had been exhibited in the company's livery at the 1931 Commercial Motor Show on the understanding that A&D would buy it afterwards. Its body was of a transitional pattern between the Strachan design for the earlier TSM's and that which was used for the numerous Dennis Lancets of 1932 onwards. When the author first explored the Halimote Road dump in 1944, the centre section of this body was in use as a shed, and the chassis was being cut up for scrap. *E. Nixon collection*

repainted in some other colours at A&D's expense. It went back to the makers and eventually became No. 21 in the fleet of Venture Ltd.

Changes were made in the A&D livery over this period. The 13 double-deckers delivered in March-April 1930, Dennis H's OU 4310-22, appeared in a lighter shade of green and had cream reliefs replacing the white of earlier years. Decisions over the single-deck livery took a little longer, and after experimenting with schemes including all-over green relieved by a red band, the outcome in October 1931 was a combination of two shades of green with a broad cream waistband.

The conversion of Service 14 to double-deck operation involved an extensive tree-lopping operation in the winter of 1930/31. Some vigorous complaints were received by the Council about the way in which the work was carried out without permission "by stealth, in the middle of the night (1.15 a.m.)" as Col. Butchart, of Worthy Park, put it. A farmer was awakened early one morning by the noise and called on the men to desist, as they could produce no authority. They went away, the farmer returned to bed, and

the men were later "again hacking away at the trees". An apology was extracted from the company, although they proved to have been acting within the law.

In 1931 it was announced that A&D had purchased shares to the value of £4,721 in London Coastal Coaches Ltd. which was engaged in the construction of a new covered coach station at Victoria, to replace the open park at Lupus Street. The new premises, in Buckingham Palace Road, were opened by Mr Pybus, the Minister of Transport, in March 1932, and all of A&D's express services were diverted there from 10 March.

Twenty-two more covered-top double-deckers were obtained during 1930-32, OU 6841-5, 7956-70 and CG 1313-4, again having 48-seat Strachan bodies on Dennis chassis, but for these batches the improved HV model was used. Early in 1932, A&D obtained a prototype of the new 30hp Dennis Lancet single-decker, with a 32-seat Strachan bus body (CG 477), and on 3 June a fleet of twelve with 30-seat coach bodies of similar profile started work on the London routes (CG 1317-28). A welcome innovation was piped hot water heating. Each pair of seats was staggered

Until Aldershot bus station was opened in 1933, the terminal was the kerbside of Station Road and the railway station approach. The Reading-bound bus in the foreground has a white-on-black destination indicator, while the three buses behind have black-on-white. This dates the picture, taken from Gale and Polden's roof, as not more than a few months before the bus station was built on the site to the right of the picture. *Aldershot Society*

by a few inches to allow the passenger adjacent to the gangway to have a view through the window, unobstructed by his neighbour. CG 1315/6 had similar bodies, but were fitted as 32-seat buses. For lightly-trafficked routes, ten Morris RP 20-seaters were acquired in 1932-3. These were CG 755-62 with Strachan bodies and CG 3006/7 with Abbott bodies, but they proved so disappointing that within two years ten of the new 24.8hp Dennis Ace chassis were bought and the original bodies transferred to them. Accommodation for the fleet was improved by the opening of a new garage at Hindhead on 1 June 1931 to replace the garage at Wey Hill, Haslemere, in addition to the new premises at Woking and Alton mentioned in Chapter 6.

In June 1931, Aldershot Football Club had its application to join the Third Division of the Football League rejected. In order that it could continue to run a team of Third Division standard, and reapply in 1932, several local bodies made donations towards expenses and wages. A&D contributed £25, and further donations were made in subsequent years when the team had achieved League status. An earlier scheme whereby two A.F.C. players were taken onto the A&D payroll to help the club's finances soon ran into trouble when the men had to be dismissed for poor timekeeping when employed as cleaners in the depot.

The second change in the chairmanship of the company in two years occurred in 1932. When Mr Myers resigned through ill-health in 1930 his place had been taken

by Mr Thomas Wolsey, a director of Tilling and BAT, and of several subsidiaries, who had joined the A&D board in 1928. However, he resigned altogether from the board at the time of the 1932 AGM and his place as Chairman was taken by the senior director, Mr Sidney Emile Garcke, who had already become chairman of the Tilling and BAT company and of the neighbouring Thames Valley company. His eminence in the transport business was to prove of value to A&D in several problem periods yet to come.

A small territorial adjustment took place early in 1932, resulting from the takeover of Mr B.H. Martin's service by East Surrey in April 1931. This service, Woking–Byfleet–Addlestone–Chertsey, known as the Red Bus, and using the fleet name 'Bus de Ville', had been the subject of an unsuccessful bid of £500 by A&D in July 1930, and they regarded the first mile of the route, to Maybury Inn, as their own territory. They suggested that East Surrey should therefore truncate their route, but the opposite solution was proposed when negotiations opened over the setting up of a London Passenger Transport Board – A&D's service 47 would be transferred to the new body. The transfer actually occurred ahead of the formation of the LPTB, and on 1 February 1932 London General Country Services Ltd took over the service, immediately upsetting local residents by reducing the frequency. The compensation payment to A&D was not finally settled until the main LPTB transaction was completed, though a 36-seater Dennis bus, PH

An interior view of the Strachan body of the first Dennis Lancet, CG 477, shows the provision for the conductor's equipment and parcels beyond the inset folding door, and the small passengers' luggage racks. The upholstery was patterned green. The bell cord can be seen along the roof.
E. Nixon collection

On 3 June 1932, a fleet of twelve new Strachan bodied Dennis Lancet coaches was placed in service on the London express routes and on the coastal express journeys. The first of the batch, CG 1317, was duly photographed in Foden Road for a press release. *A. Lawrence*

The luxurious interior of the 1932 Lancet coaches is clearly shown in this view: grey and black upholstery, staggered seating, individual light switches and a roof and luggage rack design which became the standard for all of the single-deck buses and coaches built for A&D over the next eight years. Piped hot water heating completed the new specification for passenger comfort. *A. Lawrence*

Right: The second Dennis Lancet bus, CG 1315, carried a Strachan body which followed the lines of the contemporary coaches. However, the door was inset, and there were six window bays ahead of it instead of five.   *E. Nixon collection*

Below: For its new batch of 20-seat buses for rural services, A&D chose the Morris RP chassis, eight of which arrived with Strachan bodies in 1932, and a further two appeared in 1933 with almost identical bodies by the Farnham firm of E.D. Abbott. The Morris chassis proved unreliable, to the extent that, in 1934, ten of the new Dennis Ace chassis were ordered, in order to re-mount the bodies. CG 3006, the first of the Abbott-bodied pair, is posed in Foden Road when new.
E. Nixon collection

1106, was transferred to LGCS in December 1932.

Competition on the outer end of the long 14 route to Winchester was brought under control in March 1932, when agreement was reached between A&D and the other three operators working between Alresford and Winchester. Mr Herbert Whapshare's Winchester and District Motor Services had been running co-ordinated short workings, shown in the A&D timetable, since April 1926, and now these two combined with Mr A.W. Vickers to buy out Mr W.R. Perry's service and set up three-way co-ordination of timetables and fares.

The Southern Railway closed its uneconomic Basingstoke–Alton branch to passengers on 12 September 1932. Although the traffic was extremely sparse, A&D used this closure as a pretext for an application to the Traffic Commissioners for a stage service over the parallel road. Opposition from Venture Ltd. was to be expected, and this infilling between two A&D outposts was not permitted by the Commissioners. The service was subsequently provided by Venture Ltd.

Tom Foster died after a short illness on 26 October 1932, and the contribution which he, his father and his brother (who had been Mayor in 1927-29) had made to the life of Aldershot was duly eulogised in the press reports and the funeral address at the Parish Church. No successor as Deputy Chairman was appointed, and his special position as a full-time director with a higher fee was never repeated.

On 1 July 1933 the London Passenger Transport Board was formed, absorbing the LGOC and its associates, and empowered to acquire all private operators within its area. One of the provisions of the Act was the drawing up of statutory, rather than negotiated, boundaries with neighbouring operators. That with A&D was drawn through Woking and Guildford. Accordingly, on 2 August 1933 three routes east of Guildford – 25 to Dorking, 27 to Merrow and 44 to Ewhurst – were handed over to the LPTB, together with the garage at Ewhurst and six buses (Dennis E OT 4743, 6136/7, 6914, Dennis G OT 8598 and Dennis H OU 1108). A&D received £1870 compensation, including the Maybury deal already mentioned.

The completion of negotiations between the LPTB and some of the independent operators within its area took a long time. One of the last to settle was W. Eggleton & Son, Ltd. of 57 Walton Road, Woking. This firm had started in the mid '20s and had become a limited company in April 1928. Its original route was Woking–Chobham–Burrow Hill, and subsequently routes to Chertsey, to Sunningdale and to New Haw and Addlestone had been introduced. By 1930, the Addlestone service was the principal one. As the Burrow Hill route lay outside the LPTB's area, it was transferred by the Board to A&D on 2 June 1934, when the business was taken over, and became 55c. One of Eggleton's five buses – Dennis GL PJ 7438 – was also handed over to A&D.

A bus station was opened by the company in August 1933 to relieve congestion in the vicinity of Aldershot Station. This was situated on railway-owned land in the angle between The Grove and Station Road, and included a combined booking/enquiry office, waiting room and staff rooms, with a separate block of toilets, which were open to the general public as a result of the council having contributed to their cost, since they replaced earlier conveniences on the same site. The roadway covered an area 120 by 162ft and provided for buses to enter from The Grove and then reverse up to one of nine gates in a chain barrier to load. Express and other services not terminating at the bus station drew up alongside the kerb on the public roads or at the exit from the terminal area. The first use of the new facility was for the annual outing provided for employees' families to the seaside, on 1 August. A regular feature of this event henceforth was the photograph of all the vehicles and persons involved taken from the roof of the printing works across the road, owned by Gale & Polden, who acted as the company's official photographers for many years. Public services from the bus station started on the following day.

During the 1930s, a number of hospitals were established in country areas to cater for long-term or chronic illnesses. Some were newly constructed, while others were converted from wartime military hospitals as the need for them diminished. By their very nature, many were inaccessible by normal public transport routes, but provision had to be made for relatives and other visitors from a distance on Sundays and other visiting days. The A&D's area contained the Surrey County Sanatorium and King George V Sanatorium at Milford, which were served from the summer of 1933 by a bus each from Milford Station, numbered 59. On 26 August 1934, service 19a started as a joint venture between A&D and the Southern Railway, from Haslemere Station to King Edward VII Sanatorium, Midhurst, with through tickets available from Waterloo. This service ceased, however, early in 1937. Brompton Sanatorium was given a regular daily service from Aldershot (5b) in 1928, but for some reason was also given a one-way journey to Ash Vale Station after Sunday visiting time during 1936-7, numbered 5c. In a rather different category was service 36, on which a bus ran on Wednesdays and Sundays only from Aldershot to Winchfield Infirmary, which had provided a home for the elderly since the days when it was a workhouse. This service started on 19 November 1933, after some argument as to whether the County Council should guarantee a minimum level of income.

In August and September 1931, Dennis EV OU 1806 had created what was believed to be a national record when in a period of 28 days it had carried the band of the 1st Battalion King's Own Scottish Borderers on a summer tour of 2,500 miles. 32 passengers and 1¼ tons of luggage were transported each day to the next engagement, the furthest north being Inverness. Apart from fuelling and tyre checks, the vehicle required no attention. It, and Driver Paget, were chosen again for an even lengthier tour a year later and the success of the venture encouraged A&D to purchase two coaches (CG 6357/8) specially equipped for such tours. They arrived early in 1934 and were similar to the London express coaches, but on the strengthened roof was fixed a long sheet metal luggage surround, capable of holding all the instruments of a military band. Similar long 'band boxes' were fitted to a proportion of each batch of buses, as well as coaches, acquired over the next three years, and the term came to be applied to all sheet metal luggage racks, long or short. The 1934 tour occupied 8 weeks and covered 3,760 miles in visiting 45 towns!

On 3 April 1934, an experimental express delivery service was started by the Head Postmaster at Farnham, by which mail could be delivered to any post office on or near an A&D bus route from Farnham. This was not the first time that the company's buses had been used to carry mail, as in May 1930, another experiment had been tried, namely the fixing of post boxes to the rear of the buses working into Farnham from Grayshott (17), Hindhead (19) and Whitehill (6) shortly after 7pm, so as to connect with the final despatches from the Farnham sorting office.

A&D's service 60 started on 1 October 1934, from Godalming to Dunsfold via Hascombe. This was the result of buying out the goodwill of two independent but closely associated individuals who has shared the route for just over ten years. Frank W. Kerridge of Cobden House, Milford, had been running 14-seaters over the route since 28 December 1923 and a few weeks later had also commenced a Godalming–Hambledon service. A&D immediately surrendered the license for the latter service, and did not take over Kerridge's vehicles. The other operator on the Godalming–Dunsfold route was Henry Manfield, of the Bricklayer's Arms, Dunsfold, who used the fleet name of 'Dunsfold Queen'. In his case, a 1930 Chevrolet bus, PL 4446, was handed over to A&D, but was never used by them.

A monopoly of the Farnham–London express services was finally achieved on 27 October, 1934, when Farnham Blue Coaches was taken over, at a price of £25,000. This concern had become a limited company on 13 June, 1932, and by now three of the morning journeys up to London and three evening journeys down had been extended to Bordon and Whitehill. The already-integrated timetable was continued except for one of the Whitehill extensions in each direction, and all journeys now used Victoria Coach Station. Farnham Blue's smart fleet of coaches (eleven Gilfords and two Maudslays) were absorbed into the A&D fleet, but although the garage at the top of Wrecclesham Hill was included in the deal, the new owners transferred the operation to their existing Aldershot garage.

By now, the only other A&D express services to London were the daily journey from Crookham and two journeys from Haslemere. The former survived until 1939, but the Haslemere service was abandoned in 1935, when the goodwill was sold to the Southdown company (whose Portsmouth express coaches already used the same road) for £3,500.

In addition to the rebuilding of the Morris 20-seaters with Dennis Ace chassis, 15 completely new Aces with

Right: Photographs of the Dennis Aces carrying the 20-seat bodies originally built for the unsuccessful Morris RP buses are rare. This is CG 9016, seen at Guildford garage in its declining years.
E. Nixon collection

Below: Two brand-new Dennis Aces, with 20-seat Strachan bodies pose for their portraits on the new Guildford by-pass, in 1934, with the Dennis works as a background. This model, with its extremely short wheelbase of 9ft 6in, became very popular in all parts of the country for operating rural services on narrow roads.
S. W. Stevens-Stratten

The general-purpose Dennis Lancet coaches obtained in 1934-35 introduced a facility in aid of the tours often made by Aldershot-based military bands: a long roof rack to carry all of the instruments of a full band. These were known as 'band-boxes', but in later years the term came to be used for all such luggage racks, whether long or short. CG 9597 is shown on the express service to Farnham, at Victoria Coach Station in London. The sliding door first introduced with this design is evident.
W. J. Haynes

20-seat Strachan bodies (CG 6391-6405) were obtained in 1934, and in time for the 1935 season, nine more Lancet coaches were delivered, with long 'band-boxes' (CG 9596-603/5).

The company instituted a Safe Driving Award scheme for its drivers in 1935. To qualify, a complete year of service without blame for any accident, however minor, had to be shown. Sponsored by the Road Operators' Safety Council, the presentation of these awards became an annual highlight of the A&D year, and continued as long as the company lasted. By that time the most senior driver, Mr J.R. Balfour, had progressed through diplomas, medals and bars to brooches and eventually a 35-year cross.

In addition, a pension fund was established for A&D's employees in 1936. Membership was optional, with the usual arrangement of the company and employee making equal premium contributions. Until that time, pensions had only been granted by the Board to selected long-serving employees with exemplary records.

In all parts of the country, unrest among employees of bus operators increased during the 1930s, and strikes occurred in the neighbouring LPTB and Thames Valley concerns in the early summer of 1936. A&D received demands for improved pay, overtime rates (1¼ time) and the confirmation of a 48-hour working week, and towards the end of June a strike was threatened over the slow progress of negotiations on pay, although the 48-hour week had been agreed. In order not to interrupt services, union mass meetings were called at Aldershot and Guildford to start at midnight. Negotiations dragged on for many months, and it was not until December 1937 that agreement was finally reached on all points.

After 6½ years of co-ordinated operations, the Fleet Coaching Co. sold out to A&D on 18 May 1936 for £6,750. It then had ten assorted Guy buses, acquired at various dates from 1927 onwards, with seating capacities ranging from 20 to 32. All were numbered into the A&D fleet list. The jointly-operated services were absorbed into the timetables of A&D's 8 and 9, and a rationalisation of frequencies took place in the following January. The extended journeys from Fleet Station to Bramshot Golf Club were continued. Warren's other service, from Ewshott Camp to Aldershot via Crookham Cross Roads, became 39.

September 1936 saw the most extensive private hire job ever undertaken by the Company. The situation in the British protectorate of Palestine had been tense for some time, and a rapid worsening made it necessary to recall, to a state of readiness for embarkation, the three infantry brigades of the First Division of the Army. These were at the time distributed in camps all over Sussex, on their summer manoeuvres, and A&D was asked to provide transport back to their barracks at Aldershot and Bordon at short notice. A fleet of 70 buses was mustered to assist the Army's own transport, and some of them made two journeys.

During 1936, the first steps were taken towards the modernisation of the double-deck fleet, which was to eliminate open staircases several years in advance of most other major companies. All of the new acquisitions had 48-seat Strachan bodies. Early in the year, a Dennis Lance, fitted with the German-designed 84bhp Dennis-Lanova pre-heated oil engine, was acquired. This vehicle, AOT 580, had the radiator style with which the petrol-engined Lance model had first been launched in 1930, but a second evaluation model, BAA 386, had the new Lance II parallel-sided version, and was powered by a Gardner oil engine. AOT 580 returned to the Dennis works after a year. Its engine was scrapped and its chassis modified to take the more conventional Dennis O4 oil engine, which had been specified for a production batch of 41 Lances. The rebuilt bus was registered CCG 188, and the main batch was CCG 311-351. The last member of this series was exhibited at the 1937 Commercial Motor Show at Earl's Court.

Single-deck models also underwent striking changes around this time. Most of the 1936 deliveries were Lancets with Strachan bodies of similar appearance to the coaches and buses of the previous four years: 29 appeared during the year (AOT 587-605, BAA 387-396). In December, however, the first three of an order for twenty Lancet II 32-seaters (BOT 288-307) went into service. These also had the new radiator shape, and bodies which flared outwards at the bottom, as well as having a cream relief above the cantrail. The six 20-seat Strachan-bodied Dennis Aces, AOT 581-6, delivered during the year were little different from those obtained in 1934. By October 1937 the fleet had grown to 226: 43 double-deck, 141 single-deck and 42 coaches.

The company's first venture into the economical oil (or diesel) engine was made in January 1936, when this Dennis Lance, AOT 580, was placed in experimental service. It had a Dennis Lanova pre-heated indirect injection engine, of 82bhp, built under licence. However, it was not a success, and within a year AOT 580 (shown here undergoing a tilt test at London Transport's Chiswick works) was returned to Dennis. According to Dennis records, the engine was dismantled, the chassis was reconstructed and renumbered, the original Strachan 48-seat body was remounted on the chassis, and the resulting vehicle, now with a Dennis-designed oil engine, was re-registered CCG188 in April 1937. The 'new' chassis received a new Strachan body four years later. *E. Nixon collection*

After the lack of success of the Dennis Lance with a Lanova engine, another of the manufacturer's options was tried in 1936 – the version with a Gardner oil engine. BAA 386 appeared in September, and ran for many years, although the following year's large batch of Lances used Dennis's own oil engine. They also had 48-seat Strachan bodies, but the curved rear end of BAA 386 remained unique in the fleet.

E. Nixon collection

Postcard publishers seem to have had a knack of capturing rare buses in their scenes. This view of Aldershot High Street is the only photograph known to the author of the erstwhile AOT 580 in its rebuilt form as CCG 188. The alterations to the dash panel and destination blinds, as well as the new-style Lance radiator, are evident when this view is compared with that of the original bus undergoing a tilt test.

Author's collection

CCG 334, of which this is a manufacturer's photo, was one of the batch of 41 Dennis Lance 2s delivered in 1937. All had 48-seat Strachan bodies and 6.5 litre Dennis 04 oil engines, and the new fleet permitted the complete withdrawal of all previous double-deck models, some of which were only six years old. Note the duplication of bonnet number between the fixed and removable panels, to avoid inadvertent renumbering by exchanging the latter between buses.   *E. Nixon collection*

Above: AOT 603 was one of the four Dennis Lancets of 1936 which received full-length band boxes on their 32-seat Strachan bodies. This scene was taken during a layover in Guildford station yard. It had served throughout the war years as an ambulance. Note that, because of the independent mounting of the cab, it is joined to the body by flexible material. *E. Nixon collection*

Left: In 1937, the Dennis Lancet 2, with revised radiator design, joined the A&D fleet. The body, though obviously derived from the Strachan design of the previous five years, was much more stylish, with an integral cab and flared skirt panels. BOT 291 was one of the first ten, with long band boxes, which were the most modern vehicles to be taken for military service in 1940.

E. Nixon collection

1937 was the year of King George VI's coronation, and as it was also the year of the company's silver jubilee, it was a special year for the publicity department. In February, a new hall was opened for the Sports Club, in the middle of the Halimote Road site, to replace the old Halimote Club house. The first event was the annual children's party, soon to be followed by the company's Jubilee Ball, attended by numerous local dignitaries, who were welcomed by the Chairman, Mr Garcke. As one of the largest privately-owned halls in the district, the 'Traction Hall' became a popular venue for events planned by Aldershot organisations.

As for regular entertainment, by the late 1930s cinemas at Addlestone, Alton, Bagshot, Camberley, Farnham, Fleet, Haslemere, Horsham, North Camp, Weybridge and Woking were all served by special or scheduled late services to local destinations, in addition to the long-standing cinema and theatre services at Aldershot and Guildford. No fewer than 16 special buses set out from the vicinity of the Hippodrome, Aldershot every night, including a longer-distance journey to the Army base at Bordon and Whitehill. Others waited at the Queen Hotel for patrons of the Empire cinema. The busiest time at Guildford was on Saturday nights, when ten services waited in North Street for

BOT 297 was delivered in time to be elaborately decorated for the coronation of King George VI in May 1937. Almost 1000 red, white and blue lamps were used, and the royal portraits were illuminated. The crown was illuminated from inside, showing the hundreds of glass bead 'jewels' to good effect. After the Coronation celebrations, the batteries, lamps, etc. were removed, but the painted embellishments on the band box remained for the rest of the year. *Author's collection*

The Dennis photograph of 1937 Lancet 2 BOT 300 shows the lines of its Strachan body very well: this was one of the second batch, with short band boxes. Above the cantrail a route board has been inserted into the clips: this facility was rarely used in normal service. *E. Nixon collection*

The Traction Hall, Aldershot's best civilian venue for social occasions, was constructed out of one of the former Vick's garage buildings in 1937. Its excellent dance floor is shown to advantage in this view. The green and gold decor was designed by General Manager J.B. Parker. The problems of safety and car parking in the middle of an operational garage site caused its closure in March 1955.   *Alder Valley*

passengers to various destinations. During 1936-7, a number of previously untimed special late cinema services were added to the scheduled timetables, for the benefit of users other than cinema-goers.

During what proved to be the final years of the Aldershot Tattoo, the company's organisation of the mass movement of the spectators was conducted with military precision. An operational headquarters was set up in Badajos Barracks Square, where the Traffic Manager, Mr P.N. Gray, was in touch by field telephone with his inspectors at the arena, railway stations, and bus parks. Special excursions were operated direct to the arena from most of the principal towns in A&D territory, while local passengers travelling by normal services made connections at the special bus parks with a shuttle service to the arena. After the show, which ended after normal services had concluded, passengers were returned to these parks; Badajos Square for Farnham, Shortheath, Ash, Tongham and Badshot Lea; Claycart Road for Farnborough and Cove, and from the 'Yellow F' arena bus park to Crookham Cross Roads and Fleet Station. Upwards of 200 departures were provided in the space of 1½ hours after midnight for these destinations in addition to returning passengers to the railheads for some three dozen special trains. In 1938, A&D actually had a part in the show, when driver Harold Quinn drove a double-decker full of Royal Engineers into the arena each night as

part of a battle scene. 1939 was the final year of the Tattoo, since it was never revived after the Second World War as an official Army display.

Apart from a few improvements in local services, there were not many significant changes in the route map during the second half of the 'thirties. The Royal Air Force took over the new Odiham Aerodrome in January 1937, and on 17 February a direct service 50 thence to Farnham and Aldershot was started. This ran on Wednesday, Friday and Saturday afternoons and evenings only, and was primarily a feeder to the London service from Farnham. In addition, on Saturdays and Sundays the midnight coaches down from London were extended beyond Farnham to the aerodrome. The response was not sufficient, and the service was withdrawn on 1 May. On 5 May, the licence for the Guildford–Cranleigh service run by Gastonia Motor Services (George Weller, of Gaston Gate, Cranleigh), was transferred to A&D, who gave the new service the vacant number 25. No vehicles were transferred, since Gastonia's other operations continued unchanged. An immediate replacement bus service might have been expected when the railway line through Tongham and Ash Green closed from 6 July, but in fact it was almost two years (23 June 1939) before Ash Green was given buses on Fridays and Saturdays only (Service 40).

In addition to the double-decker already mentioned,

One of the 1938 fleet of Dennis Lancet express coaches is shown here in its later years, after it had been displaced from the London service and relegated to the summer coastal services. The 'A' on the autovac was used for identification when several coaches were due to depart simultaneously. COR 158 is awaiting departure from Southsea on 4th August 1952 to return to Camberley. *D.T. Sharwood*

the 1937 Show at Earl's Court included the prototype of the new batch of 32-seat oil-engined Dennis Lancet II coaches for the London service. Registered COR 151, it had Strachan coachwork with the sweeping curves which were to distinguish coach bodies from bus bodies for the next fifteen years. A high floor level allowed luggage to be stowed below at the rear, so no roof rack was required. COR 152-63 were delivered in 1938 to complete the batch of 13.

New single-deck buses appearing in 1938 were Lancet II's COR 164-91, which, although at first glance (and indeed second glance!) similar to the previous year's series bodied by Strachan, had Dennis bodies differing in a few minor details. Although 'bandboxes' were still fitted, the inconvenience and consequent reduction of facilities for carrying large items of passengers' luggage on the roof had resulted in restriction to folding perambulators only by 1936, and in the summer of 1938 a complete ban on perambulators, non-folding wheeled chairs, invalid chairs, bicycles and heavy luggage over 56lbs was imposed.

The 1938 Lancet IIs were also fitted with Dennis 04 oil engines, and at the Annual General Meeting in July, the company reported that about £1,000 had already been

saved by conversion to oil fuel, with no adverse comments from the public, who had previously tended to associate diesel propulsion with the smelly black smoke emitted by heavy lorries. A year later it was stated that 60% of the scheduled mileage was being run on fuel oil.

Two operators were taken over in 1938. On 12 January, A.T. Locke and Son of 16 Stoke Road, Guildford, sold their business to A&D. This had been operated as the Blue Saloon Bus Service since 1925. Two of the routes lay within the London Transport area and, by prior arrangement, were immediately resold, together with seven buses, to LPTB. A&D retained Locke's service 3 (Guildford–Stoke–Sutton Green–Woking) which became 29, and also absorbed the excursion and tours side. Three vehicles were also retained – a Star PL 8827, a Dennis Ace DPD 858 and a Dennis Lancet I coach, CPH 130. Next to be absorbed was the Direct Bus Service, which had been started in April 1928 by Mr Henry Lintott, a former Yellow Bus Driver, who established his headquarters at The Garage, Lightwater. His route was Guildford–Pirbright–Knaphill–Bagshot, later extended to Bracknell. By 1937 he was a sick man, and his services and vehicles were suffering from lack of supervision, to the extent that the Commissioners were

In addition to the Dennis Lancet coaches, the company took delivery of 28 buses for ordinary stage services during the first six months of 1938. They were fitted with the Dennis O4 oil engine, and were the first single-deckers so equipped. Their bodies were all built by Dennis to A&D's standard design of the period. COR 185 stands in Farnham's Castle Street, on the 45 service to Godalming in June 1951. *P.J. Holmes*

Above: Locke's 'Blue Saloon', based at Guildford, was jointly acquired by A&D and London Transport in January 1938. Most of the vehicles were allocated to the LPTB, but this Dennis Lancet coach (CPH 130) of 1935 vintage was one of three which came to A&D. However, just two years after acquisition it was requisitioned for military service, and never returned.

Below: S. Ansell of Peckham took over Lintott's Direct Bus Service of Bagshot early in 1938, but this proved to be only a short-term salvation. Three ex-Lintott buses, plus a new Dennis Pike, were sold to A&D in June. BOR 501 is shown in A&D livery beside Woking station on service 55C: it was the only Dodge vehicle ever operated by the company, and received the bonnet number D1. It had a 26-seat Reall body.   *Both E. Nixon collection*

In 1939 orders were placed for 39 new Dennis Lancet 2s with Gardner 5LW engines, for which 20 bodies were to be built by Dennis and 19 by Strachan. The imminence of war, and the priority given to war preparations, resulted in delivery only beginning at the end of 1939, and the last of the order came over a year later. DHO 295, seen here in Woking, was one of the batch with Strachan bodies.

M.J. Stephens

The 20 Lancets with Dennis bodies are exemplified by DHO 281, seen here in Guildford. Minor differences from the Strachan batch are to be seen at the corners of the destination panel and the positions of the emergency exit door handle and driver's step beside the cab door.

V.C. Jones

The caption to this publicity postcard says 'The coach for your outing this year'. In fact, this emphasises the high standard of interior treatment of A&D's ordinary service buses, since this is one of the 1938-40 style of Dennis Lancet. Upholstery was blue leather, surrounding bluish-grey patterned moquette. The 'curtains' were for appearance only, and could not be moved. They were taken out as a wartime economy, and were never replaced. Roof and side panels were silver-grey.   *Alder Valley*

unwilling to renew his licence. At a hearing in January it was stated that A&D were helping with timetabling and fare charts, and were willing to allow one of their inspectors to be put in charge of the crews, who were by now running like the 'pirate' operators of the 'bus war' days. However, in December, Mr S. Ansell, a coach proprietor of Camberwell Road, Peckham, SE5, bought the business and its three buses, only to sell it again to A&D on 8 June 1938. By then a new Dennis Pike, EXF 377, had been added to the fleet, and this was the only bus retained by A&D for any length of time. The Guildford–Bagshot service became A&D's 62 a week later, but the new owners did not obtain a licence for the Bagshot–Bracknell section of the route.

On 10 May 1939 the last surviving independent operators in the Woking area were taken over. The first of these was the Grey Bus Service, run by Mr Francis W. Renshaw, the active partner, and Mrs Lily M. Leam, and based at Oxford House, St. John's. Starting with a route from Woking to Worplesdon Hill, a network of local routes in several directions from Woking had been established during the late 'twenties, and by the time of the takeover, they had four small buses, which A&D sold immediately. Their routes were partly reorganised: Woking to Fox Corner became A&D 63, incorporating the service taken over on the same day from a second operator, W. Bulman and Son, of Hook Heath Garage. This firm had run under the fleet

name of Bulman's Bus Service since the mid-twenties, from Woking to Hook Heath (Fisher's Hill) via Star Hill, and had been thwarted in all its attempts to expand beyond this short route. No buses were taken over, though the one driver employed was taken on by A&D.

Renshaw & Leam's more southerly route to Fox Corner via Mayford became 64. This had formerly been linked to a Woking–Knaphill–Brookwood section to form a circular route, but the latter section was now operated separately as A&D 44. A second route from Brookwood to Mayford and Woking by way of Worplesdon Golf Club was discontinued. Finally, Woking–St John's–Knaphill was absorbed into A&D's existing 34B.

The orders for new buses in 1939 were destined to be interrupted by national preparations for war with Germany. 39 Dennis Lancet II 32-seat single-deckers were to be fitted with the 7.0 litre Gardner 5LW oil engines. Strachan bodies were specified for 19 chassis (DHO 267-72/93-305), while the remaining 20 bodies (for DHO 273-92) were ordered from Dennis, and differed only in minor details. Delivery of a few of these buses was delayed until 1940, as was the batch of six 48-seat Lance double-deckers, also with Gardner 5LW engines (DOT 478-83). The nine 20-seat petrol-engined Dennis Falcons (DHO 266, DOT 470-83), all with Strachan bodies, were, however, delivered in 1939.

Above: The last buses obtained before wartime problems put an end to normal production were six Lance 2s ordered and delivered in 1940. Their 48-seat Strachan bodies had teak frames. DOT 479 is shown at Aldershot Bus Station in the summer of 1951, displaying the white destination blind for the special shuttle service 'to and from Aldershot and Frensham Pond'. *D.T. Sharwood*

Below: The 1939 successor to the Dennis Ace was the 20-seat Dennis Falcon. Nine were acquired during 1939, but they were stored during the war and they had a relatively short period of service after reinstatement. The neat Strachan body looked good enough for use as a small coach, but this picture of DOT 471 was taken on stage service, at the Woking station terminal area. *V.C. Jones*

Chapter Seven

The "Tracco" at War Again

The outbreak of war with Germany on 3 September 1939 came almost at the end of the summer season, and as it was not unexpected, contingency plans had been prepared. The coastal services were immediately cancelled, and the London service halved to an hourly frequency. A few very late workings on some services were also cancelled, and buses and crews were thus made available for military purposes and for the evacuation of children from London to Surrey and Hampshire. Shuttle services for evacuees were operated from various railheads: Farncombe station, on the Portsmouth line, became an important centre.

According to pre-arranged plans, all of the older Dennis Lancet coaches and most of their contemporary single-deckers, 45 in all, dating from 1932 to 1936, went into the workshops for removal of seats and the installation of ready-made supports for ten stretchers apiece, plus other equipment to fit them to serve as civilian ambulances. The work was completed within a few days of the outbreak of war, and at the same time the vehicles were painted grey. They were then held in readiness in various centres, including Winchester, Portsmouth and Basingstoke, for coping with the anticipated heavy toll of air raid casualties in strategic target areas in the south. A & D also provided volunteer drivers when necessary.

The first and greatest inconvenience of the busman's war was the 'black-out', designed to minimise the enemy's ability to locate towns from the air at night. The use of street lamps was banned, and the showing of interior lights from buildings became a serious offence. In common with all other vehicles used during hours of darkness, buses were fitted with headlamp masks to direct a reduced beam downwards, while the step edges on double-deckers and the bottom edges of front wings and rear panels were painted white to improve their visibility. A&D's buses had their interior lighting drastically reduced. Passenger lights were removed, the glasses of gangway 'cash lights' were painted blue, and a row of dim bulbs was fitted over each block of seats, enclosed in horizontal cylindrical shades with a narrow slot designed to point the beam vertically downwards. At the same time as these were installed, interior embellishments such as the clocks and 'flaming-torch' lamps on the front bulkhead and the dummy curtains were removed from all the single-deck fleet.

The rule for operation during periods of air raid warning was that buses would continue to run until advised by the police that enemy aircraft were in the vicinity, in which case they were to stop until danger was past. Fortunately no A&D bus was ever attacked while on the road, although one suffered some minor damage when a bomb fell near the Officers' Club at Aldershot.

The need for fuel economies, the demands of wartime movements and the general uncertainties of the first few weeks of the war led to the complete curtailment of many services and reduction in frequency or shortening of the routes of several others. All augmented 'Friday and Saturday only' services were cancelled and late night buses were severely reduced.

These changes were incorporated in an emergency timetable issued on 4 October. Of the services which ceased altogether, eight (5, 5a, 5b, 11, 26, 31b, 55 and 62) were never revived, three (38, 55b and 55c) returned with the issue of emergency timetable No. 2 on 1 November, while 22a, 40, 43, 52, 56a, 59 and 61 and 64 returned at various times during the war or soon after. The shortening of routes of 3c, 8, 9, 10a, 16, 19, 48, 48a and 55a involved, inter alia, the disappearance of A&D buses from the outposts at Bognor Regis and Weybridge until after the war. However, an improvement of a sort, introduced with the first emergency timetable, was the provision of an earlier journey than hitherto on five urban routes (2, 10, 15, 22 and 32).

In mid-May 1940, a fortnight before the evacuation of the British Army from Dunkirk, an urgent transport requirement for the forces was met by the temporary requisitioning of a considerable number of buses from Aldershot depot. Some services ceased for a few hours, until buses from other depots or borrowed from other operators' reserves could be brought in. Not all rural services could be covered, however, and some routes were without buses for a few days, while others survived on a variety of odd vehicles in strange colours and dubious condition. The loss of many of the Army's vehicles in France resulted in the Emergency Powers (Defence), Acquisition and Disposal of Motor Vehicles Order, 1940, which gave powers for compulsory purchase of civilian vehicles of all types. Many a private car owner regretted his curiosity in finding out what the mysterious 'VCC' signs meant – they were Vehicle Collection Centres, where their cars were instantly assessed for suitability and summarily requisitioned. A&D provided 49 middle-aged and older buses and non-standard coaches. Twelve of them were returned later in the war, while others were eventually sold to other operators or scrapped.

In the summer of 1940 conductresses once again started to take over the duties of men leaving for military service, while a number of conductors who were for various reasons not liable for call-up were retrained as drivers. Passenger discomforts of this era were epitomised by a popular song 'We mustn't miss the last bus home', and despite the running of as many relief vehicles as possible, many journeys were crowded with standing passengers. The annual number of passengers doubled between 1939 and 1943, from 21 million to almost 42 million.

The vehicles left after the departure of those to be used on war service sufficed to operate the reduced level of services of 1939-40. During the first few months of the war, the batches of double and single-deckers which had been in hand in the Dennis and Strachan works were completed, but then the needs of war production caused a slowing-down of manufacture for the civilian market, culminating in a 'freeze' on further work on buses throughout the country in 1941, imposed by the Ministry of War Transport. Increasing loadings, due to the curtailment of private motoring and the growth of the working population in factories, combined with the loss of vehicles to wartime employment, led to shortages of stock. These were alleviated by the hiring of twenty Dennis Lancet I's (JG 6800-19, of 1936 vintage) in the summer of 1940 from the East Kent Road Car Co. whose services in the most vulnerable area of south-east England had been greatly reduced. They had 35-seat Dennis bodies, and after arrival at Aldershot on 4-5 July, some of them ran for a few weeks in their original red livery until they could all be repainted in A&D green. All were normally allocated to the Aldershot area, and they carried the legal lettering 'On hire from the East Kent Road

The appearance of the twenty Dennis Lancets hired from East Kent in July 1940 was familiar to everyone in A&D's area during the war. They were painted plain green, with a cream waistband and no fleetname, but apart from a newspaper advertisement showing the rear of the nearside beside a bus queue, no photograph of any of these buses in A&D service has come to light.

M&D and East Kent Bus Club

Car Co.' but never carried A&D fleetnames or numbers. The hire fee was £2 each per day, later raised to £2.10s.0d. They trickled back to their proper owner at intervals during the latter part of the war, and all had returned by the end of 1945.

The fall of France increased the risks from enemy air raids in the summer and autumn of 1940, and the lower level of the main block in Halimote Road was protected by sandbags for use as a public air raid shelter for 500 people. As a means of minimising risks to buses and their crews from night raids, as well as economising on fuel and manpower, a special revision of the timetable took effect from 16 October. This virtually completed the curtailment of late night services, and with few exceptions, buses were henceforth back in their garages by 10 pm. This hit the London service, which had previously run its last down journey at 10.15 pm. In order to be home in time, the last run now left at 7.15, with a correspondingly earlier time for the last up journey.

The coastal services operated for a shortened season in 1940, with fewer vehicles and routes, but after 15 September they did not reappear until after the end of the war.

As a fuel economy measure, major operators throughout the country were instructed in 1941 to plan to power a proportion of their fleets with producer gas. This involved the provision of trailers carrying the equipment for generating the gas from coke, and installing gas pipes thence to the engines, whose fuel systems had to be modified to use the gas in place of oil vapour. Although five trailers were delivered, only one bus, Lancet DHO 279, was ever fitted (in 1943), and after a few months the

experiment was abandoned. The trailer, numbered 414 for some unexplained reason – perhaps because the bus carried body number 614 – joined its unused companions in the long grass at the back of the sports ground.

Three more buses 'joined up' in the late summer of 1941 when Dennis Aces CG 9010/2/3 were compulsorily acquired by the Air Ministry and sent to Bicester RAF station.

After restoration of some of the later journeys in May, for the lighter summer evenings, all late journeys were again curtailed from October 1941, and the last coach down from London now left at 6.15 pm.

The 'freeze' on new bus construction was relaxed in 1942, when existing component stocks and partially-completed chassis were 'unfrozen', to be completed in the most economical manner possible, with light alloys, needed in the aircraft industry, replaced by more readily available materials, while chromium plating and other embellishments were virtually eliminated. This permitted the completion of eight units of an A&D order for 25 Dennis Lancets, which were given 32-seater Strachan bodies of very plain appearance, but of similar outline to earlier models (ECG 380/1. 424. 600, 851/2, 945, EHO 162). In addition, the balance of 17 Gardner engines was acquired and put into store. Two Leyland Titan TD7s (ECG 943/4) were also obtained, with 48-seat lowbridge bodies by East Lancashire Coachbuilders, of Blackburn, thus beginning a relationship between A & D and the latter which was to last for sixteen years. None of these vehicles carried fleetnames, as these had disappeared, as an economy measure, in July 1940. From September 1942, the roofs of newly-painted buses were painted grey, to reduce their visibility

In December 1939, 25 new Dennis Lancets, to be fitted with Gardner oil engines and Strachan 32-seat bodies, were authorised by the Board. However, before any could be completed, construction was frozen, on government instructions. In the autumn of 1941, permission was given for part of the order to be fulfilled, subject to the 'austerity' restrictions on the use of light alloys and other materials in short supply. Eight of the Lancets were completed in this way, and their plain appearance is evident from this photo of ECG 852 at the rear of Guildford garage in the 1950s.

P.J. Holmes

Six more Dennis Lance double-deckers were ordered in the summer of 1939, but the war intervened. The company eventually obtained official permission to buy two new double-deckers in 1941, but by that time Lance production had ceased, and the result was the first purchase of Leyland vehicles for thirty years. The two TD7 Titans were registered ECG 943/4, and they had 48-seat bodies from East Lancashire Coachbuilders, which started a valuable contact with that manufacturer. ECG 943 is seen at Winchester bus station, the terminus of service 14, in June 1950; the Leylands were mainly used on the long-distance services to Winchester and Reading. *P.J. Holmes*

Delivery of 'utility' Guy Arabs started in September 1942, and the sixth example, EHO 587, is shown at Aldershot Bus Station. It has the obligatory headlamp and sidelamp masks and white edges to the wings. The 48-seat body was built by Strachan. *Alder Valley*

to enemy aircraft, and this practice continued until the end of 1944.

As the country's industry became adjusted to war needs, the Government permitted bus manufacture to be resumed by four firms, of which only one, Guy Motors Ltd. of Wolverhampton, supplied A&D. EHO 173, delivered in September 1942, was the first of twenty Guy Arab 48-seat 'utility' double-deckers acquired during the war, at irregular intervals. The first seven (EHO 173, 217, 286, 316, 508, 587, 695) had Strachan bodies of typical utility style – angular corners, with flat panels used wherever possible and complications such as opening windows reduced to a minimum. All of the first 500 Arabs manufactured had the 7.0 litre Gardner 5LW engine. Subsequent production changed to the so-called Arab II, which had the radiator set six inches further forward, to allow for the installation of the more powerful 8.4 litre 6LW engine if required. The front edges of the wings were curved forward to suit the new profile. A&D's first six Arab IIs also had Strachan bodies, which differed from the first batch in having wooden slatted seats. They also had windows in the emergency door at the rear of the upper deck, whereas the previous Guys had had austerely-upholstered seats and blank panel emergency doors. EHO 806, 818, 952, 983, EOR 28 and 288 constituted this group. Next came four, EOR 29-31, 373, with even more angular bodies of Roe, of Leeds, early in 1944.

Some later Guys, delivered in 1944, had bodies built by Roe of Leeds, showing a different version of utility angularity. By this time, even the upholstering of seats had to be curtailed, and until the war was over, all new buses had seats made of varnished wooden slats. These later Guys, from EHO 806 onwards, were of the Arab II variety, with a longer bonnet and wings swept forward, to accommodate a longer engine if required. EOR 373 is shown in Wellington Avenue, Aldershot, in 1950.

D.T. Sharwood

Finally, in the spring of 1945, EOR 374-6 arrived with bodies of two slightly different varieties by Weymann, of Addlestone. All A&D's Arabs had the Gardner 5LW engine.

Further vehicles became available for stage services when the fleet of 13 coaches operating the Express Service to London was taken off 'for the duration' on 29 September 1942. Service 1 to Egham Station was augmented, to compensate regular travellers from intermediate points for the loss of their through service to the capital. The coaches' luxury fittings and route boards were stored away and they were immediately set to work on more menial tasks. These, together with the 'unfrozen' buses and those hired from East Kent, enlarged the stock of full-size single-deckers, and a number of 20-seaters were consequently taken out of service over the same period and stored under cover in various places, including the company's sports ground at

At the end of the war, three Guy Arabs received bodies from yet another coach-builder. This was Weymann, whose composite construction employed a metal frame rather than the unseasoned wood which had been used for the bodies of the earlier Guys. As a consequence, these survived for a full period of service, whereas the earlier bodies had to be replaced. EOR 375 stands in Wellington Avenue, Aldershot, behind the Empire cinema, whose construction had been partially financed by some of A&D's cash reserves in 1933.

Surfleet Transport Photos

Weybourne. Included among these temporary withdrawals were the almost-new 20-seat Dennis Falcons delivered in 1939. Since their post-war reinstatement was soon followed by new regulations permitting more than twenty seats in a one-man-operated bus, their total time in normal service was destined to be very short.

A Government order of March 1942 produced a lasting change in the streets of larger towns during the succeeding months. The formation of queues became compulsory at bus stops where more than six passengers were waiting. In a number of places, A&D was obliged to set up separate bus stop signs for each group of services where one sign had previously sufficed for all destinations. Some streets did not permit this, because of obstruction of footpaths, and in these cases new locations had to be found where there was room for several queues. The problem of short-distance passengers on longer-distance services became serious, as it was illegal to differentiate (though some conductors and inspectors did so). In the Farnham area, minimum fares were applied to some services to encourage short-distance passengers to use the local services. These took effect in October 1942, and similar measures had to be applied in July 1944 to keep short distance passengers between Guildford and Onslow Village off the 31 service to Farnham.

An administrative change took place during that year when the Tilling and BAT organisation was split into two separate bodies, Tilling Motor Services Ltd. and British Electric Traction Omnibus Services Ltd. Though not all companies reverted to their original owning group, A&D remained in the BET section. Some redistribution of directors resulted from the split.

In September 1942, the company had the opportunity of purchasing properties on the corner of Park Street and Mount Street in Guildford, and applied to the council for outline approval of plans for a bus station, with shops and flats above, to be completed after the war. Events in Woking in July 1939 had clearly shown the hostility of both A&D and LPTB to municipally-owned bus stations, and this move was an attempt to ensure that the company controlled its Guildford terminus. However, the authorities stated very firmly that it was not desirable for the numerous operators to act independently, so Aldershot remained the only A&D-owned bus station.

Wartime services reached their lowest ebb on 4 January 1943, when a new timetable gave effect to a Ministry decree that Sunday morning services should be abolished, and thereafter most Sunday services started at about noon. The complete shutdown after 10 pm daily was also enforced, and in fact some services now ceased soon after 9 pm. The motive was, of course, the further saving of fuel and reduction in staff.

Despite the general application of 'utility' standards to new vehicles, it became possible to embark in 1944 on a programme of rebodying some of the 1937-38 vintage double-deckers with non-utility bodies by East Lancashire. These were similar to those which had been fitted to the two Leyland Titans in 1941. Over the period up to 1948, 22 of the CCG-registered Lances, plus the earlier singleton BAA 386, were taken out of service one or two at a time, their chassis renovated and fitted with new Gardner 5LW oil engines which had been in store since 1942, and then despatched for re-bodying. Their original Dennis engines were stored for further use. The last three Lances to be rebuilt, in 1948, were to a slightly improved design, with sliding ventilators instead of half-drop windows. The rebuilds survived until 1958, whereas their unrebuilt contemporaries were scrapped in 1950.

The company had for long been content to live in peaceful co-existence with the remaining independent firms in its area, as long as they did not attempt to encroach on its routes, undercut its fares, or make significant inroads into excursion traffic. However, in August 1944, A&D joined forces with Southdown to oppose applications from Mr Basil S. Williams, of Emsworth, to start some additional services near their agreed boundary. A&D would have found a new rival in Haslemere if he had succeeded, but the application was refused, and instead A&D was allowed

East Lancashire Coachbuilders were allowed to continue building new bodies to peace-time standards, as replacements, during the latter years of the war. A&D started a programme of rebuilding some of its 1937 Lances in 1944. Their engines were replaced by the Gardner 5LW units obtained in 1941 when the buses they were destined for could not be built. CCG 348 is shown in Castle Street, Farnham, where the introduction of double-deckers for the first time in 1950 aroused vigorous protests from the owners of houses and first-floor flats.   *P. Trevaskis*

The last three pre-war Lances to be rebuilt with East Lancashire bodies, in 1948, received an updated version characterised by sliding ventilators in place of half-drop windows, and a new pattern of front dome: this design was to be used for the company's first post-war Dennis Lances, delivered in the following year. CCG 330 is shown on August Bank Holiday, 1955, standing at Aldershot Bus Station with the white destination blind for the Frensham Pond shuttle service.   *D.T. Sharwood*

The prototype Dennis Lancet III was constructed during the last months of the war, and was delivered to A&D in February 1945. Dennis built its 32-seat body, which shows signs of uncertainty as to how to adapt a low waistline to the high radiator and bonnet of this model. Their more serious problem was a reprimand from the Ministry of Supply, because they had misinterpreted their permission to build the body as allowing full peacetime luxury standards. EOR 743 is seen standing, some years later, in The Grove at Aldershot.   *T. Wright*

to extend its service 60, Godalming–Dunsfold, onwards to Petworth from 21 August.

There was some relaxation in wartime restrictions in the second half of 1944, when the invasion of Europe had reduced the threat of enemy action. "D-day", 6 June 1944, had given the A&D ambulance buses work for a few weeks, transporting casualties returning from France from Basingstoke Station to Park Prewett Hospital. A few of the buses taken by the Army had already been returned to service, and the next one to be extensively renovated, BOT 289, reappeared in November 1944 in full peacetime livery, with fleetname, green roof and cream strip above the windows. The rest of the fleet was similarly repainted over the next two years and, moreover, better standards of lighting, both inside and out, were now permitted.

Meanwhile, Dennis Bros., whose factory had been devoted to production of armoured vehicles, had received permission to design and construct the prototype of the Lancet III model, fitted with the 7.58 litre, 110 hp Dennis O6 6-cylinder oil engine. This appeared with a 32-seat Dennis body in January 1945, and after makers' trials it went into regular A & D service on service 19 to Midhurst.

In anticipation of a rapid expansion of bus services as soon as wartime restrictions were completely removed, the A&D management negotiated a comprehensive new agreement with Yellow Bus Services to co-ordinate their activities within the Guildford area. This was signed on 10 January 1945, and ensured that on any routes which were jointly operated, no changes of fares, times or frequencies would be introduced by either company without the consent of the other. A&D also reserved the right to re-open its services 31b and 62, to Compton and Bagshot respectively, which had been stopped as wartime economies. There was discussion of a possible takeover of YBS, but the time was not yet ripe. The most important outcome of the agreement was the inauguration of a new joint local service from Guildford to Rydes Hill Estate (A&D 26), from 26 March 1945. Interworked with the existing joint service (A & D 28a) to Stoughton, Royal Hotel via Manor Road, the new service used Worplesdon Road, and the two journeys by each operator on each route per hour provided a 7-8 minute headway for the residents of Stoughton.

In May 1945, the war in Europe came to an end – a fact which was commemorated in a very small way by the Aldershot paint shop, which appended the minute letters V E (Victory in Europe) to the painting date (P545) shown on a new Guy double-decker (EOR 374) which entered service in that week!

A rear view of EOR 743, taken in Wellington Avenue in July 1955, shows the lines of this unique body, built by Dennis. Ahead of it is EOU 476, one of 102 of the Lancet III buses which received Strachan's post-war version of A&D's standard outline.   *D.T. Sharwood*

Chapter Eight

Nationalisation by Instalments

Shortly after the end of hostilities, there was a nation-wide round-up of elderly buses for use of the authorities in occupied Germany. A&D provided the eleven Tilling-Stevens buses which were still capable of running. A little-known fact is that there was a proposal to re-register all these in a series prefixed CCG (Control Commission for Germany), and the Hampshire police and licensing office were warned that it might be required to renumber all existing vehicles bearing CCG index marks. However, the requisitioned buses were rapidly shipped to Germany, and the re-registration scheme was no longer necessary in this country.

On 13 August 1945, the last remaining competition on the Worplesdon Road route out of Guildford came to an end when the long-established Blue Bus service of P. Crouch & Son from Guildford to Fox Corner was taken over and absorbed as short workings of A&D's 28. Crouch's business had recently passed out of the family to a limited company, P. Crouch and Son, Ltd., which retained the private hire side. Its two other stage services were also taken over by A&D. Guildford–Wood Street was integrated with the existing 31a to form a new service 67, Peasmarsh–Guildford–Wood Street, and Guildford–Stoke (Parrot Inn) was extended to Sutton Green and became 29a. No vehicles were involved in this transaction, or in any subsequent absorptions of small operators by A&D.

The last small batch of double-deckers delivered towards the end of 1945, Guy Arabs EOT 25-30, was fitted with Strachan bodies which were best described as 'semi-utility', but had the inestimable improvement of upholstered seats to peacetime standards.

It was some time before fuel supplies and manpower allowed services to be fully restored to peacetime levels, but some improvements were brought about on heavily-loaded routes. The majority of the suspended Sunday morning services, as well as the late evening journeys, were reinstated with the new timetables of 18 March 1946, except for a few services which had to wait until 1 July. On the former date a service to Weybridge was restored but this time it ran direct from Camberley via Chobham, numbered 58, instead of via Bagshot and Woking, as did the pre-war 48a.

Mr Sidney Garcke stepped down after fifteen years as Chairman in May 1946, though he remained a director of A&D until his death seventeen months later. He was succeeded by Mr William Thomas James, OBE.

The London express service recommenced on 3 June 1946, using the 1938 Lancet coaches which had been demoted to other duties during the war, but were now restored to their original high standards. For two years the service ran hourly, until for the summer of 1948 a half-hourly timetable was introduced. However, the single journey to and from Whitehill was not restored until the 1953 season.

The daily express coaches to the coastal resorts were reinstated for a short 1946 summer season, from 1 July to 15 September, with the usual destinations, but a rather simpler pattern of starting points than before the war. Two groups of services covered Camberley, Farnborough and Aldershot and Brookwood, Woking, Guildford and Godalming respectively, with Hindhead and Haslemere covered by the most appropriate one for the ultimate destination.

Special hospital services reappeared more slowly, and it was not until the spring of 1948 that a service from Milford Station to the Surrey County Sanatorium at Milford was advertised for Wednesday and Sunday afternoons. The service to the nearby King George V Hospital was not restored by A&D, and this was provided later by Warner's Coaches of Milford, although advertised in the A&D timetable. Brompton Sanatorium, once on a main A&D route, was never again so fortunate. A Sunday afternoon visitors' service from Farnborough and Frimley stations was started in the spring of 1952, and in the following October, two journeys of 34a (Guildford–Camberley Station–Blackdown Camp) were extended to the Sanatorium on

At the end of 1945, the last six of A&D's fleet of Guy Arabs were delivered. Bodywork was once again by Strachan, to a relaxed utility specification which allowed a domed rear end and upholstered seats to be fitted. EOT 25 is shown at Aldershot Bus Station. *D.T. Sharwood*

This rear end view of EOT 26 shows the improved appearance of the final batch of Guy Arabs. The location is Wellington Avenue, Aldershot. *D.T. Sharwood*

weekdays for the benefit of the staff. A further new hospital service, introduced in the autumn of 1949, was a Sunday afternoon shuttle service between Alton Station and Lord Mayor Treloar's Cripples' Hospital.

A notable change in staffing policy was now becoming apparent. Whereas after the 1914-18 war it was unquestioningly accepted that conductresses and other non-clerical female staff would hand their jobs over to returning ex-servicemen, there was no such attitude in 1945-6. Although many conductresses did give up their wartime duties, a number of their colleagues remained with the company, and a proportion of the crew strength has been female ever since, up to the time when women started to qualify as drivers as well.

To cope with the increasing traffic of the immediate post-war period, a rapid programme of reinstatement of the buses released from ambulance service was started. These vehicles had carried a total of 46,000 casualties during the war, and while some were fully refurbished before going into service, others ran for a short time in their grey ambulance livery. The former coaches had their hinged doors replaced by sliding doors for stage service. Of the vehicles returned from military service, three (AOT 598, BAA 390/6) were in such poor condition that they were rebodied before further service with Strachan bodies of the type which had been designed for the forthcoming new Lancets. The remainder of the AOT and BAA- registered Lancet I's continued with their original bodies until 1948/9, when most of them were sent to Vincent's of Reading, for the fitting of new bodies to a design which bore little resemblance to any other of A&D's single-deckers. They were also given the Dennis O4 oil engines originally used in the 1937 Lances before they were rebuilt.

The arrival of new buses was delayed by post-war shortages, and although Dennis started to deliver chassis in quantity, they had to be stored in every spare corner of A&D's garages until the coachbuilders were ready to accept them for bodying. Consequently, it was not until December 1946 that the first three of a large series of Dennis Lancets were completed. There were still 17 chassis to be delivered out of the batch of 25 ordered in 1940, and 100 more were ordered at the end of the war. All were of the new Lancet J3 model, with the Dennis O6 engine. 102 of them appeared with 32-seat bodies by Strachan, largely similar to their pre-war design. EOU 435-84, GAA 580-608 and GOU 801-23 entered service up to September 1949. The remaining fifteen J3s were fitted with coach bodies by Strachan's which were of a design derived from the 1938 batch, and again seating 32. They arrived in time for the 1948 improvement of the London service, and were registered GAA 609-23.

The heavy programme of making up for wartime deterioration was completed by sending some of the 1939-40 vintage double and single deckers, plus the 'unfrozen' Lancets, to Portsmouth Aviation Ltd. for extensive body overhaul. It was no more than that, however, and there were no visible changes to merit the wording of the transfers applied – 'Rebuilt by Portsmouth Aviation' – or their listing in company fleet summaries in the same category as the replacement bodies built by East Lancashire.

This picture shows the sorry state in which the buses requisitioned for army service were liable to be returned. It is a Lancet of the 1936 delivery: three of these had to be given completely new bodies to fit them for reinstatement to passenger service.

E. Nixon collection

Three 1936 Dennis Lancets, whose bodies had been irreparably damaged in war service, were rebuilt in 1946 with new bodies from Strachan. These were of the pattern which had been designed as the post-war standard for 32-seaters, but for these three it was necessary to build special cabs to suit the independent mountings. AOT 598 is shown here at Aldershot Bus Station in 1949.

D.T. Sharwood

Right: The majority of the 1936 Lancets remaining in service after the war were rebodied in 1948-9 by Vincent, of Reading, and at the same time received Dennis O4 oil engines which had been displaced, by Gardner units, from the Lance double-deckers rebuilt over the previous four years. BAA 387 shows the distinctive style of these bodies, as it passes Prince's Gardens in Aldershot. *T.L.S.*

Below: Awaiting departure for Tilford, at the Windmill Inn, Ewshot, is EOU 467, one of the first fifty Dennis Lancet J3s delivered between 1946 and 1948. For many years the Ewshot–Farnham section of this route had been separately timetabled as service 38. *P. Trevaskis*

This view of Lancet GAA 600 in Aldershot Bus Station in 1949 shows a background of Gale and Polden's works and the Hippodrome, both now replaced. A minor change of the waistline treatment on the cab front can be seen when the photo of EOU 467 is compared.

P.J. Holmes

Standing at the southern outpost of the company's services – Bognor – these two Dennis Lancet J3s on service 19 show the difference between the windows of the otherwise identical vehicles: GAA 586 has the earlier sliding ventilators, while GOU 823 (the last of the series of 102 buses) has half-drop windows. *J.H. Aston*

The London express service was resumed after the war using the thirteen pre-war coaches, fully refurbished, with stored route boards and interior embellishments resurrected. During the summer of 1948 they were replaced by fifteen new Dennis Lancet J3s, whose 32-seat Strachan bodies were obviously descendants of the 1937 design. GAA 610 is here seen soon after setting out on its journey from Victoria Coach Station to Farnham. *E. Nixon collection*

Nationalisation of the railways on 1 January 1948 brought the Southern Railway's shares in A&D into the hands of the British Transport Commission, but although the Tilling group opted to be nationalised, the BET group remained independent, and its companies thus retained their individuality in choice of vehicles, coachbuilders and liveries for a further twenty years.

In 1948 the Society of British Aircraft Constructors held the first of its annual shows at Farnborough. This event, which still takes place every two years, benefited from A&D's previous experience of handling large crowds for the Aldershot Tattoo. Aldershot and North Camp were the designated railway stations for passengers arriving on normal services, and special buses ran a shuttle service to and from each. Combined rail/road tickets were available in connection with special trains from many parts of the country. In the peak year, 1953, 84% of the passengers travelling via Aldershot held combined tickets, and over 80,000 passengers were carried during the three public days of the show. Fifty buses were in use, and shortly before the show, one was departing every 30 seconds from Aldershot.

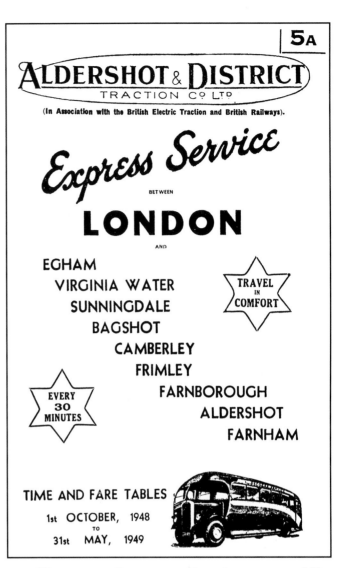

Long Service Certificate and Medal

This photograph of a Long Service Certificate and lapel badge presented in 1947 to Jim Hunt, the first driver to complete one million miles, gives some idea of the complexity of the brightly- coloured design. *Alder Valley*

The next small operator to be taken over was J.H. Stedman, of Marleycombe Road, Camelsdale (near Haslemere). He had commenced operations on 24 February 1925 with a 20-seater Dennis saloon, and for many years had run a service on two local routes, Haslemere–Hammervale and Haslemere–Kingsley Green, under the fleet name 'Progressive'. From 3 May 1948 these services were operated by A&D and became 13b and 19a respectively.

The year ending 31 May 1948 was the most profitable in the history of the company. Income increased by over £123,000 on the previous year, and the net profit was £160,898. A final dividend of 20% plus 7½% bonus was declared. Over the next few years, though income fluctuated, net profits dropped rapidly, as increased operating expenses and taxation made serious inroads.

1948 saw the retirement of the General Manager, Mr J.B. Parker, and his successor was found within the company. Mr Percy Newton Gray had been Traffic Superintendent (later Manager) since 1927, and his long experience through the difficult wartime period was an excellent recommendation. (In earlier days he had often been called by his second name, as both the late Chief Engineer Rivett and Secretary Nancarrow were also named Percy.) In recognition of the fact that many of its employees had given a lifetime's service to the company, an annual ceremony of awards for long service was instituted in December 1948. Initially, framed illuminated certificates were given to 133 people who had completed 25 or more years of service, together with enamelled lapel badges. Later, a free pass for off-duty travel on the company's buses was added, and it was decided that 40 years' service with A&D would qualify for the award of a gold watch. First to achieve this was Mr Bill Baker, in 1950, and in 1962 fitter Stanley Crick was the first to reach the milestone of 50 years with the company. Longest serving of all was another fitter, Mr Bert Lowman, who retired in 1979 after no less than 62 years' continuous service.

In the late 1940s, Guildford Borough Council entered into negotiations with the local operators over the provision of bus stations, to free several of the narrow streets of the city from the obstruction caused by buses standing at their numerous termini. Two stations, connected by a footbridge over the river Wey, were planned and were to be financed by a departure charge levied on each operator. A&D, thwarted some years earlier in its attempt to build a terminal as part of a potentially lucrative redevelopment investment, made no secret of its dislike of the municipal scheme. However, the first of the new stations, off Onslow Street, adjacent to the original Dennis works, was opened to traffic on 23 June 1949. It consisted of three 4-berth platforms and a layover area, and was to be managed by London Transport. A&D's services to the north and north-west,

and the independent operators working the same area, transferred their terminal points to this station. The second station, alongside Farnham Road, was opened to the public on 11 May 1950. This was to be managed by A&D, though also used by LPTB and independents. It had three long platforms, with continuous shelters serving 18 bus stands, and also included a booking office and public conveniences. The departure charge was set at 1¼d per vehicle in 1949, and was raised to 1½d on 1 April 1957.

Double-deckers to post-war standards started to arrive in June 1949, when A&D's first Dennis Lance K3, with O6 engine and 51-seat East Lancashire body, was completed no less than eighteen months after its chassis was delivered. A total of 40 K3s, registered GAA 624-9, GOU 824-47 and HOT 692-701, was acquired up to January 1951. At the other end of the scale, new 20-seaters began to arrive in September, 1949. They were Dennis Falcon P3s GOU 847-62, with Dennis bodies and Gardner 4LK oil engines. Later in their careers, most of them had four extra seats fitted, as the regulations for one-man operation had been relaxed.

The company's bus station at Aldershot was extended in March 1950. The original section was retained unaltered but two new through platforms, each with two shelters, were built on an area enlarged beyond the original south-

The Farnham Road bus station in Guildford catered for services running southwards and westwards from the town, and provided a base for independent operators as well as A&D, which supervised on behalf of Guildford Corporation. In this 1955 view, wartime Lancet ECG 852 is departing, while a variety of pre- and post-war A&D buses are at the stands, together with a London Transport T type bus.

Alder Valley

western boundary. The additional space allowed the terminus of the long-distance service 19 to be moved into the bus station after many years at the Queen Hotel, thus improving connections.

In 1950, the use of larger buses was legalised. Single-deckers could now be up to 30ft long and 8ft wide, and double-deckers up to 27ft 6ins long and 8ft wide. The Dennis Lancet J10B was designed to the new dimensions, and eleven chassis (HOU 899, 901-10) received suitably enlarged 38-seat versions of the familiar-shaped Strachan body. No 'band-boxes' were fitted, however, and this long-familiar but now little-used feature was removed from a large proportion of older single-deckers about this time. A less orthodox newcomer, in May 1951 was HOU 900, a prototype of the Dennis Dominant model. It had a 7.585 litre underfloor engine – a horizontal version of the Dennis O6 engine which was fitted to all the post-war Lancets – and an automatic gearbox. The 41-seat body, by Strachan, was of a unique style, and had a central entrance, just ahead of the rear wheels. However, although it served in the A&D fleet for 14 years, it suffered from high fuel consumption and other drawbacks, and only one other Dominant was ever built by Dennis.

The Guy 'utility' double-deckers had proved very useful on short-distance, heavily-loaded routes, and in 1950-1, 17 of them were given new 51-seat Weymann bodies. The later series, EOT 25-30, did not require rebodying until 1954, when they were provided with 56-seat, 8 foot wide East Lancashire bodies, which extended their lives for a further nine to ten years. The last three of the true utility series, the Weymann-bodied EOR 374-6, were never re-bodied, though EOR 376 received a completely new top deck after sustaining serious damage in 1955.

Despite an all-time peak of almost 52 million passenger journeys in 1950, the financial situation was starting to

The first batch of new Dennis Lance 3 double-deckers introduced after the war entered service on 1 August 1949, after a long delay at the coachbuilders. Their 5-speed gearboxes were an innovation, as was ducted heating for the upper deck. On the same day, service 20, Aldershot–Guildford, was converted to double-deck operation. GAA 629 was captured on film two days later, at the Wellington Avenue terminus.   *P.J. Holmes*

GOU 829, a Dennis Lance 3 of 1949 with 51-seat East Lancashire body, is shown at the Farnham terminus of service 31, which was in Great Austins, almost a mile south of the town centre.   *P. Trevaskis*

Unlike the pre-war Dennis Falcons, those delivered in 1950 had the 3.8 litre Gardner 4LK oil engine. They had Dennis bodies, and were delivered with 20 seats, though four more seats were subsequently added. GOU 862, in new condition, shows the emergency release control for the automatic door, which was an innovation on this batch of buses.   *E. Nixon collection*

The company's first buses to the newly legalised dimensions of 30 feet long and 8 feet wide were a batch of a dozen Dennis Lancet 3s on the J10 version of the chassis. Their arrival, in October 1950, coincided with the introduction of fleet numbers on A&D buses, though the familiar bonnet and body numbers continued to be displayed in addition. Their Strachan bodies seated 38, and because they were larger than anything previously in use, they received the nickname of 'Brabazons', after the contemporary airliner which was also noted for its large size. HOU 910 is shown crossing the railway at North Camp.   *P. Gascoine*

Above: In 1950, new 51-seat Weymann bodies were fitted to the oldest 17 Guy Arabs, which had previously carried Strachan or Roe utility bodies, thus extending the lives of these sturdy chassis by fourteen years. The earlier series of Guy Arabs retained their original short bonnets and wings when rebuilt, and looked rather neater than the Arab IIs, EHO 316 is shown at the Camberley Station stand, which A&D had financed in order to avoid any involvement in the suggested municipal bus station. *P. Trevaskis*

Below: For comparison with EHO 316, an Arab II, EHO 806, is shown in Aldershot High Street soon after rebuilding: at that time service 10 terminated here, due to lack of space in the bus station. *D.T. Sharwood*

Above: The 1950s saw the arrival of the underfloor engine, and Dennis exhibited their Dominant prototype in A&D livery at the 1950 Commercial Motor Show. It had a 100bhp engine and automatic transmission, and a Strachan 41-seat centre-entrance body was fitted. The slot near the front for one of the long trafficator arms is visible: they were very vulnerable, and were soon removed. Although HOU 900 ran for fourteen years in A&D service, latterly with a conventional gearbox, its complexity did not find favour and no other Dominants were ever built. The location is Aldershot Bus Station. *V.C. Jones*

deteriorate after the post-war boom years for public transport, and the impact of private motoring began to show in the statistics for subsequent years. By the time of the 1950 Annual General Meeting, about two-thirds of the mileage operated was failing to cover its costs, and that year's Budget had added no less than 9d per gallon to the fuel tax. To counteract these increasing costs and provide more revenue, two steps were taken on 2 October. Six unremunerative services (19a, 56a, 58, 59, 66 and 70 – all post-war innovations) were withdrawn and return fares were abolished for short journeys on all routes (i.e. up to 1/3d return, which represented about 7 miles each way). A general increase in fares, already planned before the 1951 Budget added a further 4½d to the fuel tax, took effect on 30 April 1951, and this enabled the company to maintain the quality of its services unchanged for a few more years. This increase was the first significant change in fares since 1928.

Expansion of the company's fleet, which in March 1952 consisted of 96 double-deckers, 215 single-deckers and 28 coaches, demanded increased accommodation. In 1952 Woking garage was considerably extended and the small garage at Alton was doubled in size. During 1952-3, the pre-war Dennis Falcons were withdrawn, thus eliminating the last petrol-engined vehicles from the fleet.

In January 1953, Mr James resigned as Chairman, and his place was taken by Mr T. Robert Williams, MA, LlB, who had been a director of A&D for the previous seven years. Living within the company's operating area, at Virginia Water, he made frequent use of the buses, becoming well known and popular among the A&D bus crews.

Small operators were by now facing the same economic problems, with less margin for absorbing increased costs. On 27 April, 1953, following the death of the proprietor Mr Whapshare, A&D took over the main route of Winchester and District, from Winchester to Alresford, which had been interworked with service 14 since 1926. The service continued under A&D as short workings of the latter, but the little red W&D buses were immediately replaced by double-deckers. Another 1953 takeover was the absorption of the stage services of B. Hammond & Sons, of Great Langley, Wonersh. Their frequent Wonersh–Guildford service was incorporated as short workings of A&D's existing 23 on 14 September.

The fifteen new express coaches (LAA 223-37) for the 1953 season took advantage of the increased dimensions now permitted, and were based on the Dennis Lancet J10C chassis. They had 38-seat Strachan bodies, similar in styling to the earlier coaches, but instead of the 'half-cab' layout, they were full-fronted. Structurally, these were noteworthy for being all-metal bodies: all previous A&D bodies had wooden frames. However, they were destined for a very short life in front-line service, as the front-engined layout was by now becoming obsolete.

In the first few months of 1953, some comparative trials were carried out with a range of underfloor engined single-deckers. Each was tried for a fortnight on the arduous 19 route to Bognor Regis. KOT 113, a 41-seat Guy Arab LUF fitted with an East Lancashire body, was subsequently taken into the company's stock. KOT 600 was a Strachan-bodied 41-seat Dennis Lancet UF, with a horizontal Dennis O6 engine. It was exhibited in A&D livery at the 1952 Earl's

Above: In June 1953, the Coronation Review of the Royal Air Force was held at Odiham. Although the authorities panicked over the possibility of large numbers of the public converging on Odiham, and made public announcements to discourage this, the logistics of transporting large numbers of additional service and civilian staff were formidable. These 29 Dennis Lancets, mostly of post-war vintage, made an impressive line-up for an amateur photographer to capture. *Alder Valley*

Right: The Lancet J10C chassis was designed to take a full-fronted body, as the advent of the underfloor engine had made an exposed radiator a symbol of obsolescence. Strachan's produced this 38-seat body, of traditional A&D coach appearance, with lines dictated by the existing curved route boards taken from earlier coaches. LAA 223, seen here in an official photo, was the first of a batch of 15 delivered for the summer of 1953. The absence of a bonnet meant that no bonnet number was allocated, and these were in fact the company's last full-sized front-engined single-deck vehicles. *E. Nixon collection*

Court show before starting trials, and was returned to its makers after a fairly short stay with A&D. The other three, all 44-seaters, bore other liveries. Two red Atkinsons from the North Western Road Car Co. (512/3, FDB 512/3) were respectively a very light weight (just over 5 tons) model PL 744H, with a 75bhp Gardner 4HLW engine, and a PL 745H with the 94bhp 5HLW engine. The third 44-seater was a 90bhp Leyland Tiger Cub demonstrator, OTD 301, in maroon livery.

In the event, none of these was adopted as the standard for the future. The honours were eventually to go to the AEC Reliance, with front-entrance bodies for stage carriage work. A demonstrator of this model, 50 AMC, carrying a cream and red 44-seat Park Royal body, was on trial on a number of routes in the first quarter of 1954.

A new batch of double-deckers was obtained in the same quarter to permit the conversion of a number of heavily-loaded single-deck services, thus reducing the number of relief vehicles and crews required. The new buses were 32 Dennis Lance K4s (the only K4s ever produced). They were fitted with Gardner 5LW engines from recently withdrawn Lances and Lancets of 1939-40 vintage, and their radiators were concealed behind a so-called 'tin front'. Twenty had 56-seat East Lancashire bodies (LOU 31-50) and twelve (LOU 51-62) had 56-seat Weymann 'Orion' bodies (modified in some details for A&D's use) which were

Above: Another venture in the cause of finding the right model of under-floor engined bus was the acquisition of KOT 113, a Guy Arab III LUF, which had a 41-seat East Lancashire body. The engine was the Gardner 5HLW – a horizontally-mounted version of the familiar 5LW. Unlike its Dennis rival, it served a full life of twelve years with A&D, and is seen here on the long service 19, a favourite haunt of the company's experimental buses.   *T. Wright*

Below: Dennis hired a Dennis Lancet LU to A&D for a year's trial in 1953. Its engine was a horizontal version of the Dennis O6, and a 5-speed gearbox was fitted. Although this design was more successful on the open market than Dennis's previous underfloor engined product, A&D were not interested in placing an order. KOT 600, with its smart 41-seat Strachan body, spent most of its life in the service of other operators.   *E. Nixon collection*

Above: The batch of Guy Arabs delivered at the end of 1945 was due for rebodying by 1954, and they received 56-seat East Lancashire bodies similar to those on recent Dennis Lances. This led to the unusual combination of a body 8 feet wide and 27 feet long and a chassis designed for a body 7ft 6ins by 26ft. EOT 26 is seen entering Aldershot Bus Station. *E. Nixon collection*
Below: Outside Reading South station, where Thames Valley had its principal terminus and booking office, a Dennis Lance K4, LOU 36, stands awaiting its return to Aldershot. The new double-deck livery, with dark green below the waistline, was introduced with this batch of 56-seat East Lancashire bodies. The white steering wheel, used to remind the driver that he was operating an 8-foot wide bus, is clearly visible. *E. Nixon collection*

The batch of 32 Lance K4s included twelve with a special version of the Weymann 'Orion' body, which was lighter and cheaper than the East Lancashire model. A&D's specification required the outswept skirt panels, the sliding ventilator on the lower-deck front window and the opening front windows to the upper deck. Relatively few double-deckers were stationed at Hindhead garage, where this photograph was taken, despite the blinds set for an Aldershot-based route. *P. Gascoine*

almost one ton lighter. In addition to a heavy programme of tree-cutting on all of the converted routes, the introduction of double-deckers on service 6, Aldershot– Petersfield, involved the raising of Wrecclesham railway bridge by one foot over the weekend before the new buses started work on 4 January, 1954. The company contributed £1,000 towards the cost of the operation.

Although the first four of the Lance K4s had appeared in the normal livery, the remainder were delivered in a completely revised scheme, which was to become the new standard. The panels below the waistline were now very dark green in colour, while the upper parts retained the familiar light green, with cream bands, and the long-established 'scroll' fleet name continued.

All the new AEC Reliance express coaches which appeared from August 1954 onwards carried this new livery. There were 25 of these coaches, MOR 581-605, fitted with 41-seat Strachan 'Everest' bodies, for the London service, as well as for other coach and private hire work. MOR 588 appeared at the Commercial Motor Show in September.

Apart from a few experiments, single-deck buses did not adopt the new colours until many years later.

An approach from Yellow Bus Services, whose proprietor Mr Hayter had died in 1951, led to A&D taking over their Guildford–Camberley route on 22 March 1954. This was replaced by a new A&D service 39, which covered the route from Camberley to Ash (Dover Arms), where connections were provided with the existing 20 to Guildford, and by augmenting 67, which covered the Guildford end of the YBS route as far as Wood Street.

A number of local route alterations, extensions and innovations had been introduced with varying success during the late 40s and early 50s, but entirely new ground was broken on 5 April 1954, when a new service 75 began between Reading and Guildford, via Wokingham, Bracknell and Bagshot. This service was operated jointly with Thames Valley, as the territory north of Bagshot was theirs,

and alternate journeys at 2-hourly intervals were run by the two companies. Interavailability of road and rail tickets was provided over the Reading–Bracknell section. A month later, on 1 May, another joint operation was started between them when A&D's service 12, Aldershot–Reading, was revised to permit one in three of the hourly journeys to be run by Thames Valley vehicles. This replaced the previous Thames Valley service 6c which ran from Reading to the territorial boundary at Hartley Row.

Since the end of the war, Mr B.S. Williams had built up a loosely-knit empire of stage and coach services, known as the Hants and Sussex group of companies. This was at first underpinned by the contracts for transporting large numbers of workers to Southampton for the post-war reconditioning of the liners *Queen Elizabeth* and *Queen Mary*. The end of these contracts and indulgence in an ambitious expansion programme brought about financial difficulties, and at the end of 1954 the business collapsed and services shut down overnight. A rescue operation had to be mounted hurriedly by neighbouring firms, and in view of the circumstances, no compensation was payable to the original operators. One of the subsidiaries, F.H. Kilner (Transport) Ltd. shut down on the evening of 21 December, and on the next day, A&D took over the operation of their Plaistow–Horsham and Plaistow–Cranleigh (Fridays only) services, which were numbered 50a and 50b respectively.

A slight contraction of the company's area resulted from the closure on 7 February 1955 of the Meon Valley railway line, between Alton and Fareham. The replacement bus service (Alton–Portsmouth) was provided by Southdown, and as it covered the route of A&D's Service 56 (Alton–East Tisted), the latter was withdrawn. Saturday services from Newton Valence into Alton were retained, and reverted to their original number, 59, which had been used for these one-time daily workings prior to their merging into the 56 timetable some five years earlier.

Although the Traction Hall was still in great demand

Tree-lopping was essential whenever a route was to be converted to double-deck operation, and provided a useful out-of-season role for the drivers of the summer coastal coaches. In March 1951, a team was at work on the A287 at Ewshot, using a converted 1937 Dennis Lance double-decker CCG 334, under trade plates 351 HO. While Inspector Jock Balfour directs the traffic, Drivers 'Digger' Stanley, Ted Price, Jasper Roberson, Charlie Shone and Sid Weston are making light work of the low branches. *Alder Valley*

Probably the most important conversion to double-deck operation scheduled for 1954 was that of service 6, Aldershot–Petersfield. As it served the military areas of Bordon, Whitehill and Longmoor, its heavy traffic of off-duty soldiers had caused many workings to consist of two (or even three) single-deckers since the war years. The company's £1,000 contribution to the cost of raising the Wrecclesham railway bridge was soon matched by the economies resulting from the abolition of the numerous relief buses. LOU 35, one of the new 'tin front' Dennis Lance K4s, was posed for this press release photograph. *Alder Valley*

Above: After only one year, the full-fronted Dennis Lancet coaches were displaced from all the principal coach services in 1954 by a much larger batch of AEC Reliance coaches, which had 41-seat centre-entrance Strachan bodies and 6.75 litre AH 410 engines. Their frames were straight, resulting in a higher floor level than users had come to expect. The new scheme of dark green below the waistline was introduced on these coaches, though its application to service buses was delayed for some time. MOR 599 is shown on a coastal service at Brighton, followed by a post-war Southdown Guy Arab. In May 1956, sister coach MOR 598 was fitted with a Wellworthy-Ricardo supercharger for some comparative trials, but it was not considered worthwhile to equip the whole fleet. *E. Nixon collection*

Left: The interior of one of the 1954 Reliance coaches shows that the traditional style of A&D comfort was maintained, though the pre-war embellishments such as dummy curtains and ornamental beading on the roof had been abandoned, and the luggage racks were cantilevered from the cantrail rather than being supported from the roof. *Alder Valley*

as a venue for company and private events, the authorities refused to renew its Music and Dancing license in 1955. New regulations on exit arrangements, fire precautions and car parking were impossible to implement in a building surrounded by an operational bus garage, and it was reluctantly decided to close the hall. In future, the three major annual events at which the company entertained its present and past employees to an official dinner – the long service award and safe driving award ceremonies, and the Benevolent Fund Annual Reunion for retired employees – were held at the Hog's Back Hotel. Other events were transferred to the clubroom at the athletics ground in Weybourne Road.

Official restrictions on the capacity of vehicles for operation by one man were relaxed at about this time, so that

crew-operated 32-seaters on a number of country routes were replaced by one-man operated (OMO) Dennis Falcon P5s. These were normal-control 30-seaters with Strachan bodies and Gardner 4LK engines. They were also used as replacements for the earlier 20-seaters on some routes. The two batches carried registrations LOU 63-77 and POR 421-8, delivered in 1954 and 1956 respectively.

An unexpected operating difficulty appeared suddenly at the end of 1956, when the international crisis over the Suez Canal led to the rationing of motor fuel. On 17 December, many off-peak journeys were cancelled, and on 31 December further wide-ranging cuts in services were introduced. These included cancellation of nearly all Sunday morning journeys, while some services lost all their

The latest oil-engined version of the Dennis Falcon was ordered to replace the small petrol-engined buses on rural routes, but their Strachan bodies now carried 30 passengers, only two less than the full-size buses of five years earlier. The distinctive sound of the Gardner 4LK engine earned the nickname of 'conker boxes' for these vehicles. This is a manufacturer's photo of LOU 73. *Author's collection*

No new vehicles were added to the fleet in 1955, and the 1956 intake consisted only of a batch of eight more Dennis Falcons, POR 421-8, identical to those of two years earlier. After withdrawal in 1967, seven of them were sold for further service in the Isle of Man. Until the 1960s, old buses were sold subject to covenants that they would not be used again in public service, and only a handful of earlier buses were ever recorded as having broken the ban. 23 HMN had started life as A&D's POR 422. *Author's collection*

Sunday workings. Inevitably, the oil companies raised their prices, and in addition the government applied a temporary surcharge to the fuel tax. A&D and other operators had to pass the cost on to passengers, but the fare increases turned out to be permanent, as basic fuel costs never returned to their previous levels.

In the expectation of achieving some fuel and staff economies by the introduction of larger-capacity buses, the company arranged to accelerate the delivery of its first batch of underfloor engined single-deckers, even though this involved writing off £10,000 as a consequence of the pre-mature withdrawal of some older buses. The new vehicles were AEC Reliances, RCG 601-30, with front-entrance Weymann bodies fitted with 43 seats for crew operation or 41 seats for one-man operation. A number of the former were later converted with the cash and ticket-issuing fitments and reversing lights which were necessary for one-man operation. Subsequent deliveries up to 1961 were SOU 421-43, XHO 370-7 and 378-93 AOU. With the similar Metro-Cammell bodied batch of seven delivered in 1967 and fifteen of the earlier AEC coaches rebuilt about the same time there were eventually 99 vehicles with this

The AEC Reliance chassis was chosen as A&D's standard for the ten years from 1957 to 1967, although minor variations of the chassis and of the Weymann body appeared from time to time. The first delivery of 30 buses appeared in February and March 1957, and were spread all over the company's area. Some were equipped for one-man operation from the start, while others were converted later, reducing the seating capacity from 43 to 41. The boards fitted to these one-man buses read 'Please pay as you enter and tender exact fare'. RCG 610 is seen outside the body shop in 1970, with the foreman of the team, Rip Coyne, beside it. It has just received the new style of fleetname, and is in the later dark green livery: all were originally delivered in the earlier lighter green colours. *P. Gascoine*

standard BET-specified design of body.

One casualty of the economy cuts was the cutting back of the long Aldershot–Bognor route to Midhurst. Although service 19 had been running since 1924, with the exception of the war years, it was recognised that the economics of running a stage service outside the company's usual area were no longer viable, and it was decided not to reinstate the Bognor extension when the crisis was over. In its place, a limited-stop service, 19a, was started in May 1957 for the summer months only. This was operated from Whit weekend until late September in each year until 1963: from 1964 until final withdrawal in 1969 the operating season was shortened to ten weeks, from early July till mid-September. Standard AEC Reliance buses were used, with specially-fitted brackets to hold boards announcing 'Limited Stop Service'.

The fuel situation had hardly recovered – some restoration of the Sunday services having become possible in April 1957 – when in July the company suffered its very first full-scale official strike. Although A&D crews had only received a pay rise in the previous November, causing an application to the Commissioners for another fare rise in February, they joined with provincial busmen all over the country to press a national pay demand. From this time onwards, wage increases occurred with increasing frequency until from the spring of 1960 an annual review became the accepted pattern. However, by exercising economies the company managed to avoid following every wage increase by a fare increase. One-man operation was greatly extended, and on 20 September 1958 a further batch of unremunerative services (57, 64, 69 and 74) ran for the last time. Also, the Wednesdays and Saturdays only service 36 ran its last journey on 17 September.

Despite the recent acquisition of 30-seat Dennis Falcons for rural services, the company carried out extensive trials of the Albion Nimbus 31-seater in 1957-8. Three different vehicles were involved. In July 1957 a demonstrator of the MR9 model, with an Alexander body, ran on 13 and 13a, and in October the exercise was repeated with the show model NS3N (XTA 839) with Alexander body and in Devon General livery. This also ran on the 65 and 66 routes. The same routes also saw NS3N 143 SMG during November and December 1958, carrying Maidstone and District livery, and this time the trial was extended to the

53 route. However, no further small-capacity buses were ever bought by A&D, which was now prepared to allow independent operators to take over some of its unremunerative routes: Odiham Motor Services provided a limited Odiham–Alton service, with A&D's blessing, after the larger company's service 57 had been abandoned.

From 30 September 1957 the express service to London, which had been reduced in frequency off-peak mid-week over the previous three winters, was cut back permanently to an hourly timetable, and the single daily journey to and from Whitehill was abolished. Journeys up from Farnham now started on the half-hour, and departures from Victoria were at ten minutes to the hour, throughout the day, with two additional journeys up in the morning and down in the evening.

The late 1950s saw extensions of the coastal express services in several directions. The 1958 season produced Saturday-only services to Hayling Island, and in 1959 the Eastbourne services were extended on Saturdays only to Bexhill and Hastings. Feeder services were introduced to permit passengers to start from places which had not previously had convenient connections to the main routes: Crookham and Fleet had been thus provided in 1951; Blackwater, Hawley and Cove were served in the 1956 season, and in 1960 the first steps were taken towards serving the area north of Woking, as well as linking Farncombe to the network. Other feeders ran on Sundays and Bank Holidays when the regular stage services did not run: Frimley Green, Ash and Tongham (1955), Wonersh (1962) and West Byfleet (1963) were among those places benefitting.

The fortunes of Yellow Bus Services Ltd. continued to decline after A&D had relieved them of the Camberley route in 1954, and on 16 June 1958 the remaining services were taken over. These were Guildford–Farnham via Seale and Guildford–Farnham via Compton (allocated service numbers 65 and 66 previously used by services to Puttenham and to Compton, respectively), Guildford–Bellfields via Woodbridge Road (which became 29c), Guildford–Stoughton and Guildford–Rydes Hill, both of which had been interworked with A&D since 1945 as 28a and 26 respectively. The last three of these services were immediately converted to double-deck operation.

Double-deckers of higher capacity were introduced in

Standing in Aldershot Bus Station, on service 6, is SOU 454, one of the 34 68-seat Dennis Lolines introduced in 1958. They were the first A&D double-deckers with power-operated doors to the rear platforms. *E. Nixon collection*

1958, when the Dennis Loline chassis became available. This was a version of the Bristol Lodekka, built under licence, as according to the rules laid down for the nationalised Bristol company, it was only allowed to sell its products to the nationalised operators of the Tilling group. The Lodekka principle involved offsetting the transmission shaft and differential housing from its traditional centre-line position, thus permitting a much lower floor level for the lower-deck gangway. This in turn enabled the floor levels of both decks to be lowered, and the 'highbridge' arrangement of central upper-deck gangway could be used, with a roof height little different from previous 'lowbridge' designs.

The Dennis product incorporated a Dennis gearbox, clutch, front axle and other components. The first 34 A&D Lolines (SOU 444-77) had Gardner 6LW engines and 68-seat East Lancashire bodies, fitted with electrically operated doors to their rear platforms.

A major extension was opened at Guildford garage during 1958. This consisted of a large and well-equipped workshop and associated offices and stores, and the area of the main garage previously used for maintenance work was freed for housing more of the buses stationed there. With a roof span of 126ft, without pillars, there was now room for 91 vehicles under cover.

In 1960, the front-entrance Dennis Loline II went into production, and during May to July of that year an exchange was arranged between SOU 459, of the original rear-entrance type, and the North Western Road Car Co's Alexander-bodied Loline II 813 (RDB 813). As a result of this trial, several orders for the subsequent Loline III model were placed for delivery over the period 1961 to 1965. Again having 6LW engines, all of these had air-operated doors, and air suspension was provided for their rear axles. As East Lancs were unable to fulfil the order for bodies, the first 56 (394-413 COR, 121-140 DOR and 449-465 EOT) were given 68-seat Alexander bodies. A novel feature of 122-40 DOR and 449-65 EOT was the provision on the offside of back-illuminated advertisement panels. These were not, however, perpetuated on subsequent deliveries, and were covered over in 1967-8. A more lasting innovation was the fitting of fluorescent interior lighting. 465 EOT, the last of the Alexander-bodied series, acted as a demonstrator when new, being loaned to East Kent and to Middlesbrough Corporation in the spring of 1963.

A&D was now following the example of a number of other major operators in booking blocks of registration numbers to coincide with the fleet numbers allocated to new vehicles. The XHO-registered Reliances were the first to be numbered in this way, in 1960, and the practice continued until the last year of the company's existence, 1971. The only exception was the 1962 batch of Loline IIIs, 121-40 DOR.

The permitted size of single-deck vehicles was increased in August 1961, to a new maximum length of 36ft, with a width of 8ft 2½ins instead of just 8ft. The new regulations came just too late for the order for new coaches for the 1962 season, so that these fifteen Reliances, 414-28 DHO, had to be built to the older specification. Fitted with 41-seat Park Royal bodies and boasting fluorescent interior lighting, they spent only one year on the London service before being superseded by 36ft long 49-seat vehicles in the spring of 1963. The first of these, 466 FCG, was on the Park Royal stand at the Commercial Vehicle Show at Earls Court in September 1962.

The remaining 49-seat coaches, 467-80 FCG, were delivered in the following March and April, and were supplemented in 1966 by a further five, FHO 531-5D, carrying almost identical Metro-Cammell bodies. Starting with the DHO-registered batch, a new coach livery was employed, being predominantly cream, with light green areas on front and side panels shaped to soften the straight lines which had now become the fashion in body design.

In May 1962 a 36-foot AEC Reliance bus, 327 NMP, with a Park Royal body seating no fewer than 54 passengers, ran as a demonstrator on the heavily-loaded Cove services from Aldershot. However, there was no urgency for the introduction of 36ft buses, and none were obtained for a further six years. Two other vehicles considered in 1962 were an Albion Lowlander, which was inspected though not operated, and in December, an AEC Renown double-decker, 7552 MX.

Turning away from vehicles, to deal with more general aspects of the early 1960s, special mention must be made of the company's golden jubilee celebration in 1962. This was marked by a special luncheon for 200 distinguished guests and long-serving employees in the Officers' Club at Aldershot on 30 October. The Mayor of Aldershot, Councillor S.C.H. Gibbs, was the principal speaker, and a well-illustrated booklet was published to coincide with the event.

The goodwill of two small operators was purchased in

Above: By 1960, the regulations which required opening windscreens had been abolished, so that year's intake of AEC Reliance buses had a more symmetrical front aspect than those of the previous 4 years. With this batch A&D began the practice of booking registration numbers to coincide with fleet numbers. XHO 376 is standing, in its original livery, in Farnham Road Bus Station at Guildford. The Setright ticket machine is visible beside the steering wheel, showing this to be a one-man-operated bus. *D.M. Studdard*

Below: 1961 saw sixteen more Reliances delivered, originally as crew-operated buses, though some were later converted to driver-only operation. 392 AOU is seen at Aldershot Bus Station in its later livery, with revised style of fleetname. *Photofive Transport Enterprises*

Over the years, many buses were offered by manufacturers as demonstration vehicles, either for inspection or for extended trials. In June 1960, however, A&D negotiated for the loan of a Dennis Loline II from the North Western Road Car Co, with the specific intention of evaluating Dennis's front-entrance double-decker model. It seated 71 passengers in its East Lancashire body, and ran on various routes based in Aldershot. Although A&D never bought any Loline IIs, this trial led to a large intake of Loline IIIs from 1961 onwards. The photo was taken in Farnham Road bus station, Guildford.   *N. Hamshere*

The first of many Dennis Loline IIIs entered service, with extensive press coverage, in September 1961. The company had to abandon its favourite double-deck body builder, East Lancashire, in order to avoid delays, and the equivalent 68-seat bodies built by Alexander were used for the first 67 Loline IIIs. 397 COR is shown at Aldershot Bus Station.   *E. Nixon collection*

Above: A short-lived venture was the illuminated advertisement panel fitted to the off side of 36 of the 1962 batch of Dennis Loline IIIs. Advertisers were not sufficiently enthusiastic, and these buses spent most of their lives with the panels blanked out and only conventional advertisements applied. 136 DOR is shown in Onslow Street bus station, Guildford.   *E. Nixon collection*
Below: A 1966 scene in The Borough, Farnham, shows 409 COR, a 1961 Loline III, approaching the bus stop in a direction which has since been banned under the one-way traffic system.   *P. Gascoine*

Above: For the 1962 season, fifteen Park Royal bodied 41-seat coaches were ordered, though by the time they were in service they were in one respect out of date, since new regulations had been introduced to permit the use of 36-foot long coaches. They had in any case been designated as dual-purpose vehicles, so though their time on the London route was short, their use on less exacting work was not inappropriate. 415 DHO is shown here in a works photograph. *E. Nixon collection*

Below: 36-foot coaches made their debut in 1963, when 15 AEC Reliances, with AH 470 engines and 49-seat Park Royal bodies, arrived. The first of these had been exhibited in the 1962 Show, and had in fact been completed in time to be featured in the A&D anniversary booklet earlier in that year. 475 FCG is seen in this view taken while manoeuvring at Victoria Coach Station. *Author's collection*

1962. On 29 January Mr Ernest R. Gudge of The Bourne, Farnham, reached agreement for his private hire and excursion business, running under the name of Comfy Coaches, to be taken over by A&D in the following April. He had bought his first coach in September 1926, and had formed a limited company in 1956. None of his final fleet of twelve vehicles was acquired by A&D, but the deal included the Farnham Travel Agency office in Castle Street, which A&D continued to run for several years. Mr Gudge continued in business for several more years as a garage proprietor at his original premises.

On 4 June 1962, Odiham Motor Services Ltd. handed over its main route from Odiham to Basingstoke via Greywell to become A&D's 7a. This company had originated in the 1920s as the 'Nancy Bus', and in 1930 was bought by William Stacey and Son. By 1950, four routes were in operation from Odiham: two to Basingstoke, one to Camberley and one to Fleet. By 1962, however, the latter two had been abandoned, and after the sale of his main route, Mr Charles Stacey was left with his subsidiary route to Basingstoke and the hire and excursion business, together with a petrol service station, created out of the former Regal Cinema at Odiham. The A&D bus working 7a was outstationed there for several years until Mr Stacey retired and sold the premises.

On 1 January 1963 the British Transport Commission's part ownership of A&D passed to the Transport Holding Company, thus severing the railway involvement which had lasted for over thirty years. Although there was a consequent change of certain Board members, no obvious operating changes resulted, since it was agreed that the Standing Joint Committee should continue in being to co-ordinate road and rail activities in the A&D area.

The accommodation at Aldershot bus station was further increased in 1964, when more land was added to allow nine end-loading gates in place of the two through platforms which were built in 1950. This enabled the transfer to the bus station of the few services still terminating elsewhere in Aldershot. Safety was enhanced by the provision of overhead lighting.

Following the lead of British Railways, a number of bus companies changed their timetables to the 24-hour clock around this time. A&D's express service times were printed in this form for the 1964/5 winter, and the company adopted the new scheme for the whole of its network with the timetable for summer 1965.

The chassis for the final order for Dennis Loline III double-deckers were delivered in 1964, but a prolonged strike at the bodybuilders, Weymann's, delayed their completion for many months. They were originally to have been registered 481-530 KOT, but Hampshire took up the year suffix system of registrations in 1965, so those entering service in that year appeared as AAA 503-30C. All fifty had 68-seat bodies. 483 KOT was exhibited on the Dennis stand at the 1964 Earl's Court Show, while AAA 530C had the double distinction of being the last double-decker and the last Dennis vehicle ever purchased by the company.

For some years, excursions to coastal resorts had been losing custom, as private car owners preferred to drive themselves for these 40 to 50 mile journeys. In contrast, long-distance excursions had been increasing in popularity, as 300 or more miles' driving was not such an attractive proposition. Consequently, for the 1965 season, there was a complete re-casting of the excursion programme, and new

A&D were able to obtain bodies from Weymann for their final batch of Loline IIIs, introduced in 1964-5. This view of 489 KOT was taken in the Onslow Street bus station at Guildford.
Photofive Transport Enterprises

destinations included Cambridge and Ely, Cardiff, Cheltenham and Tewkesbury, the Chiltern Hills, Shropshire and the Welsh Marches, while the existing Derbyshire Dales run was revised to make use of the M1 motorway and thus give more time in the destination area.

The A&D area was less affected by the 'Beeching' railway closures of the 1960s than any other major operators. Only one line, Guildford–Horsham, was closed to passengers, on 13 June 1965. On the following day, two new Lolines, AAA 528/9C, started operating an un- numbered limited stop service into Guildford from Rudgwick, Baynards, Cranleigh and Bramley stations in the mornings and outwards in the evenings. In addition, on Tuesdays and Fridays only a shoppers' journey was operated from Baynards to Cranleigh and back by a 30-seat Falcon.

On 24 July 1965, a general increase of fares took effect. Despite almost annual wage increases and the increase of fuel tax in successive budgets, fares had been held constant since July 1961, and many had been unchanged for five years. However, the percentage of mileage which was failing to cover operating costs had once again risen above 50, and a fare rise was now inevitable. This time, however, the new fares structure was short-lived, as a nationally-agreed sick pay scheme and a 40-hour working week came into force in February and April 1966 respectively, and the next general fare revision became necessary on 1 July, 1967.

The popular T. Robert Williams died in November 1965, after almost thirteen years as Chairman of A&D. His successor as director, Mr Frank Pointon, was already experienced in the bus industry, and was immediately appointed Chairman of the company.

As the FHO-registered batch of coaches was not ready in time for the 1966 season, five coaches were hired from Southdown from April until September. They were middle-aged Leyland Royal Tigers, with 41-seat centre entrance

Some of the 1964-5 Loline IIIs were delivered later than expected, with the result that instead of carrying on the allocated sequence of registrations, in the KOT series, they were the first A&D vehicles to receive registrations with year suffix letters. (Hampshire did not use the suffix letters A or B for 1963-4.) When new, these buses were sometimes used on London express duties at busy times, as with AAA 520C, shown here at Bagshot. *P. Gascoine*

Harrington bodies, carrying Southdown numbers 1675/6/89-91 (LUF 815/6/29, MUF 430/1). 1689 was exchanged in July for 1686, LUF 826. Although still in Southdown colours, they were given A&D fleet name transfers to avoid any confusion.

Five more 49-seat Reliance coaches were obtained in 1966, but though their bodies were to the same design as the 1963 examples, construction was undertaken by Weymann. FHO 534D is posed near Aldershot, with its roof ventilation panels raised. *P. Gascoine*

For the 1966 season, it was necessary to hire five coaches because the new Reliances were not yet ready. The substitutes were Leyland Royal Tigers from Southdown, with 41-seat Harrington bodies. Although they ran in Southdown colours, A&D fleetnames were applied to avoid confusion when operating excursions into Southdown territory. LUF 816 is shown parked at Aldershot garage.
L. Smith

Although a few vehicles of other makes were evaluated, such as the Albion Viking, EGG 559C, demonstrated on 13 and 14 April 1966, every new acquisition from 1965 until 1970 was on one version or another of the AEC Reliance chassis.

The Weymann works at Addlestone had closed late in 1965, so the associated Metro-Cammell works provided the familiar BET-style 41-seat bodies for HHO 536-42E in February 1967, and similar 40-seat bus bodies were built for the chassis of fifteen of the 25 AEC Reliance coaches of 1954 vintage, which re-entered service also in February 1967. The disappearance of the earlier rear-entrance single-deckers permitted a rapid conversion to one-man operation. By the spring of 1966, 53% of single-deck mileage was OMO, and in September 1967 it was reported that of all the single-deck services only 19, 33, 44, 50a and the Cove group (3b, 3d and 76) remained crew-operated.

A long-familiar feature disappeared during the months following June 1967, when the 'scroll' fleet name, surrounded by the oval flourish, was superseded by a new style in the plainer idiom of the times: 'Aldershot & District' in sans-seriffed italic letters. The normal sequence of bus repaints led to the demise of the old style within the following two years, although it was of course replaced immediately on publicity material.

In May 1968 a small batch of five Reliances arrived with the first 36-foot bus bodies in the fleet. These were MOR 558-62F, with 51-seat Willowbrook BET Federation pattern bodies, and were often used on the coastal services because of their high seating capacity. Early in the following year they were followed by thirty buses fitted with 45-seat bodies by Marshalls of Cambridge, which were 32ft 8ins in length (PHO 566-95G).

Mr Gray retired as General Manager on 31 March, 1967, and his successor, the fourth and last man to hold this office, was Mr Peter Scully, formerly Traffic Manager of the North Western Road Car Co.

A symptom of labour problems in the bus industry in the late 1960s was the difficulty of recruiting, training and retraining staff, both as crews and in workshops, due to the competition from the expanding and prospering heavy goods vehicle industry. Advertisements for the direct recruitment of drivers showed how times had changed since the 1930s, when drivers were normally found by promotion of conductors of suitable aptitude and seniority. In the workshops, arrears of maintenance led to several instances across the country of operators hiring, or even purchasing, serviceable vehicles from their colleagues who were in a more fortunate position. A&D was no exception, and loans both to and from City of Oxford Motor Services took place over the years 1968-71. From November 1968 onwards, no fewer than 17 Lolines were loaned by A&D for periods of a few months, with up to six at Oxford at any one time. Initially, front entrance Loline IIIs were provided, but later replacements were elderly rear entrance Loline Is. COMS gave them temporary fleet numbers A1-17.

Two of the DHO-registered Reliance coaches (i.e. the batch which had been superseded by 36ft coaches after a year on the London service) also went on loan to Oxford in September 1969 and were numbered AS 1/2. Before the end of the year these two, which though only seven years old were surplus to A&D's needs, were officially transferred to COMS ownership, and subsequently another eight of the same batch joined the Oxford fleet on a permanent basis. To complete the story of inter-company loans, we must look ahead to the first half of 1971, during which four 44-seat Reliances, 748/51 HFC with Weymann bodies and 753/5 KFC with Park Royal bodies, were on loan from COMS to A&D from the end of January until early June.

Some respite from the ever-increasing trend of costs

In 1967, ten years after the first AEC Reliance buses were delivered, the final batch arrived. They were the last to have the light green livery, and their bodies were built by the Metro-Cammell factory. Minor changes in the body design included the grille above the front number plate, the absence of chromed windscreen frames, and the relocation of the emergency exit from the centre to the rear of the offside. HHO 542E was one of the buses provided with slots to take the 'Limited Stop' notice used on the summer service 19A to Bognor. This picture was in fact posed at Tweseldown, whatever the destination blinds purport to show. *P. Gascoine*

Fifteen of the 25 Reliance coaches of 1954 vintage were rebodied in 1967 with Metro-Cammell bodies of the standard design. One of them, MOR 581, was privately preserved after withdrawal, and is seen here at a rally, in the old A&D livery. *N. Hamshere*

The very first of the AEC Reliance buses was used in 1967 to enable the directors to decide on a new fleetname style. They decided to use the two-line version on the front of RCG 601, rather than the single-line upper and lower case version shown on the side.   *L. Smith*

Left: When the 1962 Reliance coaches had been displaced from the principal long-distance services, they were modified for use on stage services by introducing a more bus-like destination panel. 422 DHO was photographed outside the body shop after this rebuilding, repainted with the new style of fleetname, in 1968. Most of these vehicles were hired, and later sold, to City of Oxford Motor Services in 1969-70. *P. Gascoine*

Above: The largest single-deck buses ever bought by A&D were a batch of five Reliances with 36-foot Willowbrook bodies designed to BET specifications. They were primarily for routes which needed the high capacity of 51 seats, but were fitted out to dual-purpose standards and could sometimes be seen on the London service. *P. Gascoine*
Right: Awaiting departure from The Grove at Aldershot is PHO 580G, one of the thirty Reliances of 1969, which were given 33-foot long 45-seat bodies built by Marshall of Cambridge. *P. Gascoine*

was provided by the transport Act of 1968. This enabled stage operators to receive a tax rebate on their fuel bills, so alleviating a long-standing cause of complaint raised at every Annual General Meeting since 1950. In that year the increased fuel tax had doubled the expenditure on this account to some £85,000. By 1966 the fuel tax bill was £123,000, at 3s 6.9d per gallon.

A new departure in June 1968 was the purchase of three coaches of a type suitable for long-distance touring, whereas all previous coaches had been specified primarily for the express service to London. NAA 563-5F were AEC Reliances with 36ft 49-seat Duple Commander III bodies, which were provided with a passenger address system for the driver and fleet name panels in translucent glass illuminated at night by fluorescent back-lighting. When not required elsewhere, they took their turn on the London service. A notable private hire job in 1969 was the use of thirteen coaches to transport a contingent of the 1st Battalion, Welsh Guards from their depot at Pirbright for the investiture of the Prince of Wales at Caernarvon. They left the depot on 23 June and returned on 2 July, having taken the opportunity of fitting in a short summer tour by the regimental band to various towns en route.

Major disruption was caused in the Guildford area by a downpour of 3.75 inches of rain on 15 September 1968. Not only did this completely flood the bus stations close to the river Wey, necessitating the cutting back of services to temporary termini for a few days, but the garage, also close to the river, had up to 1 foot depth of flood water inside. Other areas of West Surrey, including Farncombe, Farnham and Woking, also suffered, and many other services, notably 17, 19, 28, 28c, 45 and 55a/b/c were affected.

The last phase of A&D's separate existence had now begun. The BET group had, for some time, been campaigning against the continuing threat of compulsory nationalisation, and had backed this with widespread advertising, on its buses and in the newspapers. However, there was a sudden reversal of group policy, and on 14 March 1968 its omnibus interests were sold to the Transport Holding Co. and thus the company became a nationalised concern. For some time, the BET group had followed the same policy as the nationalised Tilling group, which was to appoint a regional chairman to head the Boards of all the companies within a geographical region. The THC adopted the same approach, so Mr Frank Pointon resigned the chairmanship of A&D, handing over to Mr David Deacon, who was a member of the council of the Tilling Association Ltd, and chairman of five ex-Tilling companies in the south-east as well as of two other ex-BET companies in the area. Mr. Pointon, an Executive Director of BET, now joined the board of the THC, and was appointed regional chairman for the West Midlands as well as becoming Managing Director of the Birmingham and Midland company.

On 1 January 1969 the National Bus Company was formed to manage the ex-Tilling and ex-BET companies, as well as the former Country Area of London Transport. In the process, the NBC was required to take responsibility for the capital debt incurred by the Government in nationalising the BET companies. Consequently each of the latter now had to bear a proportion of the interest payments (at a rate of 4.92%) in addition to capital repayments. In absence of adequate trading profits, this had to be covered by borrowing at prevailing, much higher, commercial rates. In 1980, A&D's successor, Alder Valley, was obliged to provide £1.2 million to the NBC's central account, which

For the summer of 1968, the coach fleet was augmented with three Reliance coaches with AH505 engines and 49-seat bodies of Duple's Commander III pattern. They were used for long-distance tours, but at other times were to be seen on the London service. This official photo of NAA 564F was posed near to Aldershot's Wellington monument. *P. Gascoine*

amounted to almost 3½p on every ticket issued.

The first visible effect of the NBC regime on A&D was that from 1970, all of its new buses were on chassis built by the Bristol company, which had been nationalised at the time when the Tilling Group sold out. The additions were all single-deckers, as for some time there had been a reversal of the trend of the 1950s and early 1960s, in view of the now declining traffic on many of the longer-distance routes which had then been converted to double-deck operation. For these, high- capacity one-man-operated single-deckers were now adequate and more economical. The number of passengers carried in 1969 was 39,461,455, as compared with the record level of 52 million in 1950.

The first Bristols, delivered in June-July 1970 were fifteen 36ft RELLs, UOU 601-15H, fitted with Marshall 'standee' bodies to a BET specification, seating 44 but licensed to carry 20 standing passengers in addition (RELL stood for Rear Engine, Long, Low floor height). They had central exit doors as well as front entrances and were fitted with semi-automatic gearboxes. A further fifteen appeared a year later.

The 1970 batch of coaches, VCG 596-600H, were still on AEC Reliance chassis, but had larger engines and 6-

Right: Reliance coach 427 DHO is shown here standing at Caernarvon, having transported its load of Welsh Guardsmen for the investiture of the Prince of Wales on 1 July 1969.

Alder Valley

Below: Exceptionally heavy rain resulted in this remarkable shot of an AEC Reliance (SOU 438) producing a high bow wave in Onslow Street, Guildford, in September 1968. The background consists of the bus station and Rodborough Buildings, which was the original Dennis motor works of 1902. *T.A. Wilkie*

UOU 603H was one of the first delivery of Bristol RELL 6G buses received in 1970. The 44-seat dual-door bodies were built by Marshall. This official view, in Aldershot Bus Station, appears to have been taken on a normal working day, in the correct place for a 3A bus.
Alder Valley

speed gearboxes. They had the slightly re-styled Duple Commander IV body, so in outward appearance they resembled the earlier NAA-registered batch in most respects. Only two coaches were ordered for the 1971 season, again on Reliance chassis, but this time changing to the Plaxton Panorama Elite II body. Registered YCG 101/2J, they started a new series of fleet numbers for coaches at 101.

In yet another move to maximise revenue, the long-established principle of half fares for children was abandoned in the summer of 1970, when the children's fares were raised to two-thirds of the adult rate. This was followed on 27 February 1971 by a move to reduce overcrowding at peak hours, by levying full fare for children travelling before 0915 on Mondays to Fridays. Only the regular travellers holding junior scholars' term tickets were exempted from this new rule.

A welcome measure under the 1968 Transport Act was the power given to local authorities to subsidise bus operations within their areas, and Surrey and Hampshire were persuaded in 1971 to provide grants for eight rural services to enable them to continue for at least one year more, on the grounds of social desirability. These were 47, 48b, 49, 50, 51, 53, 54 and 60.

The company's first woman driver, Mrs Yvonne Coleman, started work on Service 29c on 2 February 1971, from Guildford depot, and the next one went out on the roads only three days later. However, the staff situation was being affected by conversion to one-man (or one-woman!)

operation, and it was not possible to absorb all the redundant conductors into other vacancies, with the regrettable result that 26 conductors based on Woking and Hindhead depots received redundancy notices in the latter part of 1971.

An extensive rebuilding and re-equipment programme was carried out at the Halimote Road premises during the late 'sixties and early 'seventies. This considerably eased the problems which had resulted from years of piecemeal development of garage and workshops on the same site. On 5 July 1971 a gyratory system was introduced whereby all vehicles coming off service entered at the bottom of the site, refuelled, passed through a washing machine and thence went either into the garage or the running shed workshop for minor repairs if necessary. They then emerged for their next duty via Foden Road, near the top end of the site.

In addition to the second batch of 11-metre Bristol RELLs (YHO 616-30J) delivered in 1971, that year also produced 21 of the shorter 10-metre RESL model (the 'S' indicating a short chassis). Twelve had bodies from the nationalised Eastern Coach Works, of Lowestoft, which had been the Tilling Group's bodybuilders for many years past. They were again 'standee' bodies with 40 seats, room for 20 standing and central exit doors. Coincidence of registration and fleet numbers was abandoned. Nos. 640-51 were registered YHO 631-6J and CCG 291-6K. The remaining nine chassis, 631-9, CHO 691-9K, had a shorter

Right: A second batch of 49-seat Duple-bodied Reliance coaches was obtained in 1970, with the latest model Commander IV body. Despite the apparent similarity to the previous batch, the installation of the larger 11.3 litre AH 690 engine, with a six-speed gearbox, produced a vastly superior performance. VCG 598H is here seen awaiting departure for London from Castle Street, Farnham.   *L. Smith*

The last A&D coaches were a pair of 49-seat Reliances, this time with Plaxton Panorama Elite bodies and AH 690 engines. This vehicle, YCG 101J, was delivered for the 1971 season.
P. Gascoine

version of the Marshall body fitted to the RELLs, with the same passenger capacity as the ECW bodies. Many of the new arrivals were used to replace double-deckers (including the early Loline Is) and on 5 July services 8, 9, 12 and 35 as well as the single-decked 76 and 76a, were converted to OMO entirely, while other routes saw the partial introduction of the new regime.

Amalgamation into larger operating units had now become the fashion in the nationalised bus industry, and the NBC decided to integrate A&D with its similar-sized neighbour, the Thames Valley Traction Co., to form the Thames Valley and Aldershot Omnibus Co. Ltd. This was to operate under the coined fleet name 'Alder Valley', in the same way as contemporary amalgamations of local authorities usually chose a non-contentious title to avoid any suggestion of dominance by one partner.

In preparation for the merger, the General Manager of Thames Valley, Mr T.G. Pruett, joined the A&D Board: A&D's own General Manager, Mr Scully, had already been given a seat on the Board in January 1970. Other portents of the change appeared late in 1971, when experiments were tried to decide on a new livery. One withdrawn bus was painted in an experimental combination of 'Tilling green' and 'Tilling red' for the directors' benefit, though it never carried its livery outside the garage area. However, the choice eventually fell on a pleasant maroon livery, with cream reliefs, and fleet name lettering in the small Tilling style of seriffed gold characters.

For several years, the majority of A&D's vehicles had fleet numbers matching their registration numbers. This ceased abruptly after No. 630, YHO 630J, since although fleet numbers 631-9 had already been allocated to nine further Bristol RELL6G 44-seaters, their matching registration numbers were used for a priority delivery of 40-seaters on the shorter Bristol RESL6G chassis. The first of these, YHO 631J, thus had the fleet number 640. The dual-door bodies were built by Eastern Coachworks, which had been the builder of the majority of bodies on Bristol chassis for many years, both firms being nationalised concerns. This shot was taken at Frensham immediately after delivery.
P. Gascoine

Although ordered for 1970, and allocated fleet numbers, a batch of nine Bristol RELL6Gs was, at the company's request, not delivered until November 1971, the penultimate month of A&D's existence. They had 44-seat bodies by Marshall. They appeared in A&D colours, but soon received Alder Valley fleet number plates. When the NBC's poppy red livery was introduced a year later, they were not yet due for a repaint, and so the new fleetname was applied, above the cantrail, to the old green livery, to produce the hybrid scheme seen here on CHO 695K.
N. Hamshere

Withdrawn Reliance SOU 424 was used to demonstrate this proposed livery for Alder Valley in August 1971. Tilling light green was used above the waistline and on the skirt panels, with Tilling red in between. All photography was banned: no comment! *P. Gascoine*

Ex-A&D Reliance MOR 585, numbered 349 in the AV fleet, stands on the forecourt of Woking garage. It is in the short-lived AV livery of wine red and cream, with golden yellow fleetname, introduced at the time of the merger. Another change in appearance is provided by the advertisement on the body side: the subsequent NBC poppy red livery transferred all single-deck fleetnames to the roof, to clear the side panels. *Motorphoto*

Chapter Nine
Alder Valley

The merger took place on 1 January 1972, the legal process being accomplished by changing the name of the Aldershot company and, after taking over the assets of Thames Valley, formally winding up the latter company. Most existing officials of both companies were found suitable posts in the new organisation. Mr Scully became Director and General Manager of the combine, while Mr Pruett remained as a Director with a consultative role. The Registered Office and Head Office were established at the former Thames Valley premises at Lower Thorn Street, Reading (soon to be affected by road improvements and be renamed Thorn Walk). The two Secretarial Departments were merged, while the two Traffic Departments were combined and then re-organised into separate Operating and Commercial Departments. Although the central staffs of these were based at Reading, the bulk of A&D's Traffic Department remained at Aldershot as a Divisional organisation, mainly responsible to the Operating Manager, with its own Divisional Traffic Manager. The two Engineering Departments remained separate, with two Divisional Chief Engineers and no central organisation. Thus there was no total exodus from the Halimote Road offices, though they lost their status as Head Office and Registered Office. The combined Alder Valley staff numbered 2120, with 599 passenger vehicles based at ten main depots. A&D contributed 284 of the total vehicle stock.

The Aldershot fleet at the time of the merger consisted of 100 Dennis Loline double-deckers, all at least seven years old, 30 AEC Reliance coaches, 103 AEC Reliance buses and dual-purpose vehicles, of which the newest dated from 1969, and the latest intake of 51 Bristol RELL and RESL single-deckers. All single-deckers were fitted for driver-only operation. Both of Alder Valley's constituent companies had more of the Bristols on order, and those booked by A&D were delivered, with Hampshire registration numbers, during 1972.

Just three months after the formation of Alder Valley, an NBC reorganisation replaced regional chairmen by regional directors. The new director for the Southern Region was none other than Mr Frank Pointon, who thus resumed overall responsibility for affairs at Aldershot.

Inevitably, time and experience produced changes in the initial arrangements. Most obvious to the general public was the decision by the National Bus Company to impose one of its standard liveries, and of the limited choice available, Alder Valley eventually selected the poppy red colour, with white reliefs for dual-purpose vehicles and the NBC standard white livery for coaches.

This scheme started in December 1972, by which time less than half of the fleet had received the earlier maroon livery. Aldershot Division, no doubt retaining a loyalty to green, had laid in stocks of NBC green paint, and had to dispose of a large quantity to another company when the

Buses already ordered by A&D, but delivered after the merger, received Hampshire registrations. HOR 488L was AV 488, delivered in August 1972. It was a Bristol RESL6G, with a 40-seat ECW body, and was photographed at Guildford.

A. Lambert

Above: Former A&D buses started to appear in the NBC poppy red livery from December 1972 onwards. Loline 493 KOT, now AV No. 820, is seen in good condition at Winchester bus station in May 1975. By this time, drastic economies had been made in the amount of information displayed on the destination blinds: final destination and a three-digit service number had to suffice.

A. Lambert

Below: The NBC corporate livery for coaches was basically white, and A&D's Reliances duly appeared thus, with Alder Valley replacements for the original illuminated fleetname panels. In 1973 the NBC started to co-ordinate its tours and inclusive holidays on a national basis, with the result that the large fleetname 'National' appeared on long-distance coaches in addition to the fleetname of the owning subsidiary in smaller letters. NAA 565F and VCG 600H (AV48 and 53) are shown here at Guildford.

N. Hamshere

decision in favour of poppy red was made.

The fleet was renumbered into a combined stock list, and small cast number plates were screwed to front and rear panels. The numbers were allocated in blocks, those applied to ex-A&D vehicles lying in the ranges:

1-13	service vehicles
36-55	coaches
284-396	AEC Reliance single-deckers and demoted coaches
417-467	Bristol single-deck types
751-858	Dennis Loline double-deckers

The new fleet number plates were to be seen for some time on vehicles still in the A&D livery.

The amalgamation soon led to the extension of some routes across the A30 road (the previous boundary between the two companies), and several other route alterations and linkings of services appeared early in 1974. To avoid confusion, most of the Aldershot Division's services were renumbered on 29 September 1974. Some numbers were simply increased by 200, but the desire to eliminate suffix letters led to other new service numbers being completely different, while the non-conflicting numbers above 70 were left largely unchanged. The express service to London became service C (A and B having been used for the Thames Valley services to London) and was subsequently given the number 320 in a new series allocated to express and special services.

The NBC, in conjunction with the Leyland company, had developed a new single-deck bus, the 49-seater Leyland National. A&D had placed 22 of these on order, which entered service with Alder Valley from April 1973 onwards, again registered in Hampshire. Variants of the National became the company's standard for the next thirteen years, both as service buses and as dual-purpose vehicles. A total of 191 (fleet numbers 101-291) were acquired between 1973 and 1978, after which time vehicle requirements had started to decline and there was no need to purchase more. Nearly all of the Nationals were licensed to carry 24 standing passengers, which allowed considerable economies in relief workings during busy periods.

The ex-A&D double-deck fleet was due for replacement over the next few years, but another factor accelerated the introduction of an alternative to the Dennis Loline. The use of driver-only operation (originally called one-man-operation, and, with the arrival of female bus drivers, one-person-operation) on double-deckers was legalised in 1966. Thames Valley had already started using the 70-seat rear-engined Bristol VR, which had an Eastern Coachworks body with the entrance alongside the driver, ahead of the front wheels. This arrangement was suitable for one-person operation (unlike the Loline, with its entrance behind the front wheels and the driver), and thus qualified for the bus grants introduced by the government in 1968. Consequently, the Bristol VR, in a 74-seat version, also became the standard for new additions to the fleet of the Southern Area, as the Aldershot Division had been re-named on 1 November 1973.

It was soon apparent that the Leyland National was too large and expensive to operate on every Alder Valley route (and in a few cases too high to negotiate low bridges, because of its roof-mounted heat-exchanger pod). In 1974, therefore, the first of a batch of 25 Ford R1014 buses (Nos. 701-25) with 45-seat Eastern Coachworks bodies, was introduced. Ten more (726-35), with Plaxton bodies, were added in 1976, and the type was used all over the AV network. Another type of vehicle, of similar size, was the Bristol LH, which had been widely used by Thames Valley. Seven new ones, with 43 seats (535-41), were bought in 1975, but when fleet reductions became necessary in the later 1970s, the Fords and LHs were the first to be withdrawn, and all had gone by the end of 1980, some with as little as four years service to their credit.

Mr Scully was seconded to a bus traffic advisory post in the Department of the Environment early in 1976, and in March of that year Mr Bernard Rootham, from East Yorkshire Motor Services Ltd., came to Reading to succeed him. Under the NBC, senior management posts became part of a nationwide career structure, so that from this time onwards, they tended to be filled by relatively short-term incumbents, rather than by officers who had worked their way through the company over a long period. Only four months after taking over, Mr Rootham had to resolve a

The estate agents, Mann & Co, sponsored the painting of Loline AAA 529C in a special silver livery for the Queen's Silver Jubilee year of 1977. When not required for special duties, it worked on normal services, such as the 240 to Yateley via Camberley, where it was photographed. *Motorphoto*

Mainstay of Alder Valley's single-deck fleet from 1973 up to the present time – the 49-seat Leyland National integrally-constructed bus, in NBC poppy red with white waistband. No. 188 (GPC 737N) is shown, in 1977, at Onslow Street bus station, Guildford.   *N. Hamshere*

Battersea Bridge forms the background to this picture of a Leyland National in NBC dual-purpose livery. 245 (LPF 603P) was resting between workings of the X22 service from Farnham in the spring of 1980. The dual-purpose National, introduced to AV with this batch in 1976, had 45 seats instead of the 49 of the bus version.   *L. Smith*

709 (TRD 709M) was acquired in 1974. It was a 45-seat Ford R1014, with ECW body, and is shown at Guildford. Withdrawal occurred only five years after delivery. *N. Hamshere*

five-day strike by Aldershot bus crews, who were unhappy about the paying-in arrangements for one-person rosters.

Towards the end of 1976, a change of financial policy was introduced. From that time, an increasing proportion of the fleet was acquired under leasing arrangements with a wide variety of finance companies, rather than being bought outright. Starting with some new Leyland Nationals in 1976, the policy was extended to double-deckers and coaches by the end of the decade. After that time, all new full-size vehicles obtained during the NBC era, as well as some minibuses, were leased. Apart from improving the look of the company's balance sheet, by reducing provision for depreciation, the importance of the change lay in the fact that the cost of vehicles now appeared in the profit-and-loss account, which formed the basis of the local authority's calculations of operating costs, used in assessing the level of subsidies needed.

A further restructuring of the NBC regions followed soon after Mr Irwin Dalton became regional director in 1977. AV now came into the South-east Region, with Mr Dalton in charge until 1981, when Mr Derek Fytche became regional chairman.

The whole of the bus industry had been suffering since the 1950s from falling patronage, which combined with frequent fare increases to create a vicious spiral of cutbacks in services, reductions of manpower and difficulties in funding investment in new buses and facilities. The position had become critical by the mid-1970s, despite increasing financial support from the local authorities. A detailed study of the services which were being subsidised was carried out by Alder Valley, Surrey County Council and Hampshire County Council, the outcome being a major re-casting of

the network of services in the Blackwater Valley area – i.e. the Aldershot–Farnborough–Camberley–Yateley corridor. This took effect on 4 September 1977, and involved the withdrawal of many unremunerative journeys and abandonment of whole segments of routes in off-peak periods. The services included in the scheme were renumbered into a series 400-499. County subsidies to Alder Valley as a whole totalled £1.5M in 1977, and then rose steadily to £3.1M in 1983.

In addition to the ex-Tilling and BET companies, the NBC acquired the country area of London Transport, on 1 January 1970, to form a new company – London Country Bus Services. NBC policy allowed the breaking of the former territorial agreements between its subsidiaries where there was scope for provision of through services between major centres in different territories. As a result, A&D's service 1 from Aldershot to the relatively small London Transport boundary town of Egham was extended, as Alder Valley's 201, to a more logical terminus at Staines, on 1 February 1976, and on 4 September 1977 it was further extended to Heathrow Airport.

Collaboration with the NBC neighbour to the south-west, Hants and Dorset, resulted in the opening, also on 4 September 1977, of a new limited-stop long-distance service 324 from Guildford to Southampton. Taking just over two hours, these buses, at a two-hourly frequency, augmented the existing 214 service from Guildford to Winchester, though taking a more direct main-road route between Alresford and Winchester. The Hants and Dorset buses on this service were fully interworked, and covered some of the 214 workings as well as the limited stop journeys.

However, in less than three years, this became a wholly AV service, and all of the workings followed the 214 route, without any limitation on the stops which could be made between Winchester and Southampton.

The London express service from Aldershot, 320, was also recast to serve Heathrow airport. On 28 January 1979, it was split into 320, on the original A30 route and 322, diverting to Heathrow and thence using the M4 motorway into London. The 321, a once-daily peak-hour variant, which had for the past year been running non-stop from Bagshot to London along the M3 motorway, was included in the new timetable, as was 325, an express feeder service from Aldershot to Camberley via Yateley and Blackwater.

The layout of Aldershot bus station was again altered during a long period of closure in the summer of 1979, when the company also suffered a two-day strike of drivers against revised schedules.

Under the provisions of the 1980 Transport Act, a large degree of 'deregulation' of coach services was introduced. Tours and excursions no longer had to be authorised by the Traffic Commissioners, and scheduled coach services and other services over 30 miles in length could now be started by any operator approved by the Commissioners. The scope for other operators and British Railways to oppose these proposals was now severely limited. The result was a spate of new initiatives, and Alder Valley, as a long-established operator, was obliged to take steps to counter all of its new competitors' moves.

Essential to the process was an increase in the fleet of coaches. At the beginning of 1980, AV owned 14 Leyland Leopard coaches, of vintages between 1970 and 1979, and 18 Bristol RELH6Gs, dating from 1971-4: all of the ex-A&D AEC Reliance Coaches having been sold by 1979. After acquiring five more Leopards second-hand from

Above: 953 (VPF 283S), a standard Bristol VRT bus, is shown here in overall advertisement livery for John Farmer's shoes 75th anniversary celebration in 1979. This firm was always keen on bus publicity, as it was the first to advertise on the backs of Aldershot and Farnborough tickets in the early years of operation. Although Alder Valley did own a few VRTs with coach seats, the use of ordinary buses on the 320 express service to London was not unusual. The scene is in Castle Street, Farnham. *N. Hamshere*

Below: With the deregulation of coach services in 1980, it was necessary to enlarge the company's coach fleet very rapidly. AV was able to secure five Leyland Leopards from National Travel (West), which had been new to the now defunct North Western Road Car Co in 1971. Their 49-seat bodies were built by Alexander, and 366 (SJA 366J) was photographed in The Grove, Aldershot, in Londonlink livery, in the month in which it entered AV service. These secondhand coaches worked for four more years before withdrawal. *L. Smith*

National Travel (West) during 1980, there were three years, 1981-3, when the only vehicles of any sort added to the AV fleet were coaches, all but one being of various Leyland types. The odd one out was to remain unique in the fleet – a Dennis Falcon, with 53-seat Wadham-Stringer bodywork (1001, whose registration A101 DPB was the first 'reversed' number in the fleet).

Mr Douglas Adie, previously the Secretary of the Birmingham and Midland Motor Omnibus Company (Midland Red), took over the post of General Manager in August 1979, when his predecessor moved to the Eastern Counties company. The appointment of a Chartered Accountant to the post was a deliberate move on the part of the NBC, in view of AV's precarious financial position.

Despite the economies made over a number of years, the financial position of the NBC companies was deteriorating, and the group's solution was to carry out MAP (Market Analysis Project) surveys in most of its operating areas across the country. Starting in the spring of 1979, tens of thousands of questionnaires were directed at households within the Alder Valley area, to ascertain precisely what actual or potential demand for bus services existed. Where Alder Valley interfaced with neighbouring NBC companies, or had minor companies operating within its own area, the MAP analysis was conducted on a co-operative basis, notably in the Guildford area, where London Country Bus Services (an NBC company), Safeguard, Till-

ingbourne, Blue Saloon and Tony McCann Motors were involved.

The results of the survey were analysed by the NBC's central computer at Birmingham, and used in a radical revision of the route network. In many cases, under-utilised services were to be replaced by occasional diversions of better-patronised routes, or else abolished entirely. Most evening and Sunday operations were to be abandoned, and other measures included the reduction of full journeys to short workings where the number of passengers was insufficient to justify the full mileage, as well as the linking-up of previously separate services to achieve operational economies. An important factor in the reduction of operating costs was to be the withdrawal of the remaining Dennis Lolines and their replacement by driver-only Bristol VR double-deckers, which would allow the company to declare its last remaining conductors redundant.

The introduction of the revised services required an extensive marketing and public relations exercise. This commenced with an open day at the Aldershot depot on 1 March 1980, when the public were allowed to see some of the administrative and engineering aspects of the company at first hand. The public announcements of the new services were given a local flavour by the introduction of area names for the operations based on the various garages, providing a better identity than the name of a company covering six counties could offer. Thus, on 1 June 1980, Hindhead's

The standard coach in the Alder Valley fleet from 1975 to 1982 was the Leyland PSU3 Leopard, with a Plaxton body equipped with 46 or 49 seats. Some were allocated to Londonlink services, and this view of 1102 (originally 502, later 02) was taken on service X8 in The Grove, Aldershot, with Les Smith driving, in the summer of 1983. In the background, the rearranged bus station, with buses drawn up to a central platform spine, can be glimpsed.

L. Smith

network appeared under the 'Downsman' name, which appeared on timetable leaflets, notepaper and other material, as well as being applied as stickers alongside the Alder Valley fleet name on the buses and bus stop signs. Guildford and Woking's services became 'Weyfarer' on 31 August, at the same time as Alton took the name of 'Wessexway'. Alton, for many years the smallest A&D garage, largely populated by small-capacity buses, had now increased in importance, since staffing problems at Aldershot had encouraged AV to base more buses at Alton, where drivers were more readily recruited. Thus 207, Aldershot–Basingstoke, now became essentially an Alton–Basingstoke route, as a consequence of buses working from Alton to join the busiest Odiham–Basingstoke section.

To popularise the new services, new cheap off-peak return tickets (available after 0900 hours) were introduced under the name of 'Bargainride'. The full-page newspaper publicity for each new area network told of the number of MAP forms completed, and also highlighted the losses which it was hoped to eliminate (e.g. £822,000 and £600,000 per annum from Aldershot and Hindhead operations respectively). Where services of two participating operators covered the same route, the tickets were made interavailable.

All Shalford–Guildford services were thus integrated, and AV and Tillingbourne agreed on joint arrangements between Cranleigh and Ewhurst. 'Travelwide' tickets were also introduced in the Guildford town area. These could be used on any local bus, irrespective of its ownership, and were valid for one week, one month or three months, and for an unlimited number of journeys.

AV's Southern Area followed the lead of the Northern Area in establishing hourly motorway express services to London in October 1980, and both areas' coaches were marketed under the new name of 'Londonlink'. The new services were numbered in an 'X' series instead of the conventional 3-digit numbers, and their avowed aim was to establish the coach as a viable alternative to the commuter train. The coach route to London from the Aldershot area was now split into two, running alternately as X8 via Frimley and X7 via Cove and Yateley, combining at Camberley to provide an hourly frequency. Only two journeys now started from Farnham in the morning, with two returning there in the evening, and there was no longer a Heathrow Airport express service: this was now provided by changing to service 201 at Camberley. To compensate for the transfer of the main Londonlink service to the motorway, the original A30 route was given a twice-daily express service, X20.

The new X7/X8 service started on 5 October 1980, but changes were soon made, on 22 February 1981. Three journeys each way daily were extended to serve Farnham

A discreet advertisement formed part of the red and white livery designed for Londonlink coaches. A rear view, taken in Foden Road, shows 1103 (WJM 817T), which was a Leyland Leopard with a 49-seat Plaxton Supreme body. It was new in September 1979 as 503, and in 1981 it became 03, before acquiring its final number in 1982, which was the year in which the Camberley–London return fare was £2.50!

Alder Valley

Above: Under the MAP restructuring, Aldershot-based buses received the area name 'Aldershot & District', which was applied in the form of strips on the front panel and alongside the fleetname on the side panels (or above the cantrails of single-deckers). 964 (WJM 824T), a 1979 Bristol VRT with 74-seat ECW body, is shown in Victoria Road, Aldershot. Service 441, between Aldershot and Camberley (Old Dean Estate) via Hawley Lane Estate, was one of the new routes introduced as a result of the MAP analysis. *Alder Valley*

Below: Alder Valley employed a number of its Bristol VRTs as coaches. These had eight seats fewer than the bus version, and the NBC coach livery of white, with red reliefs, was applied. This photograph of 964 (CJH 124V) was taken early in 1981, when the 'Aldershot & District' area name had just been introduced. The location is the coach park at Battersea, used for layovers from the nearby Victoria Coach Station, at which this coach had arrived on express service X7. *L. Smith*

and Alton, in addition to the once-daily run to and from the Weydon Estate and Rowledge, on the outskirts of Farnham. A novel feature was the dual role of the X7 on the section of its route between Cove, Yateley and Camberley, where it provided a local stage carriage service over roads which had no normal bus service. Londonlink rapidly proved its value, and the effects of the prolonged rail strikes of 1982, combined with large rail fare increases, helped to ensure success to the extent that the two-millionth passenger was carried in 1983.

The final stage of MAP-based changes took place on 22 February 1981, when Aldershot garage's services revived the name 'Aldershot and District'. The allocation of buses was reduced from 45 to 32, both as a result of mileage reductions and the transfer of some duties to other garages. Simultaneously with its new network, Aldershot and District introduced its own unlimited travel tickets. Three area tickets were entitled respectively Aldershot, Camberley and District Rovers, each being available on a one-week or one-month basis.

The economies of the MAP exercise resulted in reductions in the fleet strength at every depot: even Hindhead, which took over a number of Aldershot and Guildford duties, saw its allocation drop from 52 to 36 buses. Between October 1979 and October 1980, AV's active fleet was cut from 509 vehicles to 357. Since similar cuts were being made all over the country, the second-hand market for middle-aged buses was saturated, and the company had 116 surplus buses on its hands early in 1981, parked in every available corner of its garage sites. It was some years before these could be cleared. The cuts also resulted in major reductions in manpower, and out of the workforce of about 1800, 228 were made redundant during 1980, and

the last conductors were phased out in February 1981. It was not possible to reap the anticipated financial benefits in the short term, and the heavy bill for redundancy payments resulted in a £3.3 million loss being recorded for 1980. However, in 1981, when the annual mileage had been reduced from about 21 million to some 15½ million, the effect of the measures was seen in a halving of the loss for the year, despite a reduction of annual passenger figures from 43 to 36 million.

Major road improvements in the centre of Guildford at this time necessitated some changes in the bus terminal arrangements. In addition to the Onslow Street and Farnham Road bus stations, there were a number of streets where vehicles of the six local operators were to be seen parked. The opportunity was taken by the local authorities to include a large new bus station in the redevelopment being planned for the Friary brewery site, and this was opened on 2 November 1980. It had fifteen bays in the new area, and seven more bays were provided in Commercial Road alongside. London Country Buses and Tillingbourne used the latter, while both of them shared the main station with Alder Valley and Safeguard, both of which had enquiry and administrative offices in the new premises.

The AV head office and ex-Thames Valley garage, near to the centre of Reading, offered scope for profitable lease or sale for redevelopment, and a decision was taken to move the head office to Aldershot. In preparation for this, the old A&D headquarters were completely refurbished to modern standards, and additional space was created by partitioning off the rear of the 1916 'Top Shop' and inserting an additional floor and new windows. All of this work cost some £650,000. At the same time the last stage of the transfer of overhaul and engineering activities from Reading to Aldershot was taking place, in preparation for final closure of the Reading premises on 2 January 1981. After the reconstruction of the Top Shop, the remaining part, no longer required as an engineering workshop, was reallocated as a paint shop, with a section devoted to the manufacture of glass fibre panels for bodywork repairs. Staff displaced from the former head office at Reading were provided with a daily minibus to Aldershot, so that the move entailed the minimum of disruption, and was completed by the end of April 1981. An official opening ceremony was performed on 1 June by Sir Hugh Smiley, Vice-Lord Lieutenant of Hampshire. The guests included Mr Derek Fytche, NBC Regional Director and senior officials of the company, the building contractors and the county councils, and a special place was found for Mr Bert Lowman, whose 62 years with A&D and AV had been an all-time record.

The exact 75th anniversary of the founding of the Aldershot and Farnborough company was celebrated on 6 June 1981 with a major open day at the Halimote Road premises. The workshops and garages were opened to visitors; several preserved buses were on show, and a number of stalls selling items for enthusiasts or souvenir-collectors were set up in the running shed. The administrative side was represented by exhibits of all the activities carried out in the newly-refurbished office block. In time for the event, one each of the current standard bus types was painted in the A&D livery of the late 'fifties: a Leyland National, 231 (KPA 382P) and a Bristol VR, 611 (GGM 81W). Although the former was repainted in Alder Valley colours after the anniversary year, the Bristol's special livery was retained for several years by careful touching-up, and it appeared as the

company's representative at many special events and won several trophies. Recognising the publicity value of operating such a vehicle, Alder Valley selected one of the last of the Dennis Loline IIIs (AAA 503C) for complete restoration to its original condition, and licensed it to carry passengers for publicity or private hire purposes. It has often appeared at rallies in company with its privately owned contemporary AAA 506C, and their much-travelled predecessors GOU 845, a Dennis Lance K3 of 1950 and MOR 581, a rebodied AEC Reliance of 1954. Less frequently seen preserved A&D buses include two Dennis Loline Is, SOU 456 and 465, a Dennis Lance K4, LOU 48 and a Dennis Lancet J10 of 1950, HOU 904.

Reappraisal of the company's fixed assets in the light of now reduced garage requirements resulted in the decision that it was no longer economic to retain premises at both Woking and Guildford, and eventually it was the former which was closed, on 2 January 1982. The site was sold for redevelopment and its 23 buses were transferred away, such local requirements as could not be met by workings from Guildford or Aldershot being subsequently covered by a small number of buses outstationed initially in a yard off Walton Road.

Alder Valley publicised a new 'Wheels within Wheels' scheme for disabled passengers towards the end of 1981. This was a development of the scheme which A&D had introduced some years earlier, when they made minor modifications to some of the AEC Reliance coaches and buses which had either central entrances or central emergency exits, to allow the fitting of a wheelchair ramp. The same system had been used in the Bristol RELL model. Now three Leyland National buses (275-7) were modified to allow a ramp to be fitted over the front entrance steps, and four seats on each side were made easily removable to provide space for a total of eight wheelchairs. Clamps were designed to hold these in place, and seat belts were fitted for their occupants. All of these installations were designed to allow conversion to or from normal configuration in about one hour. Two additional buses, 279/80, were converted in the spring of 1983.

Another important venture of the Engineering Department in 1982 was the installation of power steering. A system marketed by Autosteer Controls Ltd., of Leeds, was selected, and in collaboration with Bristol Commercial Vehicles, a pilot installation was successfully designed. Operated by compressed air, this system was then approved for use on 22 Bristol VRs of the earlier batches, some of which were up to twelve years old. Alder Valley was, at the same time, appointed as an area distributor and agent for Autosteer. This was only one of the Engineering Department's ventures into the open market around this time: maintenance and repair of passenger and goods vehicles for outside users, fabrication in metal and glass-reinforced plastic, vehicle painting and signwriting were making important contributions to the company's revenue.

Taking advantage of the deregulation of coach and other long-distance services, the NBC encouraged its constituent companies to collaborate in exploring joint operation of cross-boundary routes. Alder Valley shared several ventures with Green Line coaches, which, after many years of operation by London Transport, had been transferred to the NBC in 1970 as part of London Country Bus Services.

On 16 January 1982, a joint service totally outside AV's traditional area commenced between Victoria Coach Station and Heathrow, via the M4 motorway. Numbered 767, this was one of a number of Green Line's 'Flightline' services serving the major airports. Later in the year a joint long-distance stage carriage service, 762, was planned by AV, Green Line and Southdown from Reading, via Bracknell, Aldershot, Guildford, Dorking, Reigate, Gatwick Airport and Haywards Heath to Brighton. Despite the fact that the only grounds now allowed for objection were now 'against the public interest', British Rail and Surrey County Council registered objections, and the new service was not permitted to open until 22 January 1983. In the summer of the following year a companion service 763, continuing to Eastbourne, was introduced. To shorten the daily journey, this service omitted stops in the Aldershot area except on Sundays, but after the summer it was integrated into the 762 as a simple extension of one journey daily to Eastbourne. Some conventional commuter coach services were also opened as joint operations with Green Line: 740, Tongham–Guildford–Victoria, and 741, Whitehill–Hindhead–Guildford–Victoria, both originated within AV's Southern Area.

A new era of vigorous marketing, to keep the company in the public eye, began in 1983 with AV's first venture into radio and television advertising. To introduce its advertisements on TVS (Television South) and the local radio stations (210 at Reading and County Sound at Guildford), the company commissioned composer Mike Alexander to produce a special 'jingle' which, for good measure, was also printed on the plastic carrier bags used at its booking offices, travel centres and other retail outlets. Around this time, a number of models and souvenirs were introduced, to cash in on the 'collectables' movement which was rapidly expanding. Since that time, souvenir mugs and plates have been produced in limited editions, and a number of diecast models, painted in authentic A&D colours of the appropriate period, have also appeared, although since these have to be based on existing manufacturers' products, the types represented have not always been historically correct. Sales of these items have come to represent a not insignificant percentage of the annual turnover in recent years.

Another open day was held at the Aldershot depot on 4 June 1983, with a full day's programme of events, ranging from drum majorettes, through a judo display, to brass band performances. The occasion served also to introduce to the public the new generation of coaches for the London-link service. These were 73-seat Leyland Olympians, with Eastern Coachworks bodies, painted in the striking new NBC coach livery of white, with panels of red and black stripes. Five of these, 1501-5 (YPJ 501-5Y) formed the first batch, followed by two more, 1506/7 (A506/7 GPC), in 1984 and 1508-10 (B576-8 LPE) in 1985. Double-deckers with coach seats had been employed by Thames Valley for many years on its London services, but, while ordinary buses often acted as reliefs, double-deck coaches were new to the Aldershot routes. 1983 also saw a new type of coach, the Leyland Tiger, introduced on prestige services. Ten of these (1201-10, YPJ 201-10Y) were delivered in time for the summer season, and were fitted with 50-seat Plaxton Paramount 3500 bodies, of the high floor level, flat sided pattern which was rapidly gaining popularity at that time. The high floor allowed for ample luggage space and for a

1983 saw the introduction of five Leyland Olympian double-deck coaches on the Londonlink services. They had 73-seat ECW bodies, and were painted in the new striped livery introduced for NBC coaches in that year. Five more similar vehicles arrived in 1984-5. Five of the ten were allocated to Alder Valley South in the 1986 split, including 1503, shown here on the X37 service.
MB photos

toilet compartment for long-distance coaching duties, and they were frequently used for continental tours to France, Belgium and the Netherlands, as well as journeys to Scotland, Wales and Devon. By 1990, Germany, Austria and Spain had appeared on the list of itineraries.

When, in 1962, A&D had taken over a travel agency with the business of Comfy Coaches, the company decided to build up this activity. With the opening of new premises in East Street, Farnham, Farnham Travel combined the agency with the A&D enquiry office, and under its manager, Mrs Sylvia McMaster, the travel sales flourished even more in the Alder Valley era. However, in the early 1980s, the NBC set up a national chain of agencies under the name of National Travelworld. In 1983, Alder Valley was told to turn Farnham Travel, and its newly-opened branch in Woking, into branches of National Travelworld, and eventually the premises were sold to the latter firm. Thereafter, their role in connection with AV enquiries and bookings became but a small part of their all-embracing operations. However, with the dismantling of NBC starting just three years later, the new enterprise had only a short existence in Farnham.

In the Guildford area, there had already been a number of instances in the early 1980s where the independent operators had proposed to the County Council that they would be prepared to take over and operate some of the subsidised services at lower cost than the major operators – London Country and Alder Valley. The council therefore issued a Public Transport Plan Consultative Document, which in June 1983 prompted the independents (Tillingbourne, Safeguard and Blue Saloon) to devise a scheme for taking over all local services within Guildford, as well as all of the longer-distance services in the area bounded by Guildford, Cranleigh, Horsham and Shere. This would have left the major companies with only a small residual presence in Guildford, and the council authorities showed considerable interest in the plan. Independent consultants were appointed in March 1984 to examine it, together with a counter-proposal by the major operators to take over the independents. However, in July, before their report was complete, a government White Paper, 'Buses', was published. This envisaged a far-reaching restructuring of the industry, which was intended to minimise the need for subsidies by encouraging competition. With new legislation likely, Alder Valley was unwilling to accept the council consultants' recommendations in favour of the handing over of most of its Guildford operations, and commissioned its own consultants' report from Colin Buchanan and Partners. This soon concluded that while the town services should be the subject of negotiation with the independent companies, with the aim of cutting operating costs, Alder Valley ought not to relinquish its most profitable route, between Guildford and Cranleigh. The company adopted these guidelines and over the next few months it set about replanning its Guildford operations with a view to achieving major cost reductions in the area.

The county councils, faced with limits on the amounts of money available for support of public transport, had all been obliged to re-examine their commitments for the year 1983-4, with the result that in Surrey there was a major revision of services on 13 June 1983, followed by cuts to Hampshire's Blackwater Valley and Aldershot services in October, and changes in the Alton area on 29 April 1984. However, recognising that some villages would lose their already limited facilities for shopping journeys, some once- or twice-weekly 'Shopperbus' and market day services were introduced, e.g. 270 Hydestile–Northchapel–Haslemere–

Alder Valley had ten of these 1983 Leyland Tigers, of which two eventually came into the Alder Valley South fleet. 1204, shown here in Rouen, was one of them. They were fitted with Plaxton Paramount 3500 bodies, which provided 48 seats, with a toilet compartment and ample luggage space for long-distance touring. *Alder Valley*

Hindhead in September 1983 and, in mid-1984, 216 Alton–Petersfield–Chichester, 206 Alton–Odiham–Reading and X19 Badshot Lea–Aldershot–Farnham–Hindhead–Haslemere–Chichester.

In what proved to be the last major NBC reorganisation, on 1 January 1984, the operating companies were divided into only two regions. AV naturally came into the South region, with Mr John Hargreaves as its chairman, with two divisional directors under him.

On 30 April 1984, another effort was made to improve services to Heathrow Airport. The stage service 201 was cut back to Camberley, and new express coaches started to run six times per day between Farnham and the airport. Most of these were on service X28, but one journey up and two down ran as X18, by-passing the centre of Aldershot by means of the A325 road.

February 1984 saw the appointment of Mr Brian Hirst from the Yorkshire Traction Co. as General Manager, to replace Douglas Adie, on his promotion to NBC divisional director. Mr Adie's last two years had seen the company move into a period of operating profit, although interest charges were still producing an overall loss. After a £2.5 million loss in 1980, the operating profit in 1983 was £773,000, while the overall loss after interest payments had been reduced from £3.5 million to £482,000. The staff numbers had fallen to 1380 by the middle of 1983, the passenger numbers were now around 30 million per annum, and the previous year's mileage was 16½ million.

The vehicle history of the first half of the 1980s, apart from the coach fleet, remained virtually static. Reductions in requirements brought about by the MAP exercise meant that the Leyland National and the Bristol VR had a near monopoly, though withdrawal of the oldest examples of each had started in 1982. Apart from the preserved Loline, the only ex-A&D vehicles left after that year were one each of the Bristol RELL and RESL types (443 – YHO 627J and 465 – CHO 697K respectively).

A change in the management structure was introduced around this time, affecting the administrative, personnel and fleet organisation. The successful Londonlink Express operation was placed under its own manager, with part of the coach fleet now dedicated to this activity and a number of drivers permanently allocated, although when necessary for relief duties, drivers could be brought in from the local bus services. The remainder of the coach fleet, used for private and contract hire, tours and excursions, was placed under the control of a Coaching Unit, again with its own manager and having a separate team of drivers.

With driver-only operation becoming almost universal throughout the land, a new problem was arising: the security of drivers and their takings. As reports of assaults and robberies started to appear every week in national newspapers, AV decided to anticipate any trouble in its own area, and fit Klaxon alarms to all of its buses over the ensuing few months.

New initiatives continued to emerge in the cause of encouraging people to use their local buses. Flat fares for some local services were tried during 1983-84. The Farnham area was the first: on 30 October 1983, it was divided into three zones, centred on Hale, Farnham and Rowledge. Flat fares were fixed within each zone, as well as between zones. Alton's town services, on the other hand, were given a concentric zone structure, with all journeys within the inner zone at 10p and those in the outer zone at 20p,

starting on 29 April 1984. On 3 December the Bordon and Whitehill area saw the start of the 'Bordhill' service 222, which combined a flat fare with 'hail-and-ride'. Hampshire County Council undertook to cover any losses over the first six months, and to keep costs on this and other similar services down five 37-seater Bedford YMQ buses (298-302) were obtained second-hand from South Wales Transport.

The company's exploration of possible restructuring in Guildford was aided by the decision of the coach operators Gastonia, of Cranleigh, to scale down their activities. As a consequence, in December 1984, AV took over two of their existing coach routes as going concerns. Gastonia's Ewhurst–Cranleigh–Guildford–London and Dunsfold–Godalming–Guildford–London routes became X42/43 in AV's network. In the process, AV gained an operating base in Cranleigh, as it was able to lease part of Gastonia's garage at Manfield Park. This was the prelude to a plan to close the Woodbridge Road garage in Guildford. It was decided to base part of the Guildford fleet at Cranleigh, transfer some of the buses to a new depot at the Goldsworth Park Trading Estate on the outskirts of Woking, and to use the Guildford Friary bus station as a parking area for the remainder. The Area Inspector and much of the administrative work had already been transferred to the Friary premises a few years earlier. Thus, on 22 September 1985, Woodbridge Road garage was closed, and on the following day the Cranleigh and Woking premises were

Acquired from South Wales Transport, this Bedford YMQ, with a distinctive 37-seat Lex Maxeta body, was one of five obtained for use on the subsidised 'Bordhill' local service in Bordon and Whitehill. Fresh from the paint shop in November 1984, LCY 300X carried its original owner's fleet number into its new life with AV.

L. Smith

promoted to garage status, with facilities and staff for day-to-day maintenance being installed.

Meanwhile, the situation over the services south and east of Guildford remained unresolved, and the county council was faced with competing proposals from Alder Valley and Tillingbourne. Neither would give way, and the only way to settle the rival claims to operate the disputed routes appeared to be through a traffic court hearing. Eventually, it was agreed to continue in a state of competition, and in April 1985 Tillingbourne recast its services completely, so as to cover the villages in which Alder Valley had no interest, plus services on the main routes at a frequency which was acceptable to the larger company. The competition extended to pricing: AV introduced pre-paid 10 journey 'saver strips', which offered passengers one free journey, while their rivals introduced 4-weekly unlimited travel tickets, as well as 10p discount vouchers included in the advertising leaflets distributed to every house in the area. Yet another aspect of competition saw AV with a distinct advantage: it owned the bus stop signs, and attached its own timetables to them to the exclusion of the smaller company. The bus wars had started again!

A novel way of keeping Alder Valley's name in the public eye was the sponsorship arranged with the Aldershot Brass Ensemble at the beginning of 1985. The band was at first renamed the Alder Valley Aldershot Brass (though the town name was soon dropped) and it was provided with new uniforms and equipment bearing the AV emblem. The company offered the assistance of its purchasing, marketing and printing facilities, and one tangible result was the issue of a record of the band, entitled 'Reflections in Brass', promoted by the bus company.

The NBC was planning, in view of the reductions which had taken place in the fleets of all of its operators and the increasing standardisation of vehicles, to rationalise its workshop facilities and concentrate work in regional centres. In this context, AV's workshops at Aldershot, which were to lose much of the work on the company's own fleet, were to be given more opportunity to take on contract work for other operators and for commercial vehicle users such as the army. To facilitate this, an autonomous division, AV Engineering, was formed on 1 January 1985, with AV's Chief Engineer, Derek Allison, as its manager. Of necessity, this was to be a slimmed-down operation compared with maintenance of the bus fleet, and 30 redundancies were announced.

For many years, local authorities had been supporting public transport on the basis of subsidising unremunerative services, but government policy during the early 1980s was based on the belief that costs could be reduced by introducing more competition between operators for running the subsidised services. In addition to setting out a framework for managing the competition, the White Paper of 1984 also proposed the break-up and sale to private interests of the whole of the NBC, and the virtual abolition of the licensing of road services. The traffic commissioners, with reduced responsibilities, were to be reduced from three to one in each traffic area. In effect, this meant a total reversal of the principles of the 1930 Road Traffic Act, which had eliminated wasteful competition and allowed established operators a considerable degree of protection against newcomers. Despite the fears of increased congestion in towns and the loss of cross-subsidised rural services, not to mention the likelihood of companies with valuable fixed assets falling into the hands of unsympathetic owners, the proposals were enshrined in the Transport Act which

received the Royal Assent on 30 October 1985.

The NBC was to be broken up into units of what was considered to be the optimum size for 'privatisation', with safeguards to ensure that buyers were unable to reassemble the previous monopolies. For Alder Valley, which exceeded the optimum fleet size of around 250 buses, this meant a split into two separate companies, Alder Valley North and South, roughly corresponding to the pre-1972 Thames Valley and A&D areas, but with the logical change of allowing Alder Valley South to retain all of the new Aldershot-based services in the greatly-expanded area of Yateley, to the north of the A30. The Londonlink network of express services was to be left under the joint control of AV North and AV South for the time being.

The division of the fleet provided AV South with 78 Leyland Nationals (including six dual-purpose vehicles), 59 Bristol VR double-deckers (including six fitted with coach seats), 6 Bristol RELH coaches, 19 Leyland Leopard coaches, 5 Leyland Tiger coaches, 5 double-deck Leyland Olympian coaches, and 5 of miscellaneous types – two Bedford YMQ and one YMP 37-seat buses, the last remaining ex-A&D Bristol RESL bus CHO 697K and the restored Dennis Loline AAA 503C. These 177 vehicles kept their original AV fleet numbers under successive new owners of the company, while those of Alder Valley North were renumbered after privatisation in 1987.

Notwithstanding the participation of AV's staff in a national one-day strike against the Transport Bill, in October, the new AV North and South companies were inaugurated on 1 January 1986. At the same time, AV Engineering became an independent NBC company, Alder Valley Engineering Ltd., though still using a section of the Aldershot garage site.

By that time, plans had been drawn up for the 'deregulation' aspects of the Transport Act. These were to be overseen by the local authorities, and all operators were required to register with the Traffic Commissioner, during February 1986, all of the services which they were prepared to run commercially, without subsidies. The local authorities would then decide what other services were socially necessary and invite tenders for their operation under contract, which would normally be awarded to the operator submitting the lowest bid. Provision was made for the tendering process to be reopened at appropriate intervals, or if an operator was proving unsatisfactory.

In anticipation of the new competitive market, AV South launched its most extensive scheme of bargain fares on 2 May. The 'Traveller' ticket, available after 9am Monday–Friday, to individuals or to family groups, involved a single payment for the first bus journey of the day, and was then valid for any other journey made on that day, as well as giving discounts on admission to certain tourist attractions. A 'Super Traveller' ticket allowed unlimited use of the company's Londonlink coaches as well as its buses.

Although it was to be another nine months before 'D-day', when the new regime came into operation, the immediate effect on the bus fleets of all the major companies was astonishing. For twenty years or more, the economics of fleet management had demanded standardisation, with the result that numerous instances arose of 50-seat buses being used on journeys which never carried above a dozen passengers, but which were subsidised as socially necessary. Since owners of minibuses (or even large taxis) could now undercut the large operators, large numbers of inexpensive minibuses were rapidly acquired by the latter, to enable them to stand a chance of submitting competitive bids. Between March and May 1986, the Alder Valley companies together took delivery of 41 16-seat Carlyle-bodied Ford Transit minibuses (310-50), of which 23 were allocated to AV South. The majority were allocated to Aldershot garage, for use on local high-frequency services under the name of 'Whippet', in line with the fashion already set by other companies of giving distinctive fleet names to their minibus fleets, emphasising the speed and friendly nature of these services. Although a number were stored unlicensed, awaiting D-day, some entered service on 26 August, when a 'hail and ride' service was introduced between Aldershot town centre and North Town, with a 10-minute headway, to replace the less frequent larger buses. Six of this first batch of minibuses went to Hindhead garage, for use on lightly-loaded routes, and these did not carry the Whippet fleet name. All of the Ford Transits appeared in the new livery chosen for AV South, which was basically green, though there appears to have been a deliberate aim of avoiding a complete return to the traditional A&D colours.

The scheme was light green for the upper parts, with dark green skirt panels, with a light orange relief around window level. Versions of this for larger buses started to appear in June. Since the very last ex-A&D bus (465) had just been withdrawn, it missed its chance of returning to a green livery by a few months!

Publicity in public houses! An Alder Valley beer mat highlights a new social trend.

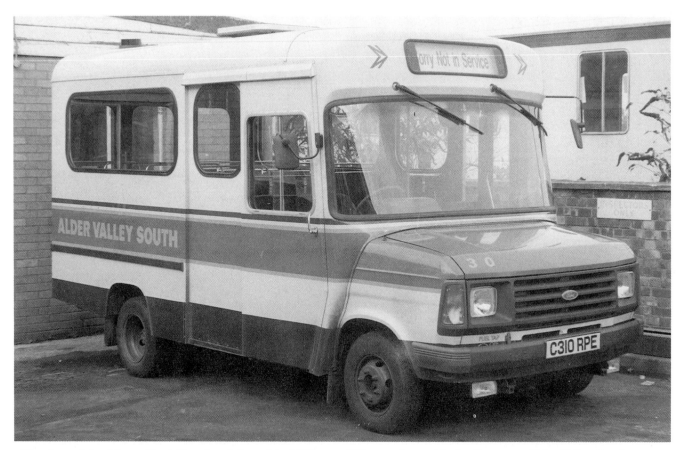

The first of the 16-seat Ford Transits, delivered in 1986, was 310, seen here with the fleetname Alder Valley South, which relatively few buses received before the northern section ceased to use the Alder Valley name. The bodies were built by Carlyle (the former Midland Red body works) at Birmingham. Interior ventilation was a problem.

Alder Valley

Chapter Ten
Deregulation and Privatisation

'**D**-day' – 26 October 1986 – saw unprecedented changes throughout the Alder Valley South area. The company and the local authorities devoted considerable expenditure to publicising the changes. AV South itself mailed a 'Newslink' newsletter to over 250,000 households in its area, while the local authorities paid for extensive advertising, the printing of free comprehensive timetable booklets and setting up telephone information lines (Surrey County Council alone spending £250,000 on these facilities). Nevertheless, there were numerous complaints about lack of information!

AV South registered 79 services for commercial operation, and while many of them departed from the long-established routes, others were still identifiable as the old A&D routes. Consequently, when new two-figure numbers were allocated to commercial services in place of the original series, some of them revived the historic numbers of the 1920s. For example, Aldershot–Guildford was once again 20, Guildford–Bagshot–Camberley became 34, Guildford–Chertsey became 48 and so on. Other unused numbers were allocated to new routes, so that 24 is now the short Camberley–Old Dean service instead of the long Guildford–Petersfield service of earlier days.

In the tendering for county council contracts for sub-sidised services, most operators gained new routes and lost others to competitors. For example, in the Alton area, AV South won two local services from Warren's Altonian Coaches, and lost one to the same competitor, which also obtained the contract to operate subsidised evening journeys on AV's trunk route 215 between Alton and Guildford. Services operated under contract were given separate numbers – Hampshire's routes taking 400-499 and Surrey's 500-599. In some cases they were allocated numbers related to previous or current A&D or AV South services so that the aforementioned Altonian evening services became 515: the passenger who might have to wait at the bus stop for a return journey on a differently-coloured bus carrying a different number perhaps had some genuine grounds for grumbling! Some new contract services in which AV took no part were given numbers based on past history: 565, a Guildford–Puttenham–Farnham shoppers' service, operated by Blue Saloon, covered the same ground as the erstwhile A&D 65. Blue Saloon, a relatively new operator reviving an old local name, was one of many which appeared in the AV area on D-day. Some were very new to the field, while others were old-established companies such as Tillingbourne and Safeguard. The latter achieved the distinction of winning a contract for an Aldershot–

In the deregulation era, Surrey County Council sponsored the provision of a number of services, numbered in the 600 series, to allow handicapped people to shop in Woking or Guildford twice a month. Alder Valley's specially equipped buses were absorbed into this 'Access Bus' scheme. 246, posed for this photograph at Guildford, had originally been allocated to Alder Valley North's 'Careline' service from Heathrow to the London rail termini, but came to AV South when that service ceased in 1987.

Alder Valley

Frimley–Camberley service (550) which involved penetrating the very heart of AV South territory, by running along Halimote Road!

As a result of tendering for contracts from West Sussex County Council, AV South gained routes in an area to the south-east of its previous territory, taking over all or part of five services previously operated by Southdown, but retaining the latter's route numbers in most cases. AV thus returned to Petworth, which it had deserted in 1980, and Pulborough became its south-eastern outpost.

A new initiative by Surrey County Council in October 1986 was the provision of a number of bus services to enable handicapped people to visit nearby towns twice a month. Under the name "Access Bus", some of these services into Woking and Guildford were operated by Alder Valley, which had been running its specially adapted "Wheels within Wheels" buses since 1981. This group of services was numbered from 601 upwards, and understandably operated on a "Hail and Ride" basis.

The division of the fleet on 1 January had left AV South with a smaller share than AV North and, despite the arrival of the minibuses, some additional full-size single deckers were needed by the end of 1986. Consequently a batch of fifteen Leyland Nationals, dating from 1974-6, was purchased from the Northern General Transport Co. in December. All but one of these entered service with AV South in their original wine-coloured Northern livery, but with AV fleet name and numbers 101-115 painted on (the use of fleet number plates having ceased some three years earlier). Eight more minibuses (469-76, D469-76 WPM) arrived at the end of 1986. These were larger than their predecessors, having 21-seat Robin Hood bodies on Fiat (Ford IVECO) chassis, and all were allocated to Woking. Six were painted in Whippet livery, and together with some of the 16-seaters, they inaugurated three new services to the Goldsworth Park estate on the outskirts of Woking. M1 ran through the estate to Knaphill every ten minutes, while M2 and M3 were peak-hour circular services running at a 4 or 5 minute headway. 'Saverstrip' tickets were introduced with these Woking minibus services. Two of the new minibuses were painted in British Rail's Network South East livery, for use on special commuter services.

Subsequent minibuses were of even higher capacities: the 1987 intake consisted of ten 22-seat Dodge vehicles with Northern Counties Bodies (401-10, E401-10 EPE) 477-80 (E201-4 EPB), which were more Fiats with Robin Hood bodies, but with 25 seats, and 411-20 (E411-20 EPE) which were Renaults with 27-seat Northern Counties bodies. Both the latter two batches had automatic gearboxes.

Alder Valley North was sold in January 1987 to a company named Q Drive Ltd. and was renamed the Berks Bucks Bus Company (using the fleet name The Bee Line). Q Drive had been founded by Isleworth coach operator Mr Len Wright, who became chairman, while the principal shareholder was his business partner Mr David Stewart. AV South thereupon dropped the 'South' from its fleet name although, in fact, relatively few of its buses had received the AVS fleet name since the 1986 split. The legal name of the company nevertheless remained as Alder Valley South Limited.

On 5 March 1987, Alder Valley Engineering Ltd., together with H&D Distribution Ltd., Kent Engineering (NBC) Ltd., and Southdown Engineering Services Ltd – i.e. all of the NBC engineering companies in south east England – were bought from NBC by a new company,

Frontsource Ltd., set up by Mr Robert Beattie, with its headquarters on the Halimote Road site. He also acquired four other NBC engineering companies as they came up for sale, to build up a leading position in public service vehicle engineering.

The sale of NBC companies was well under way by the middle of 1987, and in many cases the successful formula was a management buyout, as the White Paper had suggested. AV's management, however, were prevented from following suit by a surprise bid from Frontsource Ltd. The sale was announced in June and was completed on 1 November 1987, amid considerable speculation over the future direction of the company and its property and bus operations. The new owners retained the existing management, who endeavoured to allay the misgivings of the staff and the general public over the change. 226 vehicles and a staff of 560 were taken over. The change of ownership led to the sale of the Aldershot and Hindhead garages to a property company, and these premises were thereafter held on a short-term lease.

By this time, the 'D-day' arrangements had already been modified in the light of experience, since at the end of July, AV 'de-registered' a number of its commercial services, which therefore became eligible for open tendering, and in some cases complete re-casting. Under their powers, the county councils provided subsidies to AV to maintain the services until the tendering process could be completed. In the event, several of the contracts were awarded to AV itself, but the opportunity was taken to re-examine and amend the timetables of several other services, and between August and October 1987 the company's total vehicle requirement was reduced by ten.

In August–September 1987, the company returned briefly to its long-standing vehicle supplier, Dennis, now much re-organised under its new guise of Hestair Dennis, for the mechanical parts of six new integrally-constructed coaches. These had 57-seat Duple 425 bodies, and were for use on the Londonlink services. Nos. 1205-10 (E205-10 EPB) displaced the remaining Leyland Leopards from this duty, while in November four MCW coaches (1457-60, B457-60 WHJ) were acquired second-hand from Eastern National to replace the older Leopards from the Coaching Unit.

Towards the end of 1987, people residing in the vicinity of Alton garage escalated their long-standing complaints about the noise, fumes and traffic congestion it was causing. After over sixty years, the local press suddenly described its siting as 'controversial', and demanded its removal. AV's new owners stated that they were prepared to close and sell the premises, but at the time of the announcement to the staff, no alternative had been found, and some anxiety was expressed about the future of Alton-based operations. The garage was officially closed at the end of December, and the reduced fleet allocated thereafter was outstationed in open parking on an industrial estate on the outskirts of the town, in the care of a commercial vehicle depot.

Alder Valley's staff and customers were still assessing the merits of being owned by an engineering company with no experience of bus operation when Frontsource Ltd. decided to sell AV to a company which did have some experience. On 19 November 1988, Q Drive Ltd., which a year earlier had bought AV North, took over, and Mr Len Wright became chairman and chief executive of both companies. In the process, a management bid to buy the company had been rejected, and Managing Director Brian

Hirst and Fleet Engineer John Bryant left Alder Valley. Richard Soper, previously Traffic Manager of Alder Valley South, now became Director and General Manager. The new owner announced that, although the two companies would retain their separate identities, some of the central departments such as Accounts and Traffic Records would be merged in his Wokingham headquarters. Within the next year or so, this was carried out, although many of the staff at Aldershot decided to take redundancy offers rather than move with their work. The resulting depopulation of the Halimote Road offices provided empty office space which could be profitably let to outside users while long-term plans were worked out by the company which now owned the site. These included the submission of exploratory planning applications to redevelop part or all of the site for other purposes, including housing, but none of these proposals were accepted. Despite several major improvements over the years the site could never be described as a convenient bus depot, with such anomalies as a main traffic route through one of the garage buildings and an independent engineering works in the middle of the site. Even in the late 'forties there had been a proposal to develop a more efficiently laid-out garage on the A&D sports ground in Weybourne Road.

The Londonlink coach services, which had profitted from British Rail's problems in the early 1980s, were now experiencing a reduction in patronage. The longer journey times by road, often aggravated by London traffic congestion and motorway delays, combined with a very limited

Above: Displaying the 'Whippet' livery is Ford IVECO Diesel minibus 476. This was delivered at the end of 1986, and the 21-seat body was built by the Robin Hood works. *Alder Valley Below:* 22-seat Dodge minibus 407 is seen in Camberley on a 'Whippet' service. Bodies for this 1987 batch were built by Northern Counties. *Alder Valley*

The 57-seat Duple 425 integral coach, with mechanical parts by Dennis around a Cummins L10 engine, was introduced on Londonlink services in the summer of 1987. However, Londonlink did not use Westminster bridge, where this publicity photograph was posed. *Alder Valley*

choice of journeys on some of the routes, caused passengers to drift back to rail commuting. In September 1988, Farnham lost its service when the terminus of the main X7 and X8 routes was cut back to Aldershot, and the once-daily X35 which had served Frimley and Sandhurst ceased.

Meanwhile, the summer Sunday 'Coastal Express' services to seaside resorts continued, several now being operated by double-deck vehicles. They were still operated in two groups: X60-X65 originating at Camberley and picking up en route through Aldershot, Farnham and Petersfield, and X70-X75 starting at Horsell, and working through Woking and Guildford before diverging to their destination resorts. A new inland resort now served through the summer months was Chessington World of Adventures, which had grown out of the original Chessington Zoo of pre-war days. X77, starting at Knaphill, ran via Woking and Guildford, and initially operated to Chessington at weekends from the late May Bank Holiday until the start of the school holidays, when it became a daily service.

In February 1989, AV introduced two stage services to Brighton. Southdown had greatly reduced its presence in the Horsham area, and AV now took aboard the West Sussex County Council contract to cover the Horsham–Brighton route on Sundays. The route was extended back to start at Guildford, unsubsidised over that section, and numbered 107. At the same time, the subsidised Fridays-only 289 service from Billingshurst to Brighton, previously run on contract by Sussex Bus, was gained by AV and extended to start from Hindhead.

The first new double-deck buses to be ordered for eight years turned up in December 1988. Service reductions, and the substitution of frequent minibuses for less frequent larger buses, had meant that there were enough Bristol VRs, but with the older representatives of this type now being over ten years of age, an infusion of a newer design was desirable. A delivery of ten Leyland Olympians, F571-80

The first Leyland Olympians for local services were placed in service in December 1988. 909 is shown in Horsham, ready for departure for Guildford. The whole batch was stationed at Cranleigh. *Alder Valley*

SMG (fleet numbers 901-10), was fitted with 79-seat Alexander bodies, and the complete batch was allocated to Cranleigh garage, to the exclusion of the Bristol VRs previously based at that depot.

The 1988 intake of minibuses were all of the Fiat IVECO type, with 23-seat Carlyle bodies and automatic gearboxes. There were ten of them, F692-701 OPA, fleet numbers 482-91, delivered in November and December, and three similar vehicles, 494-6, G864-6 BPD, arrived a year later, by which time ten of the original and smaller Ford Transits had been withdrawn.

The re-tendering cycle for 1989 resulted in three of the four minibus services in the Haslemere area passing from AV to Gastonia Chauffeur Cars in May, and 1990 saw the disappearance, from 2 January, of all of AV's minibuses from local services in Fleet, as well as several in the Farnborough area. They were replaced by a fleet operated by the Tillingbourne Bus Company from a base near Farnham. The loss of some contracts is not necessarily disastrous, as others are gained elsewhere from time to time, and the availability of a pool of minibuses allows a major operator to use them on some lightly-loaded journeys instead of running 74-seat double-deckers for half a dozen passengers. Since the planned life of a minibus is shorter than that of the full-sized vehicles, the fleet strength can adjust to changed circumstances in a relatively short period, without detriment to long-term financial plans.

A type of service not previously operated by AV (though already known in other companies' areas) was the free bus from Aldershot, Farnborough and Frimley to the new out-of-town shopping centre at The Meadows, Sandhurst. Numbered T1, as it was paid for by the Tesco store,

this started on 27 March 1990, and provided four journeys each way on Mondays, Tuesdays and Wednesdays. The two principal local services were also diverted to serve the new superstores.

Cranleigh garage lost its independent status from 30 April 1990, and came under the control of Woking, with a garage foreman left to supervise operations. Both premises, plus the operations at Guildford bus station, were under the overall direction of the Guildford Local Manager, who was one of three local managers directly responsible to the General Manager.

During 1990, the break-up of the Frontsource empire gave AV the opportunity to re-acquire its engineering section and integrate its operations on the Aldershot site. However, since the rapid changes of ownership had left the company as tenant, rather than owner, of its main office building, the re-organisation of the site included the relocation of the remaining AV staff so that the office tenancy could be terminated. As a temporary measure, the displaced staff were moved into the former engineering offices, where a number of redundancies had created space, until the planned new headquarters for the Q Drive group were completed at Bracknell. The re-integration of AV Engineering took place at a time of economic recession, and it was soon decided that continuation of the contract work for outside customers was not financially justifiable. In August 1991, the management announced that AV Engineering would cease as a separate entity in November, with only the essential bus maintenance activities being retained, housed in the old body shop.

On top of the domestic upheaval of vacating the old head office building, a new and major disturbance was

Chessington World of Adventures is the location of this photograph of one of Alder Valley's last batch of touring coaches. These were five secondhand BOVA/DAF vehicles, acquired in 1989. Nos. 1403-5 (E665/7/72 JNR) seated 53 passengers, and were only one year old when they came to Alder Valley. They were very soon repainted in the new livery of yellow with diagonal green stripes, but were withdrawn from service two years later when AV cut back its coach operations. *Alder Valley*

presented to the owners and management when Mr David Stewart announced his wish to withdraw as a major shareholder in the Q Drive company. The prevailing market conditions were not propitious for the raising of new capital to buy out his holding, and the solution to the problem was the sale of parts of both the operating companies. In the case of Alder Valley, this meant the sale on 15 December 1990 of the Guildford, Woking and Cranleigh operations to Drawlane Transport PLC, owners of London and Country, the privatised successors to London Transport, which had cast covetous eyes on A&D's Guildford operations during the 1930s. As a result, London and Country itself was reorganised into two separate operating companies. Their new acquisitions were placed under the control of a company called Randomquick Ltd (Registered Office at 54 Endless Street, Salisbury – at one time better known as the headquarters of the Wilts and Dorset bus company). To reassure the travelling public, the new owners adopted the trading name of Alder Valley West Surrey, and agreed to retain the familiar Alder Valley image for the time being.

Some other consequences of this upheaval, which reduced the size both of Alder Valley proper and of The Bee Line were that Richard Soper became Managing Director of both companies, and Assistant Managing Director of Q Drive itself, and that in transferring the Cranleigh operations en bloc, AV lost its new fleet of Olympian double-deckers, which were all based there. The sale of the eastern outposts left the original Alder Valley company with a much-reduced stock list – 35 double-deck, 34 single-deck, 36 minibuses and 19 coaches – a total of 124 vehicles, based at Aldershot, Hindhead and Alton depots.

One of the new contracts won in 1991 was for one of Hampshire County Council's Sunday Rider routes. For some years, the only AV services operating in the county on Sundays had been contract services, and the council had introduced the Sunday Rider ticket to allow travel on any of its subsidised services, including those crossing into neighbouring counties. In addition to those which followed the routes of weekday services, a few gaps in the map were filled in the summer by routes, numbered in the 900 series, which were put out to tender. One of these, 906, Alton–Liss–Petersfield–Portsmouth–Southsea had been operated in 1990 by Hants & Sussex, but for the 1991 season, AV won the contract to run five journeys each way.

Other problems facing the company were disclosed to the public in the summer of 1991: the Aldershot depot was occupied on a short lease from its new owners, which were now in the hands of the receivers. The renegotiation of the lease, which was due to expire at the end of the year, was thus fraught with difficulties, and the closure of AV Engineering meant that the premises were no longer suitable for the company's current needs. At the time when this book was sent to the printers, the question of the future location of the Aldershot depot was still being resolved. In the meantime, the lease has been extended for a further short period.

Further economies were still necessary, and the Coaching Unit was disbanded at the end of the summer season of 1991. Its fleet of five Bova/DAF coaches, bought almost-new two years earlier, was immediately delicenced and put up for sale. Fortunately, it was found possible to offer most of the drivers continued employment with the minibus fleet, which was due to be strengthened.

Any thoughts of long-term co-operation with the separated Alder Valley West Surrey section were soon dispelled. West Surrey (which had very soon reduced the Alder Valley prefix to small print on its paperwork and on its buses) saw an opportunity for competition within Alder Valley's remaining area, and in October 1991 announced a new route 236 from Farnborough to Fleet, via Cove. Although there was an understanding that West Surrey would not employ any of its buses which were still in AV livery, the AV management had to issue a warning that tickets would not be interavailable over roads served by both companies. West Surrey was itself soon to disappear, as its owning company Randomquick Ltd was renamed Guildford and West Surrey Buses Ltd in January 1992, and on 14 March the new name came into full use when all West Surrey and London & Country routes in the Guildford area were extensively revised and re-registered under the G&WS name.

In September 1991, The Bee Line announced its withdrawal from Londonlink operations. These were sold to Reading Transport (formerly Reading Corporation Transport) which, when coach services were deregulated, had been quick to introduce its own Reading–London express service. As a result, Q Drive was able to reassign some of the relatively new fleet of Bee Line coaches to its other operating company, Alder Valley. These were Volvo B10Ms with 55-seat Jonckheere bodies, and they took over the majority of the AV Londonlink workings from the Duple/Dennis 425s early in 1992. Unlike the latter, whose livery was derived from the red, white and black scheme used by the NBC, the Volvos appeared in a version of AV's new green and yellow coach livery. The new era was launched on 2 February, when a new Londonlink timetable included several journeys re-routed to serve the recently-developed Southwood estate, to the west of Cove.

The 1992 round of re-tendering for county council subsidised services saw Alder Valley as the net losers of local and school services, especially to independent operators in the Alton area. Other notable changes in Hampshire were the loss of the 'Bordhill' local services in Bordon and Whitehill to Oakley Coaches, and the disappearance of the long-established Alton–Petersfield route, 226, which was divided between an Oakley Coaches service from Petersfield to Whitehill and a truncated AV service between Aldershot and Whitehill, absorbed into the existing Aldershot–Whitehill–Haslemere service 268. These changes took effect on 27 April, when AV also withdrew from the Basingstoke–Medstead–Alton route, 208. (The sharing of that route with Hants and Dorset in the late 'seventies had fulfilled A&D's thwarted ambitions for a railway replacement service in 1932!) The vagaries of the subsidised sector were highlighted around this time by a public complaint from Tillingbourne. After tendering for Fleet local services on the basis of reasonable projections of revenue, their position was seriously undermined by Hart District Council's abandonment of the issue of bus tokens to pensioners. This resulted in a sudden drop in patronage of the minibuses, and a threat to their continued operation.

As a parting comment on the fluidity of bus operations in the 1990's, it is interesting to note that the Alder Valley fleet of 1986 is now divided between five major operators. In addition to Alder Valley, Guildford & West Surrey and The Bee Line, part of the latter's fleet was transferred to form the Wycombe Bus Company in December 1990, and on 16 August 1992 the Bee Line depots at Reading and Newbury, with 55 buses and 100 drivers, were transferred to the ownership of Reading Buses – a move which General Manager Douglas Adie had fought off a decade earlier.

Chapter Eleven
Garages and Other Premises

Aldershot

The A&F company completed its garage in 1909, on a site near The Grove end of Halimote Road purchased from Alderton and Sumpster. It was designed to house four buses. In June 1910 the adjacent pair of cottages was acquired as an office building, and in October 1911 an extension onto built-up ground at the rear and an extension of the garage along the Halimote Road frontage were ready for occupation, thus providing more space for workshops to support the general motor garage side of the business.

After A&D moved out, the old garage was sold, and it was used for many years as a store by the NAAFI. It now houses the Brighton Road Garage, though the adjacent cottages were demolished in the mid-80s.

In 1914-15, A&D purchased the site of a former brickworks, at the top end of Halimote Road, with a long frontage to Grosvenor Road. The excavations had produced a level site with a steep bank against this frontage, which permitted the construction in 1916 of a garage at site level, high enough to take double-deckers, and a workshop – always known as the 'Top Shop' – at road level. The cost was £12,215. The garage was entered from a private road leading off Halimote Road. This became known as Foden Road, as it was along here that the fleet of steam wagons used to line up every morning to raise steam in the period 1914-20.

Further down Foden Road stood the sheds for the steam wagons, beyond which was the 'petrol garage' for the motor lorries. These were of brick construction, with roller doors, and were built high enough to allow for subsequent use to house double-deck buses. On the opposite side of Foden Road was the Halimote Road Garage – the private car side of the business – which was sold to Vick Bros in August 1917. They were allowed right of way over A&D's roadway. At the southern end of Foden Road were the corrugated iron canteen building and the boiler house.

In 1924 an office block was erected between the end of the main building and Halimote Road, at a cost of £5,180: part of it was increased in height five years later. Also, in September 1924 the ground between the existing site and the railway, and the buildings on it, were purchased. One of these, at one time used as a skating rink, was rebuilt in 1927 to form a new body shop, relieving pressure on the Top Shop. This building had given its name to the nearby Rink House, which was used as the residence of the Chief Engineer and was demolished in 1951. A large new garage was built on the east of Foden Road in 1926, at a cost of £4,964. This was also greatly enlarged in 1929, at a further cost of £9,711, and included docking facilities. On the opposite side of the road, the former goods vehicle sheds were linked to the main garage by roofing over the intervening yard in 1928 and an engineers' office was built between this and Grosvenor Road in 1929.

The original garage built in 1909 to house the Aldershot & Farnborough company's four Milnes-Daimler buses is still recognisable in 1992, apart from the replacement of sliding doors by roller shutters. The extension to the right was added in 1911 to provide workshop capacity for the general motor trade. From left to right, DY 118, DY 116, DY 106, DY 35 and LN 3124. Note the low radiator position on the two older Milnes-Daimlers.

Alder Valley

Above: A 1919 view of the Grosvenor Road frontage of the new building erected three years earlier shows the entrance to the 'Top Shop'. On the forecourt, Chief Engineer E.A. Eager is at the wheel of Studebaker staff car AA 8494, while his deputy and eventual successor Percy Rivitt stands in the doorway. A Daimler CC chassis, AA 5332, is being driven by Wilfred Lunn, who later became Superintendent of Docks and Running Shed, with G. Court beside him. *Alder Valley*

Below: The Steam Shed, photographed in 1919 with three Fodens just visible, as well as the ubiquitous Percy Rivitt in a light coat. Beyond is the Petrol Garage entrance, and in the distance a Belsize goods lorry stands in front of the canteen. Beside the Steam Shed is the timekeeper's hut, from which the bus crews collected the waybills and destination boards at the start of each shift, and which also served as a parcels and enquiry office for the general public. *Alder Valley*

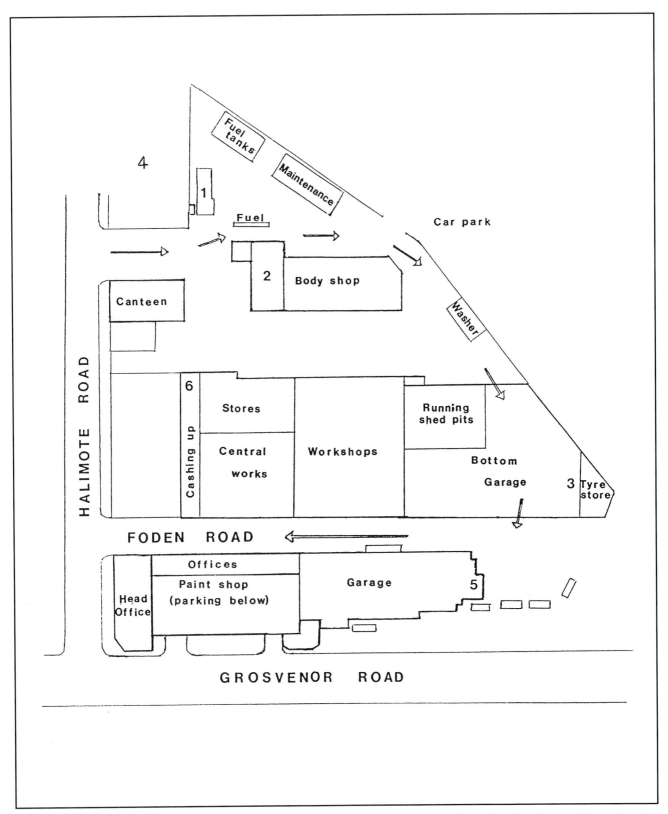

An outline plan of the Halimote Road depot in 1981. 1 – chassis washer. 2 – panel shop, trimming shop and signwriter. 3 – depot body shop. 4 – former Aldershot & Farnborough garage. 5 – old boiler house. 6 – Depot Traffic Superintendent's office.

Vick Bros sold their premises back to the Traction Company for £7,752 in 1936. By this time Vick's site was completely covered by buildings, one of which became the dance hall in 1937, while another part was converted into a mess room in the same year. These two were eventually combined into a new canteen and recreation room in 1957. The remainder of Vick's Garage (always known as such) was used as a running shed until 1980, when it was converted to become Alder Valley's central workshops.

Another major change took place in 1956, when additional land was purchased from the Co-operative Society and some buildings on it cleared to provide more parking area, as the undercover capacity of 127 vehicles had been outgrown. During the 1960s, the depot was home to around 144 vehicles, including coaches.

In 1964, the Head Office building was modernised internally and externally and in 1968, a start was made on a major programme of garage reconstruction and re-equipment. The former Co-operative shop building beside Halimote Road was first reconstructed to form a new canteen, so that the old canteen and former 'Traction Hall' could be removed and replaced by a workshop, stores and engineering offices building. Improvements were made in the running sheds, including the provision of inspection pits and sunken workshops, and the body shop was also

completely modernised, as well as being partitioned to provide a separate paint shop. When the work was completed in 1971, a gyratory system was introduced for buses using the garage between duties. Buses entered at the lower end of the site and called at the refuelling point (moved from its previous location in Foden Road). They then proceeded via the washing machine either to the garage or to the running shed workshop for minor adjustments. All outgoing vehicles then left via Foden Road.

The office block was fully modernised in 1981, when additional offices were created along the rear wall of the Top Shop. The remainder of the Top Shop now became a paint shop, with a section devoted to glass-fibre panel fabrication, and the garage below was given over to staff car parking.

The allocated number of vehicles in 1990 was 86, including 27 coaches and 32 minibuses.

In November 1990, the Alder Valley company vacated all of the office, workshop and garage space west of Foden Road.

Guildford

After the merger with Guildford & District, in 1915, a minimum of five buses was required at Guildford, until the drastic cuts at the end of 1916, after which no more

The reconstruction of 1969-70 created these sunken workshops on the site of the old Traction Hall. No. 605, UOU 605H, was a Bristol RELL6G new in June 1970.

Alder Valley

This view of the Onslow Street garage at Guildford was taken in about 1920. The offices are on the left, and a garage extension was subsequently built to the right.
Alder Valley

than two vehicles were required for the Witley Camp service. These were kept in Puttock's garage, off the High Street, in Warren Mews.

In 1919, a building on the west side of Onslow Street (roughly where the entrance to the multi-storey car park is now sited) was acquired and adapted as a garage, at a cost of £7,758. Administrative offices and an enquiry office were attached. In 1923-4 the north wall was demolished and a new section was added, including a small mess room. It was for some years the only garage apart from Aldershot

which provided docking facilities, but within a few years the vehicle capacity of 26 became inadequate for the increasing allocation and a new garage was erected in 1927 in Woodbridge Road on a site providing ample space for future needs. The Onslow Street premises thereafter became a problem. No reasonable offers were received at auction in 1931 and in January 1932 it was offered to the Town Council as suitable for a covered market, at a rental of £500 per annum, but there was little municipal enthusiasm. Eventually, in 1934, the company made alterations to

This aerial view shows the Woodbridge Road garage at Guildford in about 1960. On the left is the most recent extension of 1957-8, incorporating the new workshops. The central section, with its two large doors, was built in 1927-9, and one more garage bay and the office block to the right were added in 1940. *Alder Valley*

convert the premises into a car showroom, which was let to Jackson's Garage. This lease ended in January 1940, when A&D brought in its unlicensed vehicles for storage, but in October the Ministry of Aircraft Production requisitioned the garage as a store. (Some of the displaced vehicles were re-housed in a rented garage at Peasmarsh.) It was released on 1 October 1947, after which it was used once again for storage of unlicensed vehicles until in November 1954 it was sold to Jackson's Garage as a showroom for £22,000.

The 1927 section of the Woodbridge Road garage cost £8,878, and a £6,203 extension was opened two years later. In 1940 a third section and an office block, including a booking office, were completed, costing £7,967, on the northern end of the site. It could then accommodate 55 vehicles under cover. To the south, a further extension was erected in 1957-8 on the former bus park, including a large workshop, with three inspection pits and sunken workshops. The total capacity was thereby increased to 91 vehicles.

The garage was closed on 22 September 1985, and was subsequently sold for redevelopment, which took place in 1988.

Knaphill

A small garage for three vehicles at Highclere, near the junction of Knaphill High Street and Anchor Hill, was acquired with A.G. Smith's business in June 1926 and valued at £1,200. This served as the base for the operation of the ex-Smith Service 28b (later 4a) to Blackdown as well as the Woking end of Service 28. Initially only one bus was needed, but the introduction of services 4 (2 buses) and 41 (later 28b, 1 bus) in 1927 and 34 (2 buses) in 1928, as well as the acquisition of the routes of Ross (1 bus for 47, 2 for 48) and Tanner (3 buses for 55 and 55A) in 1928, necessitated a central garage for the Woking area. Knaphill was vacated in 1929, and was sold in 1930.

Woking

In 1929, Mr Pitcher's premises in Walton Street, near Woking station were leased. They were vacated in May 1931, by which time the acquisition of part of the Woking and District business, but not its garage, called for still larger accommodation. Walton Street was subsequently used by the East Surrey company.

A new garage for 33 vehicles in Goldsworth Road, on a site backing on to the railway, was built at a cost of £8,738 and officially opened on 1 June 1931. A temporary wooden enquiry office had already come into use two years earlier. Although the garage was built to take double-deckers, the reluctance of local authorities to allow them to be used meant that for many years most of the allocation consisted of singledeckers.

Woking garage, photographed in the late 'fifties. The newer section is on the right, and the enquiry office and bus stop are still situated adjacent to the road. In 1960 the forecourt was altered and the company-owned wooden building (which had at one time served as an inspectors' room and as an office) was removed to allow an off-street bus stop to be laid out. *Alder Valley*

An interior view of Woking garage, taken in the late 'fifties, reveals three Dennis Lancets and an AEC Reliance coach.

Alder Valley

In 1952-3 the garage was almost doubled in size, at a cost of £22,042. This extension gave a total capacity of 43 vehicles, and included offices, canteen and a recreation room at the rear. In 1960, the ground fronting the garage was cleared and a platform and queue shelter installed, to provide an off-street bus and coach loading point.

After closure in January 1982, the site was used for storage of withdrawn vehicles until sold for redevelopment.

A new, smaller, garage was established in 1985 at No. 20, Goldsworth Park Trading Estate, by adapting a standard factory unit. Maintenance facilities, including heavy lifting equipment, were installed, and up to 32 buses were allocated.

Alton

The two buses needed for service 14 were initially kept in a yard belonging to Mrs Small until November 1922, when the old fire station in Amery Street was leased. An option to purchase was exercised a year later.

The start of three new services, 53, 54 and 56 in 1928 required two more buses to be based at Alton, and the existing buildings were soon demolished prior to the building of a new shed. This was built in 1931-2 at a cost of £1,151 and consisted of a steel frame with asbestos cladding, with a capacity of seven vehicles. In 1952 a new section doubled the capacity to 13, at a cost of £8,866. The new layout included a booking office, which had been opened in 1950. Venture Ltd's Basingstoke–Alton service 7 (later Wilts & Dorset 107) used the garage as an outstation and layover point, as did the Southdown Service 38 to Portsmouth, inaugurated in 1955.

The garage was closed in December 1987, and the reduced requirements at Alton were subsequently met by basing vehicles at Hampshire Commercial's premises in Mill Lane.

Haslemere (Weyhill)

An existing motor garage site was purchased in April 1914, situated in the Clay Hill area, beside the main road to Hindhead, just west of the railway bridge: the road later took the name Wey Hill. The premises were known as 'The Motor House' (a name which was still discernible until recently painted on the brickwork above the door of the original section) or 'Clay Hill Garage' during the period when A&D carried on the motor car business.

The Haslemere section of the company's goods fleet was based here from 1914 to 1920, in addition to the single-deck buses. The garage was extended rearwards in 1919 and in May 1925 a double-deck section was built alongside the earlier building. The parcels and goods office for the local carrier business continued in use after the heavy goods contracts ceased. However, the advent of covered top double-deckers, coupled with the inconvenience of a long narrow garage, made a new depot essential, and operations were transferred to Hindhead in 1931.

Attempts to sell the property were unsuccessful, and it was eventually let to Clement Bros. Ltd., makers of metal window frames and other builders' materials in 1931. After an extension of the lease, it was sold to them in 1958.

Hindhead

This garage, built on a site off the main Portsmouth Road at a cost of £11,492, was officially opened on 1 June 1931. It had a capacity of 45 vehicles, including covered top double-deckers, although in 1936 only three out of an allocation of 32 buses were of this type.

In 1956-7 a canteen and recreation room were added, at a cost of £6,330, and in 1963 an inspection pit was installed.

The 1990 allocation of buses totalled 40.

Left: Until 1931 these two lock-up sheds constituted Alton garage. One of them houses the little Dennis, PF2077, acquired from Tanner in 1928, while the other gives shelter to Dennis G's OT 8593/7. *Alder Valley*

Below: The right-hand section of Alton garage was built in 1931-2, and was extended in 1950-2 to provide more space and a booking office. From left to right are AEC Reliances of three batches: SOU 434 (1958), HHO 540E (1967) and MOR 603 (rebodied 1967). The Denis Loline is SOU 456, of 1958, which later became a driver training vehicle and is now preserved. *Alder Valley*

Weyhill garage, at Haslemere, is seen here before the erection of an extension, in 1925, on the fire-damaged site on the left. The alterations needed to instal a door large enough for buses in the one-time motor garage are clearly visible, as are the stains on the front wall where petrol pumps once stood. The 1919 rear extension is indicated by the drop in the roofline beyond the chimney. The bus is Daimler HO 2328.   *Author's collection*

Ewhurst

The first garage, in the centre of the village, was inherited from the Surrey Hills Motor Services in January 1926, and was replaced by a brick-built garage, completed in December 1928, at a cost of £1,025 2s 0d, to take up to six buses.

On 2 August 1933 the garage and six buses were transferred to the London Passenger Transport Board, which soon sold it to Ewhurst Coaches. This operator sold out to Gastonia Coaches, Ltd. and eventually in 1974 the garage came to be used by the Tillingbourne Bus Co. Ltd. It was demolished in the early 1980s and some parts were taken to the Chalk Pits Museum at Amberley, Sussex, with a view to use in building a replica of a 1920s bus depot. However, little, if any, of the material was actually used.

Cranleigh

Part of the Gastonia garage in Manfield Park was leased in 1985. Basic maintenance facilities were provided, and Alder Valley soon became the sole occupants. 20 buses were allocated in 1990.

Hindhead garage, photographed in 1955. In 1963 the appearance was necessarily spoilt by the erection of two large fuel tanks alongside the drive. In the scene are AEC Reliance coach MOR 596, and Dennis Lance K3 HOT 697.

Outstations (listed in order of first allocation)

Dorking — (1914) one bus for the Guildford service.

Basingstoke — (1920-21) One bus for service 6.
(1928-1984) Two buses for service 7 while running to Andover in 1928, one thereafter, plus one for 52 in 1928 only.
From the 1930s the bus was kept in the Venture Ltd. (later Wilts & Dorset) bus park. In 1977 one bus each was housed for services 201 and 207, the former surviving into the 1980s.

Alton — (1922-23) Two buses for service 14, later provided with a garage (q.v.) on a site in Amery Street.

Egham — (1923-c.1972) One bus for service 1, garaged in a rented dormy shed close to the railway station.

Horsham — (1923-c.1980) One bus for service 33, kept at the Southdown garage.

Alresford — (1923-1976) One bus for service 14. Garaged in a former barn at J.C. Fairhead's builder's yard on Winchester Road.

Winchester — (1923-1980) One bus for service 14, kept in the Hants & Dorset bus station.

Woking — (1924-1926) One bus for services 28 and 28b, until Knaphill depot was acquired.
(1982-85) Winton's yard, Walton Road: open-air parking until new garage established.

Petersfield — (1924-1980) One bus for service 6, plus one for 24 (1924-27), kept at the Southdown garage.

Westcott — (1925-1933) One bus for service 25, kept in the Crown Hotel yard, until the service was taken over by the LPTB.

Elstead — (1928-1977) Buses for 45 and 46 (one each) continued to be garaged at May's Garage, Cock Hill, after these routes were acquired from May. One bus for 46 only from 1964.

Wisborough Green — (1928-1946) One bus for service 49.

Chobham — (1928-1930) Three buses for services 55, 55A, taken over from Tanner, operated from here until Woking garage was available.

Ewhurst/Cranleigh — (1933-1979) After Ewhurst garage passed to the LPTB, one bus was outstationed for services 23 and 23b, and a local poultryman, Mr J.A. Hamshire, built a bus shed to rent to A&D. When service 25 was taken over from Gastonia in May 1937, a second bus was needed, and was kept at the Cranleigh Motors garage. After exactly one year, this ceased when 23b was extended, and a single bus continued to be kept at Ewhurst until March 1964. The introduction of one-man buses, which could not be safely shunted by the driver unaided, led to the bus being kept in the public car park at Stocklund Square, Cranleigh (from which it was stolen on more than one occasion!) The double-deck railway replacement service from Cranleigh to Guildford always used a bus worked empty from Guildford.
See above for the subsequent Cranleigh garage.

Odiham — (1962-c.1981) One bus for Service 7A, kept at the Odiham Motor Services garage on Dunley's Hill.

Enquiry and Booking Offices

(also staffed waiting rooms)

Aldershot — Head office, Halimote Road.
14-16 Station Road (1923-33) with waiting room. Incorporated into the Bus Station 1933.

Alton — Garage, Amery Street (1931-1987) (enquiries only: booking and parcels facilities provided by agents until 1950).

Ewhurst garage, the second on the site, was built in 1928, but was lost when London Transport took over the area. This picture was taken soon after the new owners acquired it from A&D in 1933.

London Transport Museum

The company's Camberley office, at Yorktown, provided a waiting room and ladies cloak room for the benefit of long-distance coach passengers. Its location was inconvenient, and in the late 'twenties its replacement by an office nearer to the town centre was deemed an urgent necessity by the A&D management. Their wishes came to fruition in 1983!

Alder Valley

198 High Street, Guildford, combined the A&D enquiry office with the local inspector's residence. At the time of this photograph the legend on the door showed it to be still the registered office of Guildford and District Motor Services. *Alder Valley*

The former Comfy Coaches office in Castle Street, Farnham, became A&D's local travel agency over the period 1962-9. It is now the home of Bygone Books. *P. Gascoine*

	Mill Lane (1988-present) (telephone enquiries and bookings).
Basingstoke	10a London Street (1920-21).
Blackdown Camp	Parcels office and waiting room (c.1916-c.1923).
Bramshott Camp	Waiting room (c.1916-20).
Camberley	113 London Road, Yorktown (later renumbered 367) (c.1916-1983) Waiting room and ladies' room. Closed 11 April 1983 and replaced by a portable building in Pembroke Broadway.
Crookham	Waiting room, Cross Roads (c.1919-32).
Farnborough	Kingsmead (1988-present).
Farnham	12 East Street (1928-46).
	101 East Street (1946-67).
	Farnham Travel Agency, 5a Castle Street (ex-Comfy Coaches, 1962-69).
	12 Woolmead, East Street (temporarily shared, 1967-9).
	Farnham Travel Agency, 20 Woolmead, East Street (1969-1988).
Fleet	Tower Buildings, Reading Road (1929-40).
Guildford	Central Garage (1914).
	148 High Street (c.1915-1916).
	198 High Street (c.1916-1926).
	Garage, Onslow Street (1921-1933).
	Garage, Woodbridge Road (1933-1980).
	Park Street (1933-50) (including lavatories).

'Tin Town' was the shopping area of the wartime Bramshott Camp. Taken from a postcard marked 'passed by censor', this view shows the A&D office on the right, and Belsize AA 5644 just arrived from Haslemere station.

The 1961 booking and enquiry office at Woking, surmounted by an illuminated sign and a clock. In the background, the characteristic bracket signal gantry to the west of Woking station shows the proximity of the railway. *Alder Valley*

An interior view of the 1961 booking and enquiry office at Woking, with the slogan 'Travel in comfort' repeated all along the frieze. *Alder Valley*

	Farnham Road Bus Station (1950-1964).
	Friary Square (between Farnham Road and Onslow Street Bus Stations) (1964-1980).
	Friary Bus Station (1980-present).
Haslemere	The Motor House, Clay Hill (later known as Wey Hill garage) (1914-1931).
	Station Approach (c.1916-1923 and 1931-c.1972).
Hindhead	Waiting room, Huts Corner (1927-70).
	Garage, Portsmouth Road (c.1931-present).

Witley Camp	Waiting room (c.1916-1920).
Woking	1 Goldsworth Road (1929-c.1987) A temporary building in a corner of the garage site was followed by a permanent wooden building in April 1932, in turn replaced by a brick building when roadway alterations took place in 1961. During the transition, a wooden shop building on the garage forecourt was used for a time as the enquiry office: it also served as an inspectors' room.

Other Booking Agencies

Bognor	(Southdown Office) (1935-1940).
Chichester	(Southdown Office) (1935-1940).
Horsham	(Southdown Office) 23 Richmond Terrace, Carfax (1935-1954).
	22 The Carfax (1954-1977).
London	(London Coastal Coaches Ltd.) (1928-c.1986) Victoria Coach Station, Buckingham Palace Road (from March 1932). Also several other travel and booking agencies in Central London.
Midhurst	(Southdown Office) North Street (1935-1971).
Petersfield	(Southdown Office) The Square (1935-1972).

(*Note:* The dates given here are those for which the offices appeared in the A&D timetable. They were actually all in use at an earlier date e.g. Horsham opened in 1926.)

Other waiting rooms, not staffed as enquiry and booking offices, were provided from an early date, and the most important were listed in the timetables from 1919 until 1923. These included Aldershot Station shelter and Frimley Village. Other early locations were Farnborough Town Hall and Shortheath, where the first shelter (1914-27) was an old bus body, later replaced by the shelter moved from Frimley. Another old body served at Beacon Hill till 1927, when it was also replaced.

Most shelters were provided by local authorities (often with an A&D contribution) or by private individuals. Soon after the death of the King in January 1936, Mr C.D. Strologo offered to pay for the erection of memorial shelters in a number of parishes in his home area: Kingfield Green, Millbridge, Thursley, Farnham (East Street), Godalming (Meadrow), Yorktown and Tilford were among those which agreed on sites and benefitted. Hindhead councillors were still debating sites in 1938 when Mr Strologo died, and as he had not made provision in his will, the opportunity was lost.

Kerbside canopy shelters at queuing points were erected in most towns during and after the end of the 1939-45 war, when bus stop signs multiplied even along rural routes.

Aldershot Bus Station

The new station opened in August 1933, on land leased from the Southern Railway at a yearly rent of £100 for 42 years. Its roadway area was 120 by 162 feet, with an entrance from The Grove and exit on to Station Road. A 4,000 square foot paved area encompassed an enquiry office and public conveniences. Some existing coal order offices along the Station Road frontage were allowed to remain. There were nine passenger gates in a chain barrier, for end loading, plus another for broadside loading at the exit.

In 1950, additional land was leased at £25 per annum and two through platforms,

Left: Before the opening of Aldershot bus station in 1933, buses started from the kerbside near to the railway station entrance. A large passenger shelter was provided as the only amenity, until in December 1922 an enquiry office and waiting room was opened at 14-16 Station Road. *Alder Valley*

with concrete canopy shelters, were built to provide four new stands. The direction of flow was now reversed, from 20 March. This arrangement persisted until 1964, when the site was extended further, the through platforms were abolished, and a row of nine end loading gates was set up facing the original nine, with a long canopy shelter along the whole length of the boundary behind. The rebuilding was completed by the provision of overhead fluorescent lighting.

With front entrances becoming universal, and conductors being phased out, the reversal of buses into the bays was undesirable, and the next change, in 1979, was the building of a spine platform outwards from the enquiry office. This was provided with thirteen front-loading gates, lettered A to M.

No other bus stations were built by the company, but in December 1952, a bus departure platform was constructed in the forecourt of Camberley Station, at a cost of £1,800, shared equally between A&D and British Railways. This was to pre-empt any move by the local council to build a municipal bus station. Two queue shelters were provided five years later, but when the station was totally rebuilt in the 1970s, all this was swept away.

One more company-owned bus terminus was the passenger loading point, with platform, and shelter, laid out on the forecourt of Woking garage in 1960.

Sports Ground

This ground, situated south of Weybourne Road, near the foot of Eggar's Hill, was the property of the company's Athletic Club. Five acres were leased in 1919 and purchased in 1920. Football and cricket grounds were laid out and a spectators' stand was later erected. A further five acres were obtained for a second cricket ground, and in 1935 a pavilion with bar facilities was built.

During the 1939-45 war, the stand was cleared out and used for long-term storage of small buses, while other less fortunate delicensed vehicles stood exposed to the weather outside. The edges of the ground were brought under cultivation by a new Horticultural section. In 1947 a bowling green was opened and later three hard tennis courts were laid down.

The ground is still owned, in 1992, by the Aldershot Traction Company Athletic Club.

Above: Shortheath waiting room, with double-decker OT 319 awaiting departure on service 10, and single-decker OT 3707 passing through on the 10a to Rowledge. Originally sited beside the White Hart at Frimley, this building was moved to Shortheath in 1927 to replace an old bus body which had served as a shelter for many years. Local lads used it on occasions as a minor gambling den, and there is a tale of a bus conductor who would not allow anyone to board on the upper deck while his driver was courting a local servant girl during layover periods! *Author's collection courtesy R. Boxall*

Below: Aldershot Bus Station, photographed in about 1954, shows the nine loading gates, with the enquiry office on the left. The Dennis buses visible start with a Lance K4, two Lancet J3s, a Lancet J10 and two Lance K3s. Entering at the far end is the unique Dennis Dominant HOU 900. *Alder Valley*

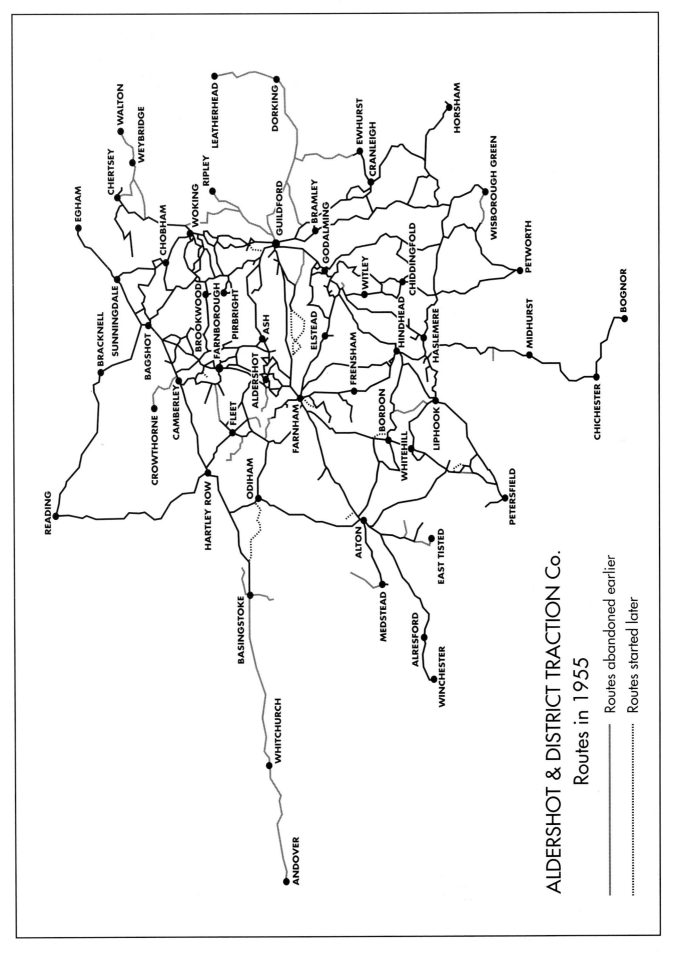

ALDERSHOT & DISTRICT TRACTION Co.
Routes in 1955

——— Routes abandoned earlier

·········· Routes started later

List of Services Operated

June 1912 (End of the Aldershot & Farnborough era)
Aldershot–Farnborough Station
Aldershot–Weybourne–Farnham
Aldershot–Deepcut

December 1916 (Prior to economy cuts due to the war)
Aldershot–Farnborough–Camberley
Aldershot–Weybourne–Farnham
Aldershot–Fleet Station
Aldershot–Farnham–Hindhead–Haslemere
Aldershot–Farnham–Shortheath
Haslemere–Hindhead–Bramshott
Aldershot–Guildford–Godalming–Haslemere
Guildford–Shalford–Dorking–Leatherhead
Guildford–Merrow
Guildford–Godalming–Witley Camp
Guildford–Godalming–Chiddingfold–Haslemere
Aldershot–Ash Vale–Blackdown
Aldershot–Upper Hale
Aldershot–Odiham–Basingstoke
Guildford–Worplesdon–Brookwood–Woking
Aldershot–Fleet–Reading
Haslemere–Hindhead Golf Club (First Class service)
Guildford–Ripley
Haslemere–Midhurst
Aldershot–Deepcut

November 1920 (Prior to economy cuts and numbering of services)

A	Aldershot–Farnham–Alton
B	Aldershot–North Camp–Ash Vale–Blackdown–Brookwood
C	Aldershot–Weybourne–Farnham
D	Aldershot–Fleet Station
E	Farnborough Station–Aldershot–Farnham–Hindhead–Haslemere
F	Aldershot–Farnborough–Camberley
G	Aldershot–Farnham–Shortheath
H	Aldershot–Guildford
I	Haslemere–Hindhead–Bramshott
J	Haslemere–Midhurst
K	Guildford–Godalming
L	Aldershot–Odiham–Basingstoke
M	Guildford–Worplesdon–Brookwood–Woking
N	Guildford–Merrow
O	Guildford–Ripley
P	Aldershot–Upper Hale
Q	Aldershot–Fleet–Reading
R	Guildford–Godalming–Haslemere
S	Guildford–Shalford–Dorking
T	Guildford–Shalford–Cranleigh
U	Guildford–Stoke–Woking–Knaphill
V	Basingstoke–Old Basing
W	Basingstoke–Cliddesden

August 1939 (At the outbreak of war)

1	Aldershot–Farnborough–Camberley–Sunningdale–Egham
2	Aldershot–Farnborough–Camberley
3	Aldershot–Farnborough Station
3a	Aldershot–Farnborough–Cove (Olden's Stores)
3b	Aldershot–Farnborough–Cove (Plough & Horses)
3c	Aldershot–Farnborough–Farnborough Street
4	Aldershot–Blackdown–Brookwood–Woking
5	Aldershot–North Camp–Blackdown–Brookwood (SuO)
5a	Aldershot–Farnborough–Blackdown–Camberley
5b	Aldershot–Farnborough–Brompton Sanatorium–Camberley

6	Aldershot–Farnham–Whitehill–Petersfield–Steep
7	Aldershot–Farnham–Odiham–Basingstoke
8	Aldershot–Fleet Station–Bramshot Golf Club
8a	Aldershot–Pondtail–Fleet
9	Aldershot–Crookham Village–Fleet Station–Bramshot Golf Club
10	Aldershot–Weybourne–Farnham–Shortheath
11	Aldershot–Weybourne–Farnham
12	Aldershot–Fleet–Reading
13	Alton–Whitehill–Haslemere
14	Aldershot–Farnham–Alton–Alresford–Winchester
15	Aldershot–Upper Hale–Farnham
16	Farnham–Dockenfield
17	Farnham–Hindhead–Grayshott
18	Grayswood–Haslemere–Hindhead–Whitehill
19	Aldershot–Farnham–Hindhead–Haslemere–Midhurst–Chichester–Bognor
20	Aldershot–Ash–Guildford
20a	Aldershot–Tongham
20b	Aldershot–North Town
21	Guildford–Godalming–Chiddingfold–Haslemere
21a	Guildford–Godalming–Chiddingfold
21b	Guildford–Godalming–Grayswood–Haslemere
22	Guildford–Godalming–Eashing Lane Estate
22a	Guildford–Godalming Station
23	Guildford–Shalford–Cranleigh–Ewhurst
24	Guildford–Godalming–Hindhead–Liphook–Petersfield
24a	Guildford–Godalming–Hindhead
25	Guildford–Shalford–Cranleigh
26	Aldershot–Ash–Ash Station–Aldershot (FSO)
27	Guildford–Dennisville
28	Guildford–Worplesdon–Brookwood–Knaphill–Woking
28a	Guildford–Stoughton
28b	Woking–Horsell
29	Guildford–Stoke–Woking
30	Guildford–Onslow Village
31	Guildford–Hog's Back–Farnham
31a	Puttenham–Peasmarsh–Guildford–Wood Street
31b	Compton–Peasmarsh–Guildford
32	Aldershot–Badshot Lea
33	Guildford–Shalford–Cranleigh–Horsham
33a	Guildford–Shalford–Run Common–Cranleigh–Horsham
34	Guildford–Stoke–Woking–Bagshot–Camberley–Hawley–Cove
34a	Guildford–Stoke–Woking–Bagshot–Camberley–Frimley–Blackdown Camp
34b	Woking–Knaphill–Bisley
35	Aldershot–Ash–North Camp–Farnborough
35a	Aldershot–Ash–Mytchett–Coleford Bridge Road
36	Aldershot–Fleet–Winchfield Infirmary (WSuO)
37	Farnham–Crondall–Crookham Village–Fleet
38	Farnham–Ewshot
39	Aldershot–Ewshot Camp (FSO)
40	Aldershot–Ash–Ash Green (FSO)
42	Aldershot–Aldershot Park–Gloucester Road junction
42a	Aldershot–Guildford Road–Gloucester Road junction
43	Aldershot–Badshot Lea–Farnham
44	Woking–Star Hill–Knaphill
45	Farnham–Elstead–Godalming
46	Elstead–Godalming–Farncombe
47	Witley Station–Godalming–Farncombe
48	Guildford–Stoke–Woking–Ottershaw–Chertsey Bridge

48a	Camberley–Bagshot–Woking–Ottershaw–Weybridge
49	Guildford–Bramley–Wisborough Green
51	Petworth–Haslemere–Critchmere
52	Basingstoke–Hartley Row
53	Alton–Greatham–Hillbrow–Petersfield
54	Alton–Medstead–Bentworth
55	Woking–Burrow Hill
55a	Woking–Windlesham–Sunningdale
55b	Woking–Windlesham–Bagshot
55c	Woking–West End
56	Alton–Farringdon–East Tisted
56a	Alton–Farringdon–Upper Farringdon
59	Milford Station–Milford Sanatoria (SuO)
60	Godalming–Dunsfold
61	North Camp–Coleford Bridge Road–Frimley (FSO)
62	Guildford–Brookwood–Knaphill–Bagshot
63	Woking–Brookwood Cemetery–Fox Corner
64	Woking–Mayford–Fox Corner

December 1971 (Eve of merger into Alder Valley)

1	Aldershot–Farnborough–Camberley–Sunningdale–Egham
2	Aldershot–Farnborough–Camberley–Old Dean Estate
3a	Aldershot–Farnborough–Cove–Ively Park Estate
3b	Aldershot–Farnborough–Cove–Pyestock Estate
3c	Aldershot–Farnborough–Farnborough Street–Camberley–Old Dean Estate
3d	Aldershot–Farnborough–Cove–Minley Estate
6	Aldershot–Farnham–Whitehill–Petersfield–Steep
7	Aldershot–Farnham–Odiham–Basingstoke
8	Aldershot–Fleet Station
8a	Aldershot–Pondtail–Fleet
9	Aldershot–Crookham Village–Fleet Station
12	Aldershot–Fleet–Swallowfield–Reading
13	Alton–Whitehill–Haslemere
13a	Alton–Oakhanger–Whitehill–Haslemere
13b	High Lane Estate–Haslemere–Woolmer Hill Estate/Hammervale
14	Aldershot–Farnham–Alton–Alresford–Winchester
14a	Farnham–Lower Froyle (SO)
15	Aldershot–Upper Hale–Farnham–Shortheath
16	Fleet–Crondall–Farnham–Dockenfield
17	Ewshot–Farnham–Hindhead–Grayshott
18	Guildford–Godalming–Grayswood–Haslemere–Hindhead–Whitehill
19	Aldershot–Farnham–Hindhead–Haslemere–Midhurst
20	Aldershot–Ash–Guildford
20a	Farnborough–Aldershot–Tongham
20b	Aldershot–North Town
20c	Farnborough–Aldershot–Ash–Guildford
20d	Aldershot–Ash Road–North Town
21	Guildford–Godalming–Chiddingfold
22	Guildford–Godalming–Eashing Lane Estate
22a	Guildford–Godalming Station
22b	Guildford–Godalming–Aarons Hill Estate
23	Guildford–Shalford–Cranleigh–Ewhurst
24	Guildford–Godalming–Hindhead–Liphook–Petersfield
25	Guildford–Shalford–Cranleigh
26	Guildford–Rydes Hill Estate
27	Guildford–Dennisville–Guildford Cathedral
28	Guildford–Worplesdon–Brookwood–Knaphill–Woking
28a	Guildford–Stoughton
28c	Guildford–Worplesdon–Brookwood–Woking

28d	Guildford–Stoughton (Grange Road)
29	Guildford–Stoke–Barnsbury Estate–Woking–Knaphill–Lightwater
29b	Guildford–Stoke–Bellfields Estate
29c	Guildford–Woodbridge Road–Bellfields Estate
30	Guildford–Onslow Village
30a	Guildford–Onslow Village (Manor Way)
31	Guildford–Hog's Back–Farnham
33	Guildford–Shalford–Cranleigh–Horsham
34	Guildford–Stoke–Woking–Bagshot–Camberley–Hawley–Cove
34a	Guildford–Stoke–Woking–Bagshot–Camberley–Frimley–Blackdown Camp
35	Aldershot–Ash–North Camp–Farnborough–West Heath–Camberley
35a	Aldershot–Ash–Mytchett–Coleford Bridge Road/Keogh Barracks
39	Camberley–Yorktown–Mytchett–Ash
39a	Camberley–Ravenswood–Mytchett–Ash Vale–Ash
39b	Camberley–Chobham Road–Mytchett–Ash Vale–Ash
41	Farnham–Farnborough Station
42	Aldershot–Aldershot Park–Bathing Pool
42a	Aldershot–Guildford Road–Heron Wood Estate
44	Woking–Star Hill–Knaphill–Brookwood–Blackdown–Aldershot
44a	Woking–St John's–Brookwood (NSSu)
45	Farnham–Elstead–Godalming–Farncombe
46	Elstead–Godalming–Farncombe
47	Witley Station–Godalming–Farncombe
48	Guildford–Stoke–Woking–Ottershaw–Chertsey Bridge
48a	Camberley–Bagshot–Woking–Ottershaw–Chertsey Bridge
48b	Chertsey–Longcross
49	Guildford–Bramley–Wisborough Green
50	Hindhead–Haslemere–Plaistow–Horsham
51	Petworth–Chiddingfold–Haslemere–Critchmere–Woolmer Hill Estate
52	Basingstoke–Hartley Row–Camberley
53	Alton–Greatham–Hillbrow–Petersfield
54	Anstey Manor Estate–Alton–Medstead
55a	Woking–Windlesham–Sunningdale
55b	Woking–Windlesham–Bagshot
55c	Woking–West End
59	Alton–Farringdon–Newton Valence (SO)
60	Godalming–Dunsfold
63	Woking–Brookwood Cemetery–Fox Corner
65	Guildford–Puttenham–Farnham
66	Guildford–Compton–Farnham
67	Guildford–Wood Street
71a	Hawley Lane Estate–Hawley School
75	Guildford–Worplesdon–Knaphill–Bagshot–Bracknell–Wokingham–Reading
76	Aldershot–North Camp–Farnborough–Cove–Farnborough–North Camp
76a	Aldershot–North Camp–Farnborough–Cove–Farnborough Street–North Camp

June 1983 (After MAP revisions)

200	Basingstoke–Odiham–Hartley Wintney–Camberley–Staines–Heathrow
201	Basingstoke–Hartley Wintney–Camberley–Staines–Heathrow
202	Alton–Selborne–Liss–Petersfield
203/4	Alton–South View Rise–Anstey Manor Estate–Alton (circular)
205	Alton–Farringdon–East Tisted–Droxford
206	Basingstoke–Greywell–Odiham

207 Aldershot–Folly Hill–Farnham–Odiham–Basingstoke
208 Alton–Lasham–Basingstoke
209 Alton–Medstead–Lasham–Basingstoke
210 Alton–Upton Grey–Basingstoke (WSO)
211 High Lane Estate–Haslemere–Woolmer Hill Estate
212 High Lane Estate–Haslemere–Liphook–Whitehill–Oakhanger–Alton
213 High Lane Estate–Haslemere–Liphook–Whitehill–Kingsley–Alton
214 Guildford–Farnham–Alton–Alresford–Southampton
217 Farnham–Tilford–Hindhead–Grayshott
219 Aldershot–Weybourne–Farnham–Hindhead–Haslemere–Midhurst
222 Rowledge–Shortheath–Farnham–Farnborough–Frimley
223/4 Aldershot–Upper Hale–Farnham–Shortheath–Rowledge
225 Aldershot–Heron Wood Estate–Badshot Lea–Farnham
226 Aldershot–Weybourne–Farnham–Whitehill–Liss–Petersfield
228 Guildford–Stoughton–Grange Park Estate–Guildford (circular)
229 Bellfields Estate–Guildford–Guildford District Hospital
230 Bellfields Estate–Guildford–Onslow Village
231 Guildford–Rydes Hill Estate–Guildford (circular)
232/42 Guildford–Wood Street Green–Fairlands Estate–Guildford (circular)
233/43 Guildford–Rydes Hill Estate–Wood Street Green–Fairlands Estate–Guildford (circular) (Evgs/SuO)
244 Fairlands Estate–Wood Street Green–Park Barn School (school days)
245 Farnham–Seale–Elstead (TuFO)
246 Cranleigh–Dunsfold–Godalming–Elstead–Cock Hill
247 Godalming–Hambledon–Witley (MThO)
250 Camberley–Frimley–Kingfield Green (school days)
251 Camberley–Knaphill–Kingfield Green (school days)
252 West End–Brookwood–Winston Churchill School (school days)
253 Bisley–Benner Lane School (school days)
260 Guildford–Compton–Godalming–Home Farm Road
265 Guildford–Puttenham–Farnham
268 Guildford–Brook–Haslemere–Whitehill–Farnham–Weybourne–Aldershot
269 Guildford–Bramley–Cranleigh–Plaistow–Horsham
271 Guildford–Godalming–Witley–Chiddingfold
273 Guildford–Bramley–Cranleigh–Grove Road/Ewhurst
274 Guildford–Godalming–Hindhead–Liphook–Petersfield
279 Guildford–Grange Park Estate–Pirbright–St John's–Woking
280 Guildford–Pirbright–Horsell–Woking
281 Guildford–Grange Park Estate–Pirbright–Horsell–Woking (Evgs)
283 Guildford–Bramley–Wonersh–Cranleigh–Buck's Green–Horsham
284 Guildford–Bellfields Estate (Evgs/SuO)–Woking–Bagshot–Camberley

285 Guildford–Barnsbury Estate–Woking–Chobham–Camberley
286 Guildford–Barnsbury Estate–Woking–Ottershaw–Chertsey–Thorpe Park–Staines
289 Guildford–Bramley–Plaistow
290 Guildford–Bellfields Estate–Barnsbury Estate–Woking–Bagshot–Camberley (Evgs)
292 Guildford–Godalming–Eashing Lane Estate
293 Guildford–Bramley–Cranleigh–Ewhurst–Horsham
294 Guildford–Godalming–Aaron's Hill Estate–Hindhead–Liphook–Petersfield
295 Guildford–Bramley–Wonersh–Wonersh New Road–Cranleigh
296 Guildford–Bramley–Wonersh–Cranleigh
297 Guildford–Bramley–Cranleigh/Ewhurst
410/411/412 Aldershot–Fleet–Hartley Wintney–Swallowfield–Reading
413/414/415 Fleet Town services (Tu Th FO)
416 Aldershot–Pondtail–Fleet Station
419 Aldershot–Farnborough–Fleet–Crookham
420 Ewshot–Fleet–Farnborough Schools (school days)
421 Aldershot–Farnham–Crondall–Fleet–Farnborough–Aldershot (school days)
430 Aldershot–Farnborough–Cove–Frimley–Camberley (-Reading SuO)
431 Aldershot–Farnborough–Cove–Frimley–Camberley–Old Dean Estate
433 Aldershot–Farnborough–Camberley–Yateley–Reading (school days)
434 Aldershot–Farnborough–Yateley–Reading
436 Aldershot–North Town–Farnborough–Minley Estate–Farnborough–Aldershot (circular)
437 Aldershot–North Town–Field Way
438 Aldershot–Tongham
439/40 Aldershot–Farnborough–Cove–Hawley Lane Estate–Farnborough–Aldershot (circular)
441 Aldershot–Farnborough–Hawley Lane Estate–Frimley–Camberley–Old Dean Estate
442 Aldershot–Farnborough–Frimley–Camberley–Old Dean Estate
443 Aldershot–Farnborough Street–Frimley–Camberley–Old Dean Estate
444 Aldershot–Farnborough Street–Frimley–Camberley–Yateley–Reading
448/9 Camberley–Brompton Hospital–Frimley–Camberley–Old Dean Estate
450 Aldershot–Ash–Frimley–Camberley–Yateley
451 Guildford–Ash–Farnborough–Cove Estates–Farnborough
452 Guildford–Ash–Aldershot
453 Guildford–Rydes Hill Estate–Ash–Tongham–Aldershot (Evgs/SuO)
454 Aldershot–Ash Vale–Blackdown–Knaphill–Woking
455 Aldershot–Farnborough–Blackdown–Knaphill–Woking
456 Aldershot–Bathing Pool–North Town–Farnborough–Blackdown–Knaphill–Woking
460 Aldershot–Ash–Frimley–Camberley

Aldershot & District Fleet List

Date	Registration No.	Chassis	Co. Chassis No.	Co. Bonnet No.	Body Builder	Type	Co. Body No.	Notes
Aldershot & Farnborough Vehicles								
1906	DY 116	Milnes-Daimler 20hp			?	O28R		New 1904
	DY 118	Milnes-Daimler 20hp			?	O28R		New 1904
	LC 4466	Leyland-Crossley 28hp						Exchanged Sept 1906 for DY 35 and DY 106
	DY 35	Milnes-Daimler 20hp			?	O36R		New 1903
	DY 106	Milnes-Daimler 20hp			?	O28R		New 1904
1911	LN 3124	Commer			?	Ch		
Aldershot & District Vehicles								
1912	AA 5040-3	Leyland			?	O . . R		
1913	AA 5076	Leyland			?	O . . R		
	AA 5162-3	Leyland			?	O . . R		
	AA 5164-5	Daimler CC	247/?	CC1,2	Brush	B34R	118/09	
	AA 5166-7	Daimler CC	248/?	CC3,4	Brush	B34R		5166 rebodied 1922 with Ex-LGOC O34R (193)
	DB729	Dennis 28hp			?	Ch		
	LN344	Commer			?	B . .		
Vehicles taken over from London & South Western Railway Co., 12/6/13								
1913	AA 2139	Thornycroft			?	B16R		New 1906
	AA 2186	Thornycroft			?	B16R		New 1907
	AA 2187	Thornycroft			?	B16R		New 1907
Vehicles taken over from B. Chandler, Hindhead 29/10/13								
1913	P 3769	Commer			Bayleys	B28R		New c.1909
	DB 285	Dennis 40hp			?	Ch		New 1909
1913	AA 5228/9	Dennis 25hp			Bayleys?	B . .		
	AA 5239	Dennis 40hp			?	B . .		
	AA 5267	Daimler CD	264	CD14	Brush	B32R	120	Rebodied 1926 with Strachan & Brown B26 (120)
	AA 5268	Daimler CD			?	B . .		
1914	AA 5269	Daimler CD	265	CD15	Brush	B32R	105	Rebodied 1926 with Strachan & Brown B26 (105)
	AB 3342	Daimler CD	256	CD13	Brush	B32R	101	Rebodied 1926 with Strachan & Brown B26 (101)
	AA 5307	Daimler CC	263	CC5	?	B . .		Rebodied c.1920 with ex-B.A.T. O34R (182)
	AA 5308	Daimler CC			?	B . .		
	AA 5332	Daimler CC	251	CC7	?	B . .	188	Rebodied c.1920 with ex-B.A.T. O34R (188)
	AA 5367	Daimler CC	257	CC9	?	B . .	183	Rebodied c.1920 with ex-B.A.T. O34R (183)
	AA 5368	Daimler CC			?	O . . R		
	AA 5369	Daimler CC	245	CC10	?	B . .	106	Rebodied c.1920 with ? B . . R
	AA 5376-7	Daimler B			?	B . .		
	AA 5447	Daimler CD			?	?		
	AA 5454	Daimler B			?	B26R	113	
Guildford & District vehicles absorbed								
1914	P 5388	Dennis 30hp			Bayleys	B28R		New 1914
	LH 9020	Dennis 30hp			?	B . . R		New 1914
	LH 9026	Dennis 30hp			Bayleys	B . . R		New 1914
1915-6	AA 5519	Belsize 3 ton			?	B . . R		
	AA 5521	Belsize 3 ton			?	B . . R		
	AA 5523-4	Belsize 3 ton			?	B . . R		
	AA 5527	Belsize 3 ton			?	B . . R		
	AA 5530	Belsize 3 ton			?	B . . R		
	AA 5643	Belsize 3 ton			?	O . . R		
	AA 5644	Belsize 3 ton			?	B . . R		

Note: There were almost certainly other Belsize buses, but only those for which there is documentary or photographic evidence are listed.

Date	Registration No.	Chassis	Co. Chassis No.	Co. Bonnet No.	Body Builder	Type	Co. Body No.	Notes
	AA 5645	?			?	?		
	AA 5647	?			?	?		
	AA 5659-60	Belsize 3 ton			?	B . . R		
	AA 5662	Belsize 3 ton			?	B . . R		
1919	HO 2320	Dennis Subsidy	202	D17	Ex-NGT	O34R	194	Rebodied 1925 with Strachan & Brown O48R, 77
	HO 2325	Daimler Y	246	Y42	?	B . . R	184	Rebodied 1923 with Arnold & Comben B32, 17
	HO 2326	Daimler Y	260	Y43	?	B . . R		Rebodied 1924 with Strachan & Brown B30, 44
	HO 2327	Daimler Y	258	Y44	?	B . .		Rebodied 1924 with Strachan & Brown B30, 43
	HO 2328	Daimler Y	242	Y45	?	B . .	123	Rebodied 1924 with Strachan & Brown B30, 46
	HO 2329	Daimler Y	254	Y46	?	B . .		Rebodied 1924 with Strachan & Brown B30, 42
	HO 2330	Daimler Y	244	Y47	Bayleys	B26R	114	Rebodied 1924 with Strachan & Brown B32, 67
	HO 2331	Daimler Y	241	Y48	Bayleys	B26R	112	Rebodied 1924 with Strachan & Brown B32, 68
	HO 2332	Daimler Y	259	Y49	Brush	B32R	121	Rebodied 1925 with Strachan & Brown B30, 100
	HO 2333	Daimler Y	243	Y50	?	B . .		Rebodied 1924 with Strachan & Brown B30, 40
	HO 2334	Dennis Subsidy	212	D18	A&D	B . . R	2	
	HO 2335	Dennis Subsidy	209	D19	Immisch Launch	O34R	191	Rebodied 1925 with Dennis O48R, 83
	HO 2336	Dennis Subsidy	205	D20	?	O34R	111	Rebodied 1924 with Strachan & Brown O48R, 74
	HO 2337	Dennis Subsidy	200	D21	Ex-NGT	O34R	189	Rebodied 1924 with Strachan & Brown O48R, 75
	HO 2338	Dennis Subsidy	203	D22	Birch	O32R	172	Rebodied 1925 with Dennis O48R, 78
	HO 2339	Dennis Subsidy	211	D23	Ex-BMMO	O34R	174	Rebodied 1925 with Strachan & Brown O48R, 81
	HO 2340	Dennis Subsidy	201	D24	?	O34R	188	Rebodied 1924 with Strachan & Brown O42R, 52
	HO 2341	Dennis Subsidy	204	D25	Ex-BMMO	O34R	192	Rebodied 1925 with Dennis O48R, 79
	HO 2342	Dennis Subsidy	206	D26	Ex-BMMO	O34R	177	Rebodied 1925 with Strachan & Brown O48R, 80
	HO 2343	Dennis Subsidy	207	D27	Dennis	Ch28	124	
	HO 2344	Dennis Subsidy	208	D28	Ex-BMMO	O34R	173	Rebodied 1925 with Strachan & Brown O48R, 89
	HO 2460-2	Dennis Subsidy	218/3/4	D30-2	Dennis?	B . . R	?	Rebodied 1923-4 with Strachan & Brown B30, 37/8/41
	HO 2463	Dennis Subsidy	215	D33	Ex-BMMO	O34R	175	Rebodied 1925 with Dennis O48R, 88
	HO 2464	Dennis Subsidy	216	D34	A&D	Ch26	1	
	HO 2465	Dennis Subsidy	217	D35	Immisch Launch	O . . R	190	Rebodied 1924 with Strachan & Brown O48R, 70
	HO 2466	Dennis Subsidy	219	D36	Birch	O38R	176	Rebodied 1925 with Dennis O48R, 91
	HO 2467	Dennis Subsidy	220	D37	Ex-Tilling	O34R	180	Rebodied 1925 with Strachan & Brown O48R, 92
	HO 2468	Dennis Subsidy	221	D38	Ex-NGT	O34R	179	Rebodied 1924 Strachan & Brown O48R, 69
1920	HO 2469	Dennis Subsidy	222	D39	Immisch Launch	O34R	181	Rebodied 1924 with Strachan & Brown O48R, 71
	HO 2470	Dennis Subsidy	223	D40	Immisch Launch	O34R	187	Rebodied 1924 with Dennis O48R, 73
	HO 2471	Dennis Subsidy	224	D41	Ex-NGT	O34R	178	Rebodied 1924 with Strachan & Brown O48R, 72
	HO 2472-7	Daimler Y	225-30	Y51-6	A&D	Ch28	3-8	
	HO 2478	Daimler CC	231	CC11	Immisch Launch	O34R	185	
	HO 2956	Daimler CC	232	CC12	Ex-NGT	O34R	186	
1922	HO 6088	Daimler Y	262	Y57	Arnold & Comben	B34R	10	
	HO 6091	Daimler Y	266	Y58	?	Ch . .	?	Rebodied 1922 with Arnold & Comben B34, 14
	HO 6092	Daimler Y	267	Y59	Arnold & Comben	B . .	?	Rebodied 1922 with Arnold & Comben B34, 13
	HO 6099	Daimler Y	268	Y60	Arnold & Comben	B . .	?	Rebodied 1922 with Arnold & Comben B34, 15
	HO 6100	Daimler Y	269	Y61	Arnold & Comben	B34R	11	
	HO 6155	Daimler Y	271	Y66	Strachan & Brown	B32R	16	
	HO 8855	Daimler Y	253	Y62	Arnold & Comben	B32R	9	
	HO 9696	Daimler Y	270	Y63	Arnold & Comben	B34	12	
1923	HO 6163	Daimler Y	272	Y67	Strachan & Brown	B32R	18	
	HO 6172/3	Daimler Y	275/4	Y65/4	East Kent	Ch 32	21/0	Body started by A&D
	HO 6174	Daimler Y	276	Y68/9	Strachan & Brown	B32	23	
	HO 6175/6	Daimler Y	273/8	Y70	Arnold & Comben	B34	19, 22	
	HO 6177	Daimler Y	279	Y71	Strachan & Brown	B32	24	

ALDERSHOT & DISTRICT TRACTION Cº LTD

NOVEMBER, 1928
until further notice.

OFFICIAL MOTOR OMNIBUS TIME TABLE
and Connections with Railway and other Services.

—o—

Printed by Wm. MAY & CO., LTD., ALDERSHOT,
AND
Published by THE ALDERSHOT & DISTRICT TRACTION
CO., LTD., ALDERSHOT.

GRATIS

Date	Registration No.	Chassis	Co. Chassis No.	Co. Bonnet No.	Body Builder	Type	Co. Body No.	Notes
	PD 8344	Dennis 4 ton	291	D16	Hickman	O48R	39	
	HO 6207	Daimler Y	280	Y72	Strachan & Brown	B32	30	
	HO 6208	Daimler Y	282	Y77	Arnold & Comben	B34	29	
	HO 6218	Daimler Y	285	Y78	Arnold & Comben	B34	31	
	HO 6219	Daimler Y	286	Y79	Strachan & Brown	B32	32	
1924	HO 6221-3	Dennis 4 ton	287/9/8	D80/2/1	Strachan & Brown	B36R	33/5/4	
	HO 6268	Dennis 4 ton	290	D83	Strachan & Brown	B36R	36	
	HO 6271-5	Dennis 4 ton	292/1/3/5/4	D85/4/6/8/7	Strachan & Brown	B36R	47/5/8,50,49	
	HO 6278	Dennis 4 ton	296	D89	Strachan & Brown	B36R	51	
	HO 6285-7	Dennis 4 ton	298/7/9	D91/0/2	Strachan & Brown	O48R	54/3/5	
	HO 6298	Dennis 4 ton	300	D93	Strachan & Brown	O48R	56	
	HO 6299	Dennis 4 ton	303	D96	Strachan & Brown	B36R	59	
	HO 6300	Dennis 4 ton	301	D94	Strachan & Brown	O48R	57	
	HO 6301/2	Dennis 4 ton	304/5	D97/8	Strachan & Brown	B36	60/1	
	HO 6303	Dennis 4 ton	302	D95	Strachan & Brown	O48R	58	
	HO 6306/7	Dennis 4 ton	307/6	D100,99	Strachan & Brown	B36R	63/2	
	HO 6312	Dennis 4 ton	308	D101	Dennis	B36R	64	
	HO 6327/8	Dennis 4 ton	309/10	D102/3	Strachan & Brown	B36R	65/6	
1925	OR 6049	Morris 1 ton	311	M2	Morris	Ch 14	76	
	PE 1213	Dennis 2½ ton	312	D104	Dennis	B30R	82	
	PE 1345	Dennis 2½ ton	313	D105	Dennis	B30R	84	
	PE 1472/6	Dennis 2½ ton	314/5	D106/7	Dennis	B30R	85/6	
	PE 1748	Dennis 2½ ton	316	D108	Dennis	B30R	87	
	PE 1851	Dennis 2½ ton	317	D109	Dennis	B30R	90	
	HO 6403-5	Dennis 4 ton	318-20	D110-2	Strachan & Brown	B32R	93-5	
	HO 6410-2	Dennis 4 ton	321-3	D113-5	Strachan & Brown	B32R	96-8	
	PE 2898	Dennis 2½ ton	324	D116	Strachan & Brown	Ch 30	99	
	PE 6859	Dennis 2½ ton	325	D117	Dennis		103	
	Vehicle sold to A&D by Thames Valley 11/25 on takeover of T. Spragg, Bracknell							
1925	MO 6184	Dennis 2½ ton	326	D118	Dennis	B30R	102	New 1925
1926	Vehicles taken over from A.G. Smith, Knaphill, 9/6/26							
	PD 2642	Overland				B..F		New 1923
	PE 6488	Republic				B..F		New 1925
	PE 7415	Republic				B20		New 1925
1926	PE 7878	Dennis 2½ ton	328	D120	Strachan & Brown	B30	106	
	HO 6492/3	Dennis 4 ton	330/29	D122/6	Strachan & Brown	B36	108/7	
	OT 315	Dennis 4 ton	341	D133	Strachan & Brown	O48R	119	
	OT 316/7	Dennis 4 ton	353/40	D145/32	Strachan & Brown	B36R	134/18	
	OT 318/9	Dennis 4 ton	333/2	D125/4	Strachan & Brown	O48R	111/0	
	OT 320	Dennis 4 ton	331	D123	Strachan & Brown	B36R	109	
	OT 321-5	Dennis 4 ton	334/5/7/8/6	D121/7/9/30/28	Strachan & Brown	O48R	112/3/5/6/4	
	OT 932	Dennis 4 ton	339	D131	Strachan & Brown	B36	117	
	PF 1792	Dennis 4 ton	342	D134	Strachan & Brown	O48R	121	
	PF 1793	Dennis 2½ ton	343	D135	Strachan & Brown	B30R	122	
	PF 1794/5	Dennis 30 cwt	344/5	D136/7	Strachan & Brown	B18F	123/6	
	OT 1430-3	Dennis 2½ ton	349/8/7/6	D141/0/39/8	Strachan & Brown	B30	130/29/8/7	
	PF 2404	Dennis 2½ ton	350	D142	Strachan & Brown	B30	131	
	PF 2405	Dennis 30 cwt	351	D143	Strachan & Brown	B18F	132	
	PF 2598	Dennis 30 cwt	352	D144	Strachan & Brown	B18F	133	
	OT 1707/8	Dennis 4 ton	355/4	D147/6	Strachan & Brown	B36	136/5	

Date	Registration No.	Chassis	Co. Chassis No.	Co. Bonnet No.	Body Builder	Type	Co. Body No.	Notes
	OT 1794	Dennis 30 cwt	356	D148	Strachan & Brown	B18F	140	
	OT 1964	Dennis 30 cwt	359	D151	Strachan & Brown	B18F	137	
	OT 1965/6	Dennis 4 ton	357/8	D149/50	Strachan & Brown	B36	138/9	
1927	OT 3707/51	Dennis 2½ ton	212/3	D30/1	Strachan & Brown	B30R	37/8 }	Took over numbers from HO 2460-2, with their bodies.
	OT 3979	Dennis 2½ ton	214	D32	Strachan & Brown	B30R	41 }	
	PF 7695-9	Dennis 4 ton	360-4	D152-6	Strachan & Brown	B36R	141-5	Rebodied 1929 with Strachan B26F, 294/2/3. Later B20F.
	OT 4377	Dennis E	365	D157	Strachan & Brown	B32R	146	
	OT 4378/9	Dennis E	367/6	D159/8	Strachan & Brown	B35R	148/7	
	OT 4380/1	Dennis 4 ton	368/9	D160/1	Strachan & Brown	B36R	149/50	
	OT 4743	Dennis E	370	D162	Strachan & Brown	B35R	151	
	PH 1105	Dennis E	372	D164	Strachan & Brown	B35R	153	
	PH 1106	Dennis E	371	D163	Strachan & Brown	B36R	152	
	PH 1107	Dennis E	373	D165	Strachan & Brown	B35R	154	
	OT 4950	Dennis 4 ton	374	D166	Strachan & Brown	B36	155	
	OT 4951/4	Dennis F	380/79	D172/1	Strachan & Brown	C28R	161/0	Rebuilt as Dennis E, 1931: D321/4. Strachan B30R, 334/7
	OT 5410	Dennis F	382	D174	Strachan & Brown	C28R	163	Rebuilt as Dennis E, 1931: D319, Strachan B30E, 332
	OT 5706/7	Dennis F	384/3	D176/5	Strachan & Brown	C28R	165/4	Rebuilt as Dennis E, 1931: D323/0, Strachan B30R, 336/3
	PH 1454-7	Dennis E	368/6/7/5	D170/68/9/7	Strachan & Brown	B35R	159 7/8/6	
	PH 1458	Dennis E	381	D173	Strachan & Brown	C28R	162	Rebuilt as Dennis E, 1931: D322, Strachan B30R, 335
	PH 2656/7	Dennis 30 cwt	386/5	D178/7	Short	B19F	167/6	
	OT 5910	Dennis 30 cwt	387	?	Short	B19F	168	
	OT 6136/7	Dennis E	388/9	D179/80	Dennis	B35R	169/70	
	OT 6861/2	Dennis G	390/1	D181/2	Hoyal	B20F	171/2	
	OT 6914	Dennis E	392	D183	Strachan & Brown	B32	173	
1928	Vehicles taken over from D. May, Elstead, 1/1/28							
	PF 8777	Guy B	251	G1	?	B24F	183	New 1927
	PH 4623	Dennis 30 cwt	407	D197	Spicer	B18	192	New 1927
	CB 2803	Fiat	—	—	?	Ch 14	—	Not used by A&D
1928	Vehicles taken over from C. Ross, Woking, 13/1/28							
	PE 7147	Republic	—	R1	?	B20	—	New 1925
	PE 9181	Morris 25/30 cwt	207	M3	Dennis	Ch28	125	New 1926
1928	Vehicles taken over from Farnham Coaches, 23/1/28							
	PH 4233	Gilford	460	G11	Arnold & Comben	C20D	185	New 1927
	PH 3795	Dodge A	—	—	?	B20F	186	New 1927
	PF 1107	Chevrolet	—	—	?	B14	—	Not used by A&D
	LP 8090/4	Daimler CC	—	—		O .. R	—	Not used by A&D
	LP 8357/61/3/4	Daimler CC	—	—		O .. R	—	Not used by A&D
1928	PH 6549/50	Dennis E	394/3	D185/4	Dennis	B32	175/4	
	PH 6693-5	Dennis E	401, 396/5	?, D187/6	Dennis	B32	182/77/6	
	PH 6696-9	Dennis G	400, 398/9/7	D191/89/90/88	Strachan & Brown	B18F	181/79/80/78	
	PH 6734-6	Dennis G	403/4/2	D193/4/2	Strachan & Brown	B18F	189/90	
	PH 6883/4	Dennis E	405/6	D195/6	Dennis			
	PH 7533-7	Dennis E	412/1/3/08/9	D202/1/3,198/9	Strachan & Brown	B32R	196/5/7/1/3	
	PH 7628-30	Dennis E	410/8/4	D200/8/4	Dennis	B32R	194, 202, 198	
	OT 7917	Gilford LL15SD	419	G1	Strachan & Brown	C20D	203	
	OT 7918/9	Dennis F	422/7	D209/13	Strachan & Brown	C28R	206/11	Rebuilt as Dennis E, 1932: D342/4, Strachan B30R (380/2)
	OT 7920/1	Gilford LL15SD	420/1	G2, 3	Strachan & Brown	C20D	204/5	
	OT 7922/3	Dennis G	416/5	D206/5	Strachan & Brown	C18R	200, 199	
	OT 8282	Dennis G	417	D207	Strachan & Brown	C18R	201	
	OT 8283/4	Dennis F	423/4	D210/1	Strachan & Brown	C28R	206/8	Rebuilt as Dennis E, 1932: D345/3, Strachan B30R (383/1)
	OT 8375-7	Gilford LL15SD	429/8/6	G6, 5, 4	Strachan & Brown	C20D	213/2/0	
	OT 8378	Dennis E	425	D212	Strachan & Brown	B32	209	

Date	Registration No.	Chassis	Co. Chassis No.	Co. Bonnet No.	Body Builder	Type	Co. Body No.	Notes
	OT 8590/1	Dennis F	438/0	D222/14	Strachan & Brown	C28R	222/14	Rebuilt as Dennis E, 1932: D346/7, Strachan B30R (354/5)
	OT 8592	Dennis E	433	D217	Strachan & Brown	B32	217	
	OT 8593-8	Dennis G	436/4/7/1/5/2	D220/18/21/15/9/6	Strachan & Brown	B18F	220/18/21/15/9/6	
	OT 8898-901	Dennis E	442/1/0/39	D226/5/4/3	Strachan & Brown	B32	226/5/4/3	
	OT 8902	Dennis E	451	D235	Dennis	B32	235	
	OT 8903	Dennis E	443	D227	Strachan & Brown	B32	227	
	OT 8915	Dennis E	444	D228	Strachan & Brown	B32	228	
	OT 8993	Dennis E	452	D236	Dennis	B32	236	
	OT 9062	Dennis H	449	D233	Strachan & Brown	H56R	233	
	OT 9063/4	Dennis E	446/5	D230/29	Strachan & Brown	B32R	230/29	
	OT 9150	Gilford 166SD	454	G8	Arnold & Comben	C25D	238	
	OT 9151	Dennis E	448	D232	Strachan & Brown	B32R	232	
	OT 9152	Gilford 166SD	453	G7	Arnold & Comben	C25D	237	
	OT 9153	Dennis E	447	D231	Strachan & Brown	B32R	231	
	OT 9350	Dennis H	450	D234	Strachan & Brown	H56R	234	
	OT 9351/2	Gilford 166SD	456/5	G10, 9	Arnold & Comben	C25D	240/39	
1928	Vehicles taken over from S. Tanner, Chobham, 8/10/28							
	PF 5831	Dennis 30 cwt	457	D238	Strachan & Brown	B18	241	New 1925
	PE 9850	Dennis 30 cwt	458	D239	?	B18	242	New 1926
	PE 2077	Dennis 21/2 ton	459	D240	?	B20F	243	New 1926
1929	OU 860	Dennis E	461	D241	Dennis	B31R	244	
	OU 1091-5	Dennis E	462-6	D242-6	Dennis	B31R	245-9	
	OU 1096-1101	Dennis E	467-72	D247-52	Arnold & Comben	C30R	250-5	
	OU 1102-7	Dennis E	473-8	D253-8	Strachan	B31	256-61	
	OU 1108-11	Dennis H	479-82	D259-62	Strachan	L22/26R	262-5	
	OU 1112/3	Dennis H	483/4	D263-4	Hall Lewis	L22/26R	266/7	
	OU 1114-7	Dennis EV	485-8	D265-8	Dennis	B32R	268-71	
	OU 1118/9	Dennis EV	489/90	D269/70	Strachan	B32R	272/3	
	OU 1120/1	Dennis EV	491/2	D271/2	Arnold & Comben	C32R	274/5	Later C30
	OU 1122	Dennis EV	493	D273	Arnold & Comben	C31	276	Later C30
	OU 1123-5	Dennis E	494-6	D274-6	Arnold & Comben	C27R	277-9	Later C30
	OU 1799-1810	Dennis E	497-508	D277-88	Strachan	B32R	280-91	
1930	OU 4310-22	Dennis H	509-21	D289-301	Strachan	L22/26R	295-307	
	OU 4323-34	Dennis EV	522-33	D302-13	Strachan	B32	308-19	
	OU 6241-7	TSM B10A2	534-40	TS 1-7	Strachan	C30R	320-6	
	OU 6841-5	Dennis HV	541-5	D314-8	Strachan	L22/26R	327-31	
1931	Vehicles taken over from Woking & District, 14/1/31							
	VB 4060	TSM B10A2	547	TS22	Wilton	B32R	363	New 1928
	VB 1272	TSM B10A2	548	TS21	Wilton	B32R	362	New 1927
	PG 9382-4	TSM B10A2	549-51	TS23-5	Petty	B32R	364-6	New 1930
1931	OU 7944-55	TSM B10A2	552-63	TS8-19	Strachan	B31R	338-49	
	OU 7956-70	Dennis HV	564-78	D325-39	Strachan	L22/26R	350-61/7-9	
1932	CG 477	Dennis Lancet	589	D348	Strachan	B32R	386	
	CG 755-62	Morris RP	581-8	M1-8	Strachan	B20F	372-9	Rebuilt on new chassis CG 9010-7, 1934
	CG 763	TSM B10A2	590	TS20	Strachan	B32	387	
	CG 1313/4	Dennis HV	579/80	D340/1	Strachan	L22/26R	370/1	
	CG 1315/6	Dennis Lancet	591/2	D349/50	Strachan	B32R	388/9	
	CG 1317-28	Dennis Lancet	593-604	D351-62	Strachan	C30R	390-401	
1933	CG 3006/7	Morris RP	605/6	M9, 10	Abbott	B20F	402/3	
	CG 6357/8	Dennis Lancet	608/7	D364/3	Strachan	C30R	405/4	Rebuilt on new chassis CG 9018/9, 1934
1934	CG 6391-405	Dennis Ace	609-23	D365-79	Strachan	B20F	406-20	

Date	Registration No.	Chassis	Co. Chassis No.	Co. Bonnet No.	Body Builder	Type	Co. Body No.	Notes
1934-5	CG 9010-7	Dennis Ace	581/4/8/5/ 3/7/6/2	D381-8	Strachan	B20F	372/5/9/6/ 4/8/7/3	Rebuilt from CG 755-62
1934	Vehicle acquired from W. Eggleton & Son Ltd., 1/6/34							
	PJ 7438	Dennis GL	624	D380	Dennis	B20	421	New 1932
1934	Vehicles taken over from Farnham Blue Coaches, 27/10/34							
	GO 4013	Gilford 1680T	625	G1	Abbott	C28	423	New 1931
	YX 9515/6	Maudsley ML3	626/37	M11/2	Duple	C30	424/35	New 1928
	UL 8634/5	Gilford 1680T	627/8	G2/3	Abbott	C30	425/6	New 1929
	GK 8611/2	Gilford 1680T	629/30	G4/5	Abbott	C28	427/8	New 1930
	GF 5202/3	Gilford 1680T	631/2	G6/7	Abbott	C28	429/30	New 1930
	GO 6464	Gilford 1680T	633	G8	Abbott	C28	431	New 1931
	GX 1240/1	Gilford 1680T	634/5	G9, 10	Abbott	C30	432/3	New 1931
	GY 176	Gilford 1680T	636	G11	Abbott	C30	434	New 1932
1935	CG 9018/9	Dennis Ace	605/6	D389/90	Abbott	B20F	402/3	Rebuilt from CG 3006/7
	CG 9596-603/5	Dennis Lancet I	638-46	D391-9	Strachan	C30R	436-44	
1936	AOT 580	Dennis Lance	647	D400	Strachan	L22/26R	445	Rebuilt on new chassis CCG 188, 1937
	AOT 581-6	Dennis Ace	648-53	D401-6	Strachan	B20F	446-51	
	AOT 587-605	Dennis Lancet I	654-72	D407-25	Strachan	B32R	452-70	AOT 602-5 had long 'band boxes' AOT 598 rebodied 1946 with Strachan B32R 713 AOT 587-97/9-601 rebodied 1948-9 with Vincent B32R 822-35
	BAA 386	Dennis Lance	673	D426	Strachan	L22/26R	471	Rebodied 1944 with E. Lancs L22/26R 689
	BAA 387-96	Dennis Lancet I	674-83	D427-36	Strachan	B32R	472-81	BAA 390/6 rebodied 1946 with Strachan B32R 714-5 BAA 387-9 rebodied 1949 with Vincent B32R 819-21
1936	Vehicles taken over from A.J. Warren (Fleet Coaching Co.), Church Crookham, 18/5/36							
	OF 3967	Guy C	684	G12	Guy	B32	482	New 1929
	ACG 559	Guy Conquest	685	G13	?	B32	483	New 1935
	OF 6081	Guy C	686	G14	Guy	B32	484	New 1930
	CG 4113	Guy FC	687	G15	?	B31	485	New 1933
	CG 7096	Guy FC	688	G16	?	B31	486	New 1934
	RO 7188	Guy BB	689	G17	?	B31	487	New 1927
	BCG 591	Guy Vixen	690	G18	?	B20F	488	New 1936
	UK 6151	Guy BA	691	G19	?	B20	489	New 1928
	UK 5465	Guy FBB	692	G20	?	B31	490	New 1928
	RO 8075	Guy BB	693	G21	?	B30	491	New 1927
1936-7	BOT 288-307	Dennis Lancet 2	694-713	D437-56	Strachan	B32R	492-511	BOT 288-97 had long 'band boxes'.
1938	CCG 188	Dennis Lance	647	D400	Strachan	L22/26R	445	Rebuild of AOT 580. Rebodied 1941 with Strachan L22/26R 655.
1937-8	CCG 311-51	Dennis Lance	714-54	D457-97	Strachan	L22/26R	512-52	Rebodied with E. Lancs L22/26R 1944: bodies 686/7/8/90 CCG 324/17/43/37 1945: bodies 691-5 CCG 331/9/49/6/8 1946: bodies 697-701 CCG 347/36/12/26/8 1947: bodies 702-6 CCG 338/27/51/41/31 1948: bodies 816-8 CCG 313/4/30
1936-7	COR 151-63	Dennis Lancet 2	755-67	D498-510	Strachan	C32R	553-65	
	COR 164-91	Dennis Lancet 2	768-95	D511-38	Dennis	B32R	566-93	
1938	Vehicles taken over from A.T. Locke (Blue Saloon), Guildford, 12/1/38							
	PL 8827	Star VB4	796	?	Duple	B25	594	New 1931. Not used by A&D.
	CPH 130	Dennis Lancet I	797	D539	Dennis	C32F	595	New 1935.
	DPD 858	Dennis Ace	798	D540	Dennis	B20F	596	New 1935.
1938	Vehicles taken over from S. Ansell (ex-Lintott, Lightwater), 6/38							
	EXF 377	Dennis Pike	799	D541	Dennis	B20F	597	New 1938.
	UR 5780	Chevrolet LO	800?	?	Thurgood	B14	600?	New 1930. Not used by A&D.
	ACG 89	Bedford WLB	801?	B1	Thurgood	B20F	598	New 1935.

Date	Registration No.	Chassis	Co. Chassis No.	Co. Bonnet No.	Body Builder	Type	Co. Body No.	Notes
1939	BOR 501	Dodge RBF	802?	D1	Reall	B26	599	New 1936.
	DHO 266	Dennis Falcon	803	D542	Strachan	B20F	601	
	DHO 267-72	Dennis Lancet 2	804-9	D543-8	Strachan	B32R	602-7	
	DHO 273-92	Dennis Lancet 2	810-29	D549-68	Dennis	B32R	608-27	
	DHO 293-305	Dennis Lancet 2	830-42	D569-81	Strachan	B32R	628-40	
	DOT 470-77	Dennis Falcon	843-50	D582-9	Strachan	B20F	641-8	
1940	DOT 478-83	Dennis Lancet 2	851-6	D590-5	Strachan	L22/26R	649-54	
1941	ECG 380/1	Dennis Lancet 2	859-60	D598/9	Strachan (U)	B32R	658/9	
	ECG 424	Dennis Lancet 2	861	D600	Strachan (U)	B32R	660	
1942	ECG 600	Dennis Lancet 2	863	D602	Strachan (U)	B32R	661	
	ECG 851/2	Dennis Lancet 2	864/2	D603/1	Strachan (U)	B32R	662/3	
	ECG 943/4	Leyland Titan TD7	857/8	L1/2	E. Lancs	L22/26R	656/7	
	ECG 945	Dennis Lancet 2	865	D604	Strachan (U)	B32R	664	
1943	EHO 162	Dennis Lancet 2	866	D605	Strachan (U)	B32R	665	
	EHO 173	Guy Arab I	867	G1	Strachan (U)	L22/26R	666	Rebodied 1950 with Weymann L25/26R 898
	EHO 217	Guy Arab I	868	G2	Strachan (U)	L22/26R	667	Rebodied 1950 with Weymann L25/26R 899
	EHO 286	Guy Arab I	869	G3	Strachan (U)	L22/26R	668	Rebodied 1950 with Weymann L25/26R 900
	EHO 316	Guy Arab I	870	G4	Strachan (U)	L22/26R	669	Rebodied 1950 with Weymann L25/26R 901
	EHO 508	Guy Arab I	871	G5	Strachan (U)	L22/26R	670	Rebodied 1950 with Weymann L25/26R 902
	EHO 587	Guy Arab I	872	G6	Strachan (U)	L22/26R	671	Rebodied 1950 with Weymann L25/26R 903
	EHO 695	Guy Arab I	873	G7	Strachan (U)	L22/26R	672	Rebodied 1950 with Weymann L25/26R 904
	EHO 806	Guy Arab II	874	G8	Strachan (U)	L22/26R	673	Rebodied 1950 with Weymann L25/26R 905
	EHO 818	Guy Arab II	875	G9	Strachan (U)	L22/26R	674	Rebodied 1950 with Weymann L25/26R 906
	EHO 952	Guy Arab II	876	G10	Strachan (U)	L22/26R	675	Rebodied 1950 with Weymann L25/26R 907
	EHO 983	Guy Arab II	877	G11	Strachan (U)	L22/26R	676	Rebodied 1950 with Weymann L25/26R 908
1944	EOR 28	Guy Arab II	878	G12	Strachan (U)	L22/26R	677	Rebodied 1950 with Weymann L25/26R 909
	EOR 29-31	Guy Arab II	879-81	G13-15	Roe (U)	L22/26R	678-80	Rebodied 1950 with Weymann L25/26R 910-2
	EOR 288	Guy Arab II	883	G17	Strachan (U)	L22/26R	682	Rebodied 1950 with Weymann L25/26R 914
	EOR 373	Guy Arab II	882	G16	Roe (U)	L22/26R	681	Rebodied 1950 with Weymann L25/26R 913
1945	EOR 374-6	Guy Arab II	884-6	G18-20	Weymann (U)	L22/26R	683-5	(EOR 376 partly rebuilt 1955 as L25/26R)
	EOR 743	Dennis Lancet 3	887	D606	Dennis	B32R	696	
	EOT 25-30	Guy Arab II	888-93	G21-6	Strachan	L22/26R	707-12	Rebodied 1954 with E. Lancs L28/28R 1002-7
1946-8	EOU 435-84	Dennis Lancet J3	894-943	D607-56	Strachan	B32R	716-65	
1948-9	GAA 580-608	Dennis Lancet J3	944-72	D657-85	Strachan	B32R	766-94	
1948	GAA 609-23	Dennis Dominant	973-87	D686-700	Strachan	C32R	795-809	
	GAA 624-9	Dennis Lancet K3	988-93	D701-6	E. Lancs	L25/26R	810-5	
1949	GOU 801-23	Dennis Lancet J3	101-23	D707-29	Strachan	B32R	836-58	
1949-50	GOU 824-47	Dennis Lance K3	124-47	D729-49/65-7	E. Lancs	L25/26R	859-82	The duplication of D729 and consequent wrong numbering of D730 onwards was never corrected.
1950-1	GOU 848-62	Dennis Falcon P3	148-62	D750-64	Dennis	B20F	883-87	
1950	HOT 692-701	Dennis Lance K3	163-72	D768-78	E. Lancs	L25/26R	915-24	
	HOU 899	Dennis Lancet J10	173	D778	Strachan	B38R	925	
1951	HOU 900	Dennis Dominant	174	D779	Strachan	B410	926	
1950-1	HOU 901-11	Dennis Lancet J10	175-85	D780-90	Strachan	B38R	927-37	
1953	KOT 113	Guy Arab LUF	186		Strachan	B41R	938	
	KOT 600	Dennis Lancet UF	187		E. Lancs	B41R	939	On loan from Dennis.
	LAA 223-37	Dennis Lancet J10	188-202		Strachan	C38R	940-54	Later B24F.
1954	LOU 31-50	Dennis Lance K4	203-22		E. Lancs	L28/28R	970-89	
	LOU 51-62	Dennis Lancet J10	223-34		Weymann	L28/28R	990-1001	
	LOU 63-77	Dennis Falcon P5	235-49		Strachan	B30F	955-69	
1954-5	MOR 581-605	AEC Reliance	250-74		Strachan	C41C	1008-32	15 rebuilt with B40F bodies and given new fleet numbers – see 1967.

Date	Registration No.	Chassis	Co. Fleet No.	Co. Bonnet No.	Body Builder	Type	Co. Body No.	Notes
1956	POR 421-8	Dennis Falcon P5	275-82		Strachan	B30F	1033-40	
1957	RCG 601-30	AEC Reliance	283-312		Weymann	B41F (OMO) or B43F	1041-70	
1958	SOU 421-43	AEC Reliance	313-35		Weymann	B41F (OMO) or B43F	1071-93	SOU 438-43 OMO from outset.
1960	SOU 444-77	Dennis Loline	336-69		E. Lancs	H37/31RD	1094-1127	
	XHO 370-7	AEC Reliance	370-7		Weymann	B40F (OMO)	1128-35	
	378-93 AOU	AEC Reliance	378-93		Weymann	B43F	1136-51	
1961-2	394-413 COR	Dennis Loline III	394-413		Alexander	H39/29FD	1152-71	
1962	414-28 DHO	AEC Reliance	414-28		Park Royal	C41F		
	121-40 DOR	Dennis Loline III	429-48		Alexander	H39/29FD		
	449-65 EOT	Dennis Loline III	449-65		Alexander	H39/29FD		
1963	466-80 FCG	Dennis Loline III	466-80		Park Royal	C49F		
1964	481-502 KOT	Dennis Loline III	481-502		Weymann	H39/29FD		
1965	AAA 503 30 C	Dennis Loline III	503-30		Weymann	H39/29FD		
1966	FHO 531-5D	AEC Reliance	531-5		Metro-Cammell	C49F		
1967	HHO 536-42E	AEC Reliance	536-42		Metro-Cammell	B41F		
	MOR 581/3/5-8/90-3/5/600/1/3/4	AEC Reliance	543-57		Metro-Cammell	B40F		Rebuilt from 1954 coaches.
1968	MOR 558-62F	AEC Reliance	558-62		Willowbrock	DP51F		
	NAA 563-5F	AEC Reliance	563-5		Duple	C49F		
1969	PHO 566-95G	AEC Reliance	566-95		Marshall	B45F		
1970	UOU 601-15H	Bristol RELL 6G	601-15		Marshall	B44D + 20		
	VCG 596-600H	AEC Reliance	596-600		Duple	C49F		
1971	YCG 101/2J	AEC Reliance	101/2		Plaxton	C49F		
	YHO 616-30J	Bristol RELL 6G	616-30		Marshall	B44D + 20		
	YHO 631-6J	Bristol RESL 6G	640-5		ECW	B40D + 20		
	CHO 691-9K	Bristol RESL 6G	631-9		Marshall	B40D + 20		
	CCG 291-6K	Bristol RESL 6G	646-51		ECW	B40D + 20		

Foden Steam Wagons

Fleet numbers appear to have been allocated from 1 up to 20, in order of purchase, and subsequently 300 was added. The known dates of purchase allow for some informed guesswork about the missing fleet numbers where there is no firm photographic evidence.

Date	Fleet No.	Reg. No.	Type
1914	301	M4142	5 ton
	302	M4128	5 ton
		M4718	5 ton
		M4393	5 ton
		M4370	5 ton
	306	M6328	5 ton
		M3198	3 ton
		M5317	5 ton
	309	M5248	5 ton
		M4134	5 ton

Date	Fleet No.	Reg. No.	Type
1914	311	M4569	5 ton
	312	M5352	3 ton
1915		M3200	5 ton
		M7112	5 ton
	14	M7214	5 ton
	315	M5446	3 ton
	316	M6652	3 ton
	317	M2114	5 ton
	319	M7345	5 ton
1916		M6656	3 ton

Alder Valley Fleet List

Not all of the vehicles shown actually saw service in AV's Southern Area.

Year / Fleet No.	Registration	Chassis	Body	Notes
1972				
468-70	DOU 491-3K	Bristol RESL6G	ECW B40D	
480-94	DRX 628-33K	Bristol RELL6G	ECW B49F	
482-5	EBL 439-41/61K	Bristol RELL6L	ECW B50F	
486-90	HOR 486-90L	Bristol RESL6G	ECW B40D	
923-5	FBL 115-7K	Bristol VRT/SL2/6G	ECW H39/31F	
926-8	LBL 585-7L	Bristol VRT/SL2/6G	ECW H39/31F	
65-7	KBL 226-8L	Bristol RELH6G	ECW C47F	
1973				
101-5	LMO 223-7L	Leyland National	B49F	
106-27	KCG 606-27L	Leyland National	B49F	
68-72	NDP 68-72M	Bristol RELL6G	Plaxton C49F	
881-4	NGM 158-61G	Bristol VRT/SL6G	ECW H43/34F	Acquired
887/90/1	OCS 595/8/9H	Bristol VRT/SL6G	ECW H43/32F	Acquired
893/4	LFS284/5F	Bristol VRT/SL6G	ECW H47/36F	Acquired
1973-4				
128-62	NRD 128-62M	Leyland National	B49F	
1974				
73-7	SJB 113-7M	Bristol RELH6G	Plaxton C49F	
163-77	TBL 163-77M	Leyland National	B49F	
701-19	TRD 701-19M	Ford R1014	ECW B45F	
720-5	TRD 720-5N	Ford R1014	ECW B45F	
501	UJB 501N	Leyland 440EA	Asco B19F	
502/3	GPC 728/9N	Leyland 440EA	Asco B19F	
178-80	UMO 178-80N	Leyland National	B49F (179 B52F)	
181-8	GPC 730-7N	Leyland National	B49F	
399	KUF 236F	Bristol RESL6G	Marshall B45F	Acquired
885	NAG 590G	Bristol VRT/SL6G	ECW H43/32F	Acquired
886-9/92	OCS 594/6/7/600H	Bristol VRT/SL6G	ECW H43/32F	Acquired
397/8	MTR 422/3F	AEC Swift	Strachan B47D	Acquired
751-60	SKO 802/4/6/7/15/ 21/3/5/7/30H	Daimler SRG6/36	Marshall B45D	Acquired
1975				
189-98	GPJ 889-98N	Leyland National	B49F	
199-203	HPK 501-5N	Leyland National	B49F	
929/30	HPK 506/7N	Bristol VRT/SL2/6G	ECW CH41/25F	930 converted to open-top 047/29F in 1987
535-41	KPA 346-52P	Bristol LH6L	ECW B43F	
1975-6				
204-39	KPA 355-90P	Leyland National	B49F	
931-4	LPF 594-7P	Bristol VRT/SL3/6LXB	ECW CH41/25F	
1975				
36-40	RUF 800-4H	Leyland Leopard PSU3A	Duple C44F	Acquired
1976				
240-9	LPF 598-607P	Leyland National	DP45F	
726-35	LPK 981-90P	Ford R1014	Plaxton B43F	
78/9	MPM 388/9P	Leyland Leopard PSU3C	Plaxton C49F	
935/6	MPM 390/1P	Bristol VRT/SL3/6LXB	ECW H43/31F	
251-64	NPJ 472-85R	Leyland National	B49F	
1976-7				
937-40	OPL 213-6R	Bristol VRT/SL3/6LXB	ECW H43/31F	
1977				
250	NPJ 471R	Leyland National	DP45F	
80-4	PPM 887-91R	Leyland Leopard PSU3E	Plaxton C49F	
265-9	PPM 892-6R	Leyland National	B49F	
941-5	PPM 902-6R	Bristol VRT/SL3/6LXB	ECW H43/31F	
679	HPN 79D	Bristol FLF6G	ECW H38/32F	Acquired
680-2	JPM 80-2D	Bristol FLF6G	ECW H38/32F	Acquired
683/4	KPM 83/4E	Bristol FLF6G	ECW H38/32F	Acquired
504	NEL 107P	Ford AO609	Alexander B27F	Acquired
270-4	TPE 147-51S	Leyland National	B49F	
1978				
946-50	TPE 152-6S	Bristol VRT/SL3/6LXB	ECW H43/31F	
281-91	TPE 157-67S	Leyland National	B49F	
275-8	TPE 168-71S	Leyland National	DP45F	
279/80	VPF 295/6S	Leyland National	DP45F	
951-8	VPF 281-8S	Bristol VRT/SL3/6LXB	ECW H43/31F	
685/6	GPN 76/7D	Bristol FLF6G	ECW H38/32F	Acquired
687	HPN 78D	Bristol FLF6G	ECW H38/32F	Acquired
1978-9				
85-94	WJM 805-14T	Leyland Leopard PSU3E	Plaxton C46F	
501-3	WJM 815-7T	Leyland Leopard PSU3E	Plaxton C49F	
959-72	WJM 819-32T	Bristol VRT/SL3/6LXB	ECW H43/31F	
1979-80				
973-80	CJH 113-20V	Bristol VRT/SL3/6LXB	ECW H43/31F	
981-6	CJH 121-6V	Bristol VRT/SL3/6LXB	ECW CH41/25F	
601-5	CJH 141-5V	Bristol VRT/SL3/6LXB	ECW H43/31F	
606-20	GGM 76-90W	Bristol VRT/SL3/6LXB	ECW H43/31F	
623-30	GGM 103-10W	Bristol VRT/SL3/6LXB	ECW H43/31F	
631-44	HJB 451-64W	Bristol VRT/SL3/6LXB	ECW H43/31F	
1980				
621-2	KKK 887-8V	Bristol VRT/SL3/6LXB	ECW H43/31F	Acquired

Fleet No	Registration	Chassis	Body	Notes
895/6	LFS 288/96F	Bristol VRT/LL6G	ECW H43/31F	Acquired
363/4/6/7	SJA 363/4/6/7J	Leyland Leopard PSU3A	Alexander C49F	Acquired
403	SJA 403K	Leyland Leopard PSU3B	Alexander C49F — Converted to open-top O47/31F in 1983	Acquired

1981

Fleet No	Registration	Chassis	Body
95-9	GGM 95-9W	Leyland Leopard PSU3F	Willowbrook C46F
04-15	GGM 64-75W	Leyland Leopard PSU3F	Plaxton C49F
16-20	HJB 466-70W	Leyland Leopard PSU3F	Plaxton C49F

1982

Fleet No	Registration	Chassis	Body	Notes
21-5	RPB 951-5X	Leyland Leopard PSU3G	ECW C49F	
1126-30	WPD 26-30Y	Leyland Leopard PSU3G	ECW C49F	
65/6	LHL 250/46P	Leyland Leopard PSU3C	Alexander C49F	Acquired
47-50	MNK 427-30V	Leyland Leopard PSU3E	Duple C53F	Acquired

1983

Fleet No	Registration	Chassis	Body
1201-10	YPJ 201-10Y	Leyland Tiger	Plaxton C50F
1211-5	A211-5 DPB	Leyland Tiger	Plaxton C51F
1501-5	YPJ 501-5Y	Leyland Olympian	ECW CH45/28F
1001	A101 DPB	Dennis Falcon	Wadham Stringer C53F

1984

Fleet No	Registration	Chassis	Body	Notes
1506/7	A506/7 GPC	Leyland Olympian	ECW CH45/28F	
298-302	LCY 298-302X	Bedford YMQ	Lex B37F	Acquired
675-8/84/5	HKE 675-8/84/5L	Bristol VRT/SL2/6LX	ECW H43/34F	Acquired

1985

Fleet No	Registration	Chassis	Body	Notes
1508-10	B576-8 LPE	Leyland Olympian	ECW CH45/28F	
303-4	B918/9 NPC	Bedford YMP	Lex B37F	Acquired
1295/6	SGS 499/504W	Leyland Tiger	Plaxton C50F	Acquired
1297	XGS 762X	Leyland Tiger	Plaxton C50F	Acquired
680	HKE 680L	Bristol VRT/SL2/6LX	ECW H43/34F	Acquired

1986
(Only minibuses allocated to Alder Valley South are shown)

Fleet No	Registration	Chassis	Body	Notes
310/1	C310/1 RPE	Ford Transit	Carlyle B16F	
312-8	D312-8 WPE	Ford Transit	Carlyle B16F	
320/1/4/7	D320/1/4/7 WPE	Ford Transit	Carlyle B16F	
330/3-5/8	D330/3-5/8 WPE	Ford Transit	Carlyle B16F	
336/9/46-50	C336/9/46-50	Ford Transit	Carlyle B16F	
340/1/3-5	D340/1/3-5 WPE	Ford Transit	Carlyle B16F	
469-76	D469-76 WPM	Fiat (Ford IVECO)	Robin Hood B21F	Acquired
101-6	PCN 424/5/9-32M	Leyland National	B49F	Acquired
107-9	GPT 94/7/8N	Leyland National	B49F	Acquired
110-5	MGR 531/26-8/30/2P	Leyland National	B49F	Acquired

1987

Fleet No	Registration	Chassis	Body	Notes
1205-10	E205-10 EPB	Dennis 425	Duple C57F	
1457-60	B457-60 WHJ	MCW Metroliner	MCW C51F	
477-80	E201-4 EPB	Fiat (Ford IVECO)	Robin Hood B25F	Acquired

1987-8

Fleet No	Registration	Chassis	Body
401-10	E401-10 EPE	Dodge	Northern Counties B22F
411-20	E411-20 EPE	Renault	Northern Counties B27F

1988

Fleet No	Registration	Chassis	Body
482-91	F692-701 OPA	Fiat (Ford IVECO)	Carlyle B23F
901-10	F571-80 SMG	Leyland Olympian	Alexander H47/32F

1989

Fleet No	Registration	Chassis	Body	Notes
494-6	G864-6 BPD	Fiat (Ford IVECO)	Carlyle B23F	
1401	KEP 640X	BOVA/DAF	C49F	Acquired
1402	A665 EMY	BOVA/DAF	C49F	Acquired
1403-5	E665/7/72 JNR	BOVA/DAF	C53F	Acquired

1990

Fleet No	Registration	Chassis	Body
502	H402 KPY	CVE Omni	B23F

1991

Fleet No	Registration	Chassis	Body
497	J416 TGM	Fiat (Ford IVECO)	Reeve Burgess B25F

1992

Fleet No	Registration	Chassis	Body	Notes
782/3/6/8/9	F772/3/56/8/9 OJH	Volvo B10M-60	Jonckheere C55F	Acquired
323	C323 RPE	Ford Transit	Carlyle B16F	Acquired
801-5	K801-5 CAN	Leyland Lynx	B51F	

This 1978 Leyland National, 274 (TPE 1515) carries all-over advertising for Sheerwater Motors of Woking, and is posed for its photograph in the Friary bus station at Guildford.
P.J. Holmes

Liveries

Buses

1912

Body: dark green, white above waistline (including roof). Double-deckers light green for upper decks. White lining-out of body and bonnet sides. Fleetname and other lettering in white.

Wheels: banana yellow, or dark green (or black?) on some buses.

Frames: black.

Radiators: metallic or painted (black?)

1923

Colour scheme unchanged, but fleetname style changed to the company name, surrounded by an oval loop starting from the 'A' of 'Aldershot', all in gold.

On the rear of single-deckers and charabancs, an oval heraldic garter device, enclosing a monogram of ornate and intertwined letters A, D, T. The garter itself was inscribed 'The Aldershot and District Traction Co. Ltd.', and by 1928-9 the monogram was omitted.

Some radiators of this era were of polished aluminium.

c.1927

White lining-out omitted.

1928

New single-deck vehicles appeared with light green roofs and bonnet sides.

Covered-top double-deckers (introduced from this year onwards) had black lining applied to the white areas, outlining the upper and lower deck waistbands and also forming an intermediate band from the white area above the lower deck windows. A thin gold line was painted about an inch inside these outlines. Roofs were white.

March 1930

Revised colour scheme for double-deckers in lighter green and cream.

Body: green, with cream bands below windows on each deck and a broader band above the lower deck windows. The beading defining these bands was picked out in black (though this may not always have been applied to the intermediate and upper bands). The black lines were still painted in where no beading existed, as on some 'utility' buses of 1941-5, and on the cab fronts of certain types.

Roof: silver.

Wheels: green (or black on some new deliveries from Dennis).

Mudguards: black.

Radiators: polished aluminium.

Lettering: white (apart from fleetname).

October 1933

Following experiments with a green livery with a red relief, a new colour scheme for single-deckers and coaches was adopted.

Body: green, with a darker shade of green above a cream waistband. Black beading outlining waistband.

Roof: green.

Other details as for 1930 double-deckers, except that a smaller version of the fleetname transfer was applied to the rear end.

December 1936

The BOT-registered series of single-deckers introduced an additional cream relief strip, without black beading, above the cantrail. From autumn 1937, bright aluminium radiator shields were supplied to replace the unsightly cardboard or newspaper which drivers had used to reduce cooling in cold weather.

July 1940

Fleetname omitted, radiators painted green.

September 1942

Grey roof, except for rear dome. (The front destination panel of single-deckers remained green.)

November 1944

Return to pre-war livery, with radiators still green. Fleetnames reappeared (with grey roofs) in the previous August. Radiators capable of being re-polished were unpainted from February 1945.

January 1947

Double-deck roofs painted silver.

November 1948

All lettering in yellow.

November 1950

White lettering again. Fleet numbers applied in 3-inch cream/gold figures. All but the first four of the LOU-registered double-deckers delivered from December 1953 onwards had dark green bonnets and 'tin fronts'.

January 1954

Livery reversed for coaches and double-deckers. Much darker green below cream waistband, light green above. The black outline to the cream bands disappeared from double-deckers about this time, but was still painted on the Lolines delivered in 1958 by East Lancashire.

Yellow lettering resumed.

This reversed livery was only applied to single-deckers in January and February 1954, after which they reverted to the previous style.

March 1958

Silver roof discontinued on double-deckers. (The first Loline was delivered with a silver roof, but this was painted green before entering service.)

c.1965

Single-deck livery changed to the much darker 1954 green above the waistband, while retaining light green below.

June 1967

Single-deck livery reversed to conform with double-deckers. New fleetname style.

January 1972

Alder Valley 'Ribble Red' – a wine-colour livery, with cream reliefs and fleetname in golden yellow.

December 1972

NBC poppy red, with white waistbands. Many Leyland Nationals entered service without these bands, but all received them subsequently.

June 1986

Light green, with dark green skirt panels. Yellow-orange relief at window level of single-deckers and lower window level of double-deckers. On some full-size vehicles, a narrow line of the same colour separated the two shades of green.

Advertisements

A&F, A&D and AV double-deck buses have always carried appropriate-sized advertisements on the front, sides and rear of the upper decks, and on the lower rear panels. Smaller items often appeared at an intermediate height on the rear offside corner panel. Interior advertising was sometimes applied above the side windows.

A&D single-deckers, by contrast, hardly ever carried advertisements, perhaps because of their frequent use on coach and excursion duties. However, in the latter part of 1947 a few buses had orange backgrounds painted on their rear ends to take 'Brobat' cleaning fluid advertisements, and a number of others had a 'British Buses' symbol applied in black and white transfer in 1944 on the bottom back panel. During the 1980s, advertising on the side, rear and front panels of Alder Valley single-deckers has become increasingly common.

Although the 'all-over' advertising bus was not invented until after Alder Valley took over, an early A&D essay on this theme was the appearance of a Dennis Lance carrying Bateman's (Opticians) material in every available conventional advertising space, including the stair risers and seat backs.

From 1973 onwards, two or three buses per year have received overall advertising liveries. Some of these, such as those for the local radio stations, have been perpetuated for a number of years, though others have only lasted for a year or so.

Coaches

Until the 1960s, there were only a few instances of special liveries being used for coaches. At least one of the Gilford coaches purchased for the London service in the summer of 1928 sported a novel cream livery with green relief for its first season, but the majority were dark green, with white above the waist.

A few acquired vehicles in the late '30s had bodywork with a streamline flash, outlined by beading, which A&D painted cream, and one acquired coach, BCG 591, was painted in a cream livery, with green waistband broadening towards the all-green rear panel in January 1939.

Post-war express coaches of the 1948 GAA series had a cream flash, as did their LAA-registered successors in 1953. From November 1948, mudguards of coaches were painted in the same green as the lower body panels. The AEC Reliance express coaches delivered in 1954-5 were all painted in the new livery of dark green below the waistband, which had also appeared, as remarked above, on a small number of earlier coaches repainted early in 1954.

In January 1962, the next batch of coaches, 414-28 DHO, appeared in cream, with shaped light green areas on the front and side panels. (422 DHO had dark green instead, until repainted.) Green upholstery replaced the normal A&D blue-grey pattern. The subsequent 36-foot coaches, 466-80 FCG and FHO 531-5D, were also painted in the same style.

In the spring of 1968, the Duple-bodied long distance coaches, NAA 563-5F, went into service with a broad dark green band half-way up the otherwise cream-painted body. Upholstery was in red patterned moquette, and the fleetnames on the sides were on back-illuminated translucent glass panels. On the next batch, VCG 596-600H, delivered in 1970, the green was confined to the lower third of the sides, with cream the dominant colour.

Alder Valley coaches were initially cream with wine-red reliefs, supplanted in December 1972 by the National Coach all-white livery or the NBC dual-purpose livery of poppy red with white above the waistline. The introduction of Londonlink services coincided with the appearance of the NBC's new coach livery which was basically white, but with extensive areas of the company colour (in AV's case poppy red), interleaved with thinner black stripes. This livery survived privatisation until October 1990, when a change to a predominantly yellow colour, with slanting green striped reliefs, was gradually introduced for the 1991 season.

Paint Shop Practice

In the early 1920s, bodies were separated from their chassis for reconditioning, but this practice later ceased as unnecessary damage was occurring.

Vehicle painting at Aldershot was manned by a staff of experienced men, working in teams of three in the combined paint and body shop, using hand painting rather than spray guns until many years into the Alder Valley era. This permitted bodywork renovation and painting to be carried out simultaneously. The normal turnround time, including varnishing, lettering and application of fleetname transfers and advertisements, was one week, and in the between-wars period, repainting intervals settled down to around 18 months. Coaches were usually touched-up, or even given a new top coat, before the start of the summer season.

The month of painting (e.g. 1045 for October 1945) was shown at the rear of each A&D bus, in very small characters in a nearside corner of one of the panels. It was prefixed by a letter code to show the type of paint employed (P – Parsons 'Parsolac', N – Nobles & Hoare 'Nulux', B – Brolac). Vehicles delivered ready-painted from their bodybuilders either had no date shown, or else were marked, in the late 1940s, with a date prefixed by the appropriate initial (S – Strachan, EL – East Lancashire).

Some 'utility' buses of 1942-5 were delivered from their makers in a grey or brown undercoat. Unlike some other operators, A&D always painted such buses in their own livery before they were put into service, and made other modifications such as the replacement of the builders' rear number 'plates' painted in stencil form on the rear window by proper number plates on the back panels.

Some of the 1988 Leyland Olympians received overall advertisement liveries. This shot of 905, advertising H.A. Fox of Guildford, distributors for Jaguar cars, was posed in the town's Friary bus station. *Alder Valley*

Dennis Ace bus CG 6403 provided the basis for this crane used in the workshops for transporting engines and other heavy components. The chassis was shortened and a steel floor fitted under the gantry when it was converted for its new duties in 1947. It received the service stock number 12, and survived into Alder Valley ownership, a life of over forty years since the chassis was new in 1934. This view was taken in the Top Shop. *G.R. Mills*

All three generations of Dennis Falcons (the 1939, 1949-50 and 1954-56 types) found their way into the A&D service fleet. POR 421, the only one of its batch not sold to the Isle of Man, was totally rebuilt in 1967 as a treecutter, No. 46, and served Alder Valley until 1978. *Alder Valley*

JHO 152, outside the door of the Top Shop, was a Morris van bought for the Publicity Department in 1951. It was fitted with racks to hold timetable boards, and was given the fleet number 24. It carried one of the oval illuminated fleetname boxes dating from the Tilling-Stevens coaches of 1930. *P.J. Holmes*

This AEC Matador breakdown lorry, No. 32, was an ex-Army vehicle bought in 1958. Unlike A&D's other Matador, this one never had a normal registration number. It went on to become Alder Valley's No. 1 (later 1052), and was finally withdrawn around 1980, by which time it was running on trade plates 141AA. *P.D. Moth*

Two of the 1949-50 Dennis Falcons were rebuilt after withdrawal ten years later as service lorries for A&D. This one was No. 34, GOU 862, which had, before its bus body was scrapped, been used for roll-over experiments in the garage yard at Aldershot, where it is shown here in its new incarnation. *P.D. Moth*

One of the 1949 Dennis Lancets was converted in 1961 for further duty as a towing lorry, and numbered 38. It always ran on trade plates 141AA, and never revealed its identity as the former GOU 814. *Author's collection*

Summary of Operators Taken Over by A&DTC

	Operator	Routes taken over and operated	Vehicles and premises acquired
24 July 1912 (backdated to 1 June)	Aldershot & Farnborough Motor Omnibus Co.	Aldershot–Farnborough Aldershot–Farnham Aldershot–Deepcut	4 Milnes-Daimler dd 1 Commer chara.
12 June 1913	London & South Western Railway Co.	Farnham–Haslemere	3 Thornycroft sd
29 October 1913	B. Chandler (Hindhead)	Grayshott–Haslemere	1 Commer sd 1 Dennis chara.
April 1914	Haslemere Motor Co. Ltd.	Wey Hill garage business	
15 December 1914	Guildford & District Motor Services Ltd. (continued separate identity till 29 October 1926)	Already acting as A&D's operating subsidiary	3 Dennis sd (+1 more later)
31 March 1916	M. Larbey (Haslemere)	Haslemere carrier service	1 Dennis van
7 January 1924	W.G. Dowle (Chilgrove)	(Contribution to takeover by Southdown)	–
October 1925	T. Spragg (Progressive Motor Services, Bracknell)	(Contribution to takeover by Thames Valley)	1 Dennis sd (via TV)
16 January 1926	G. Readings (Surrey Hills Motor Services) (Joint purchase with LGOC and East Surrey)	Guildford–Ewhurst–Cranleigh Guildford–Gomshall–Ewhurst	5 Lancia sd Ewhurst garage
February 1926	A.E. Cowley	Aldershot–Ash Vale	–
9 June 1926	A.G. Smith (Blue Omnibus, Knaphill)	Blackdown–Woking	2 Republic sd 1 Overland sd Knaphill Garage
15 December 1926	S. Spooner (St John's)	Woking–Lower Knaphill	–
11 February 1927	Col. Moffatt (Onslow Village)	Onslow Village–Ripley Road	–
19 February 1927	F. Pullen (Purchased from Mr Pullen's widow)	Guildford–Puttenham	–
1 January 1928	D. May (Elstead)	Farnham–Godalming Elstead–Godalming	1 Fiat sd 1 Guy sd 1 Dennis sd
14 January 1928	C. Ross (Maybury)	Woking–Chertsey	1 Republic sd 1 Morris sd
November 1926	H. Tanner (Blackwater)		–
23 January 1928	Farnham Coaches Ltd.	Farnham–London Farnham–Rowledge & Frensham	6 Daimler dd 1 Gilford coach 1 Chevrolet sd 1 Dodge sd
11 February 1928	W. Avann (Tilford)	Farnham–Churt	–
8 October 1928	S. Tanner (Chobham)	Woking–Windlesham Woking–Burrow Hill	3 Dennis sd
25 March 1929	J.F. Hampton (Woking)	Woking–Knaphill	3 Ford sd 1 Caledon chara.
16 March 1929	A. Payne (Ewshot)	Farnham–Ewshot	–
14 January 1931	J.R. Fox & Sons (Woking & District) (Joint purchase with LGOC and East Surrey)	Woking–Knaphill Woking–Camberley	5 Tilling-Stevens sd
7 March 1932	W.R. Perry (Winchester) (Joint purchase with Winchester and District and A.W. Vickers)	Winchester–Alresford	–

22 April 1932	A.G. & H. Lintott (Local Omnibus Service, Petersfield) (Joint purchase with Liss & District)	Petersfield–Longmoor	–
2 June 1934	W. Eggleton & Son Ltd. (Woking) (Joint purchase with LPTB)	Woking–Burrow Hill	1 Dennis sd
1 October 1934	F.W. Kerridge (Royal Blue Buses, Milford)	Godalming–Dunsfold	1 Chevrolet sd
1 October 1934	H. Mansfield (Dunsfold Queen, Dunsfold)	Godalming–Dunsfold	–
27 October 1934	Farnham Blue Coaches Ltd. (Farnham)	Whitehill–Farnham–London	11 Gilford coach 2 Maudslay coach Farnham garage (not used by A&D)
18 May 1936	A.J. Warren (Fleet Coaching Co.)	Aldershot–Fleet–Bramshot Aldershot–Crookham–Fleet–Bramshot Aldershot–Ewshott Camp	10 Guy sd
5 May 1937	G. Weller (Gastonia Motor Services, Cranleigh)	Guildford–Cranleigh	–
12 January 1938	A.T. Locke & Sons (Blue Saloon Bus Service, Guildford) (Joint purchase with LPTB)	Guildford–Stoke–Woking	1 Star sd 1 Dennis sd 1 Dennis coach
8 June 1938	S. Ansell (Direct Bus Service, Lightwater)	Guildford–Bagshot	1 Chevrolet sd 1 Bedford sd 1 Dennis sd 1 Dodge sd
10 May 1939	F.W. Renshaw & L.M. Leam (Grey Bus Service, St John's)	Woking–Fox Corner Woking–Mayford–Fox Corner Woking–Knaphill	1 Dennis sd 3 Bedford sd
10 May 1939	W. Bulman & Son (Hook Heath)	Woking–Hook Heath	–
13 August 1945	P. Crouch & Son Ltd. (Blue Bus, Guildford)	Guildford–Fox Corner Guildford–Wood Street Guildford–Stoke	–
3 May 1948	J.H. Stedman (Progressive, Camelsdale)	Haslemere–Hammervale Haslemere–Kingsley Green	–
27 April 1953	H. Whapshare (Winchester & District) (Purchased from Mr Whapshare's family)	Winchester–Alresford	–
14 September 1953	B. Hammond & Sons (Wonersh)	Guildford–Wonersh	–
16 June 1958	Yellow Bus Services Ltd. (Stoughton)	Guildford–Camberley (in 1954) Guildford–Seale–Farnham Guildford–Compton–Farnham Guildford–Bellfields Guildford–Stoughton Guildford–Rydes Hill	–
16 April 1962	Comfy Coaches Ltd. (Farnham)	Private hire, tours and excursions	Farnham Travel Agency
4 June 1962	Odiham Motor Services Ltd. (Odiham)	Odiham–Greywell–Basingstoke	–

Tickets

In the early years, the A&F and A&D companies employed the almost universal Bell Punch tickets. The principle of this system was that each value of ticket had its own distinctive colour, and when the ticket was issued, it was punched in a space corresponding to the fare stage most recently passed. The small circular patches thus cut out were accumulated in the body of the machine for possible subsequent cross-checking against the number of tickets issued, as indicated by the record of serial numbers entered on the waybill at each fare stage. An inspector discovering passengers with uncollected fares or uncancelled tickets was empowered to give the conductor notice of instant suspension or dismissal, and cases of deliberate fraud, rather than negligence, were often taken as far as prosecution in the courts.

The original 1906 Aldershot–Farnborough service only required 1d, 2d and 3d tickets, and even after a few other services were introduced there was enough space to print all possible journeys: for example, in 1911 the violet 3d tickets had spaces for both 'North Camp to Aldershot Station' and 'Aldershot Station to North Camp'. When services proliferated in the early A&D years, there was only room to print the starting points, and as time went on, the tickets had to grow in length from the common size of 6.1cm. A 1913 2d ticket showed 36 stages and was 8cm long (though not covering the Hindhead area), while a 1915 2d ticket was 12cm long and showed 60 stages. The logical next step with these geographical tickets was to print separate ones for each area: examples are known of Farnham, Frimley, Camberley, Godalming, Haslemere, Liphook and Witley area tickets.

Colours of tickets appear to have changed quite frequently, and complete listing would be beyond the scope of this short account. However, a 1916 waybill showed the following:

1d	salmon	8d	grey
2d	green	9d	buff
3d	cerise	1s 0d	sage green
4d	white	1s 3d	apple green
5d	magenta	1d (soldier)	salmon
6d	blue	2d (soldier)	green
7d	lilac	6d (soldier)	blue

Advertisements were printed on the back of many tickets: all of the earliest known examples were for Farmer's shoes, of Aldershot.

Eventually, the complications of revising tickets to cover places not previously served by the company resulted in a change to numbering of the fare stages on each route, which of course allowed one set of tickets to be used all over the A&D system. The transition is believed to have taken place shortly after the First World War.

Day return tickets were introduced gradually from June 1925 onwards, and three years later their validity was extended to one month. Advertising was placed in the hands of agents: in 1932 Frank Mason & Co paid £6 per million tickets for the privilege of putting their clients' publicity on the backs.

In February 1937, after a trial period, the company

Daimler Y HO 2329, a chassis bought after the war, carries a body which may well have come from one of the 1913 Daimler CC buses. The driver is Fred May, and Conductor Miles is equipped with the tools of his trade – cash bag, bell punch, ticket rack and fare table in his top pocket – although he has not yet been provided with a cap to complete his uniform.

E. Nixon collection

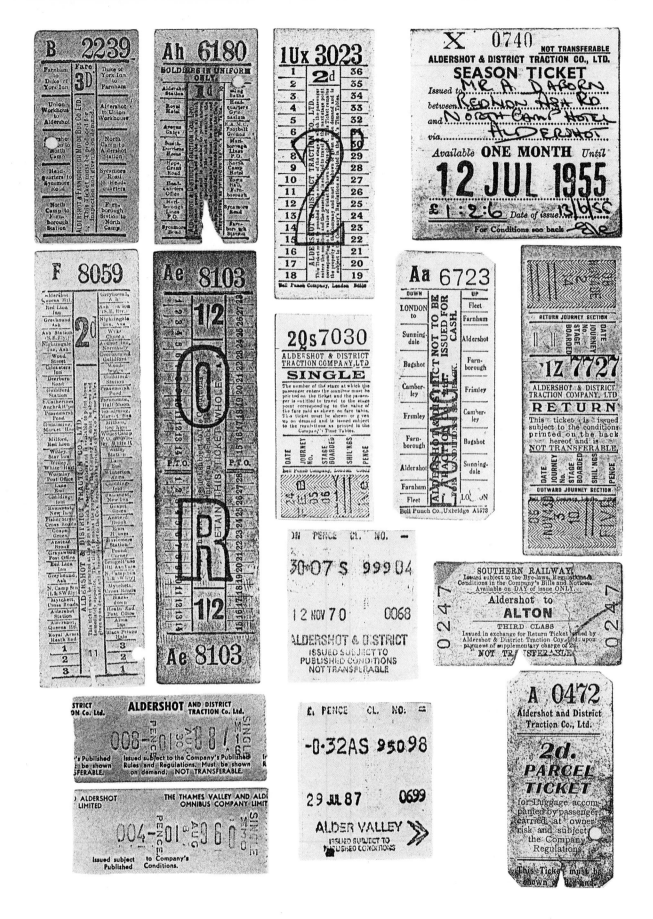

Left to right, top to bottom: Aldershot & Farnborough 3d single, 1911; A&D 1d soldiers, 1912; 2d single, c.1918; monthly season, 1955. 2d geographical single, 1915; ½d return, c.1926; Setright single, 1937; London exchange, 1929; Setright return, 1937. Setright speed, A&D and Alder Valley; Almex, A&D and Alder Valley; Southern Railway exchange, c.1945; 2d parcel ticket.

Three conductresses are posed in 1960 in their smart summer uniform, and are equipped with insert Setright ticket machines. The background is one of the 1957 AEC Reliance buses.

Alder Valley

decided to introduce the Setright system. This involved insertion of the blank end of a single, ½d single or return ticket (respectively white, mauve and yellow) into a slot in a machine, which was set by thumbwheels to the correct fare and fare stage before turning a handle to print the details. Audit was achieved by means of a corresponding print on a paper roll within the machine.

Several drivers and conductors were retrained as Setright mechanics when they were retired as unfit for further duty on the buses.

Although the changeover to the new system was largely completed over the next two years, Bell Punch tickets were retained on some services based on Guildford for many years more, and the last examples (on service 28a, Guildford–Stoughton, interworked with Yellow Buses, which also used Bell Punch) were not phased out until the spring of 1959.

In 1960, when driver-only operation was becoming widespread, the company introduced the faster Setright Speed system, and over the next few years it completely replaced the insert Setright machines. The tickets from the Speed machines were printed on a continuous roll of blanks, pre-printed along the edges with the company's name, and contained within the machine. The Northern area of Alder Valley later took up the same system, but in

1970 A&D had experimented with a small number of Almex machines. In this system, the machine printed all of the information, including the company's name, onto a completely blank square of thin yellow paper. The introduction of decimal currency on 15th February 1971 gave an impetus to the wider adoption of the Almex, but it was not in universal use in the Aldershot division of Alder Valley until some years later. The system continued in use until, in the last quarter of 1988, a complete change was made to an electronically operated machine, the Wayfarer.

Season tickets were introduced by the Aldershot and Farnborough company, and took the form of permits issued from a booklet with counterfoils, the details of name, journey and period of validity being entered by the booking clerk. By the 1930s, A&D season tickets took the form of squares of thick card, with rounded corners. 3-month tickets were pale yellow, and the corresponding 'Junior scholars' term tickets' were similar but salmon in colour, again with the details entered by hand. In the post-war period the cards were smaller, thinner and square-cornered, but it was left to Alder Valley to introduce seasons completed and recorded by computer, and sealed in a plastic cover.

A&D arranged through ticket facilities with two neighbouring operators, Southdown and Hants and Dorset.

No. 300

The Aldershot and Farnborough Motor Omnibus Co., Ltd.

Permit issued to......................

....

...avel between......................

....

...and......................

....

...191......

...191......

No. 300

The Aldershot and Farnborough Motor Omnibus Co., Ltd.

Permit......................

to travel as a passenger by the Company's ordinary service Omnibuses between......................

and......................until......................191...

......................*Secretary.*

Aldershot,......................*191...*

The Company reserve the right to cancel this Permit at any time. It is issued subject to all the Company's regulations and on condition that it be used only by the person in whose favour it is issued. Its use by such person will be taken to be an acceptance of these conditions, and as evidence of an agreement that the Company are not to be held liable for any pecuniary or other responsibility to the holder or his or her representatives for any loss of life, personal injury, or for delay or loss of or damage to property, however caused, whether by gross negligence or otherwise, that may be sustained by such person using this pass.

If this Pass be lost, a Reward of Five Shillings will be given to the finder for its immediate return to the Secretary, and the loser will be charged.

Gale & Polden, Ltd., Printers, Aldershot. 3,405-4.

Towards the end of 1928, the latter provided connections at Winchester, and reciprocal arrangements were made by the two companies to issue tickets between Southampton and Alresford, Alton and Aldershot. Each company designed its own tickets for this purpose. Through single tickets had to be exchanged for a new ticket on the connecting bus. Returns were exchanged for a return on the connecting service, while the passenger retained a portion which was to be exchanged for a single on the second leg of the return journey. Similar arrangements applied with the Southdown company (Aldershot, Bordon, Hindhead or Guildford to Southsea and Guildford to Brighton or Worthing). Corresponding tickets were designed for use with Setright machines when they came into use, though the values were pre-printed. However, in the post-war period, when fares started to rise frequently, it became common for the printed values to be amended by hand until new stocks became available. Eventually, in the late 'sixties, thin paper tickets from a duplicate pad were filled in by hand when passengers were travelling to a Southdown connection, although tickets to Hants and Dorset remained as insert Setrights.

The through ticketing facility necessitated the provision of exchange tickets, which were usually of the Bell Punch type. These, because of the range of values which had to be shown on one ticket, tended to be longer than most other tickets. This was particularly true when provision was made on the same ticket for the names of all of the principal stops on the A&D express services to London, which originally had their own entirely geographical tickets. The passengers on these journeys usually booked in advance, and were issued with written receipts, to be collected en route by a conductor who only travelled on the coach for part of the journey. Early in the Alder Valley period, the pre-booking arrangements ended, and thereafter the driver issued tickets from a normal Almex machine.

Another type of ticket which had to be punched was the emergency ticket, which A&D conductors carried in case of failure of their Setright machines. These were printed in mirror-image pairs, which were folded so that each half was punched in the appropriate place and one half could be retained by the conductor for record purposes.

Yet another area for exchange tickets was to be found in the interavailability of road and rail tickets: here it was usually necessary to pay a surcharge when the original ticket was exchanged. The Farnborough air show brought thousands of rail passengers on special inclusive return fares from Waterloo and other stations. In the A&D period the outward part of the return ticket was exchanged on the connecting bus, but Alder Valley arranged with British Railways for the bus journey to be covered by a separate control ticket, which was issued when the special return rail ticket was purchased. For many years, both were of the standard Edmondson pasteboard type.

A full account of all of the special tickets produced under successive marketing initiatives would justify a booklet of its own. Some of them have been mentioned in the main narrative – Bargain ride (1980), Travelwide (1980), Rovers (1981), Saverstrips (1985), Traveller and Super Traveller (1986) – and in addition there have been the NBC initiatives taken up countrywide during the 'seventies as the Wanderbus and Explorer tickets. Then there were tours and excursions…!

Printed Matter

Timetables

The first A&F services were advertised by handbills, and by the time that A&D was formed in 1912 the tables were combined into a small folding sheet, set out in six pages, with the 'front cover' divided vertically to enable it to be folded again to fit a breast pocket. From August 1913 booklet timetables were published, containing both time and fare tables in full, as well as the company's regulations and details of the goods and parcels services. The format was upright, 16.4 x 9.1cm, and the covers appeared in varying shades of sage green. The printers were W.L. Hunt of Aldershot, who were also the publishers on behalf of the Company.

In 1916 Bradley and Son, of Reading, took over the printing and publishing and the size increased slightly to 16.5 x 10.0cm. After the 1914-18 war, the index was expanded to include a list of particular points of interest for each town and village, as well as golf courses, hospitals, theatres and picture palaces, although these were soon squeezed out by the rapidly expanding tables.

After the introduction of route numbers, a route map once again became a regular feature, and in April 1921, the cover acquired its first illustration, of a Dennis bus of the HO 2460-2 batch. The colour of the cover changed from one issue to the next. This continued until a change of format, printer and arrangement of contents occurred with the issue of November 1923. The new format was of pocket size, 12.3 x 9.8cm, with a cream paper cover, and Wm. May & Co. of Aldershot replaced Bradley & Son as the printers. The cover illustration was now a broadside view of Dennis HO 6222 in the new livery, and the new style fleet name with ornamental loop was henceforth used above the picture. The principal internal change was the omission of full fare tables. Only a single column of fares from the starting point was now included in each timetable, while the route map was redrawn in a diagrammatic form.

By 1929, the numerous service expansions and additions had resulted in quite a thick booklet, arranged in an order of tables determined more by geography and history than by numerical order. The introduction of return fares had resulted in a new section detailing all that were available, and the cover photograph had been changed in June 1928 to show a more modern pneumatic-tyred bus, Dennis E OT 4379. Re-issues had been frequent, since all but the most minor alterations in services had been commemorated thus.

22 January 1930, however, brought a new, slightly larger format (13.7 x 10.9cm) with green paper covers but the same illustration, printed by John Drew & Co. of Aldershot, and instead of being free, sold at a price of one penny. This was the result of a suggestion made at the A.G.M. by an angry shareholder who had received no dividend for two years running! Except where convenience of grouping services partly covering the same route was concerned, the tables were now arranged in numerical order, and complete fare tables were included once again, grouped at the back of the booklet. Issues were increasingly dated for a specific period, rather than 'until further notice', doubtless because of the need to plan in advance for the seasonal coastal services and other changes to accommodate those who used the buses for pleasure outings in the summer season. New cover pictures appeared in October 1930 (Dennis EV OU 4328) and December 1931 (line drawing of Dennis HV OU 7957).

In September 1936, Drew's completely reset the whole timetable in a new style and typeface, with a cream paper cover printed in black with bright green framing round the legend and the illustration, which was now of Dennis Lancet coach CG 6357.

After the emergency issues at the outbreak of war, the same cover was restored, but after stocks of route maps were used up, this feature disappeared until 1948. More significantly, fare tables ceased to be published and were never restored for public sale. In fact the company later went as far as denying the right of passengers to consult the conductor's copy, and introduced a policy that they should pay the fare asked and address any disputes to head office. In June 1948, the pre-war illustration was replaced by one of the new express coach GAA 609, and then in 1951 the first of a series of views of A&D buses in picturesque settings appeared. These were based on original photographs, suitably coloured (and heavily retouched in some cases, even to the extent of changing the bus while retaining the setting, on one issue!). Two issues per year became the regular practice.

The move towards national standardisation of timetable formats reached A&D in May 1965, and the 21.4 x 13.9cm cover now had a coloured photograph of one of the bus stations as its central feature. Inside, a new style of layout was adopted, with 24-hour clock timings used.

Nationalisation brought no change to format or style, though the new fleet name style was used on the March 1968 issue. The January 1969 issue carried a black and white photograph of the five 36ft buses, MOR 558-62F, lined up at Aldershot Bus Station. This continued till the last A&D issue in 1971.

Prices increased, naturally, as the years passed. The first timetables were gratis, with a 1d charge introduced temporarily in 1916-20. 1d became the standard price in 1930, 2d in 1931, 3d in 1946, 4d in 1948, 6d in 1951, 9d in 1961, 1s in 1962 and 2s (10p) in 1970.

Alder Valley continued to issue timetable booklets of the same format during the 1970s, at a price of 10p, though the cover was simplified to show a diagrammatic map of the principal towns served. In 1977, the complete network timetable was replaced by area timetables of similar format, priced at 25p, but with the introduction of the new era of MAP-based services in 1980-81, each service or group of services was covered by a separate folder which could be opened out into a strip for use on timetable display boards. This continued until the formation of Alder Valley South in 1986. From that time onwards, thin booklets, containing the timetables for individual towns or areas, became the normal pattern.

Display Timetables and Notices

Timetables (road sheets) for display at A&D bus stops were of standard layout and typeface. The same type was often used, with suitable headings, for notices on coloured paper announcing alterations and new services. Often the latter had fare tables printed on the back. A small proportion of notices used the type set for use in timetable booklets, though the displayed tables subsequently posted were in the standard typeface.

For a number of years subsequent to the introduction of the A&D fleet name surrounded by oval loop, the headings on notices appeared indiscriminately in that style or in ordinary type with 'The Aldershot and District Traction Company Ltd' spelt out in full, complete with definite article.

As stated above, Alder Valley's display timetables have usually consisted of reprints of pages from timetable booklets, or the folders issued for individual areas. Scheduled coach services and excursion programmes have always been publicised by brochures available from a wide range of booking agents, etc. These advertise details of booking agencies as well as fares.

Route Guides

From the mid-1920s until the Second World War, a booklet was published annually by the New Centurion

Publishing and Publicity Co. of Derby and Cheltenham, entitled 'Omnibus & Express Coach Services by the Aldershot & District Traction Co. Ltd.' This consisted of a brief description of the principal points of interest to be seen along every one of the Company's routes, with a number of illustrations. The need to say something about every service produced two pages of text describing Service 1, Aldershot to Egham, but only two lines on 10a, Farnham to Rowledge – 'A useful short route starting from the Town Hall and running through picturesque scenery'.

In the period 1953-62, similar booklets were produced to publicise the attractions of the routes taken by the Company's coach services to London and the coast, as well as the regular excursions.

Anniversary Commemorations

A pamphlet was produced in 1927 in commemoration of the A&F company's 21st anniversary. This consisted of a number of photographs and a short text outlining the Company's history and extolling its virtues such as the fact that 'In all 21 years there has been only one fatal accident to an actual riding passenger on the Company's vehicles'.

This pamphlet was given to passengers who boarded buses on the anniversary day, and on that day every bus was decorated with a green and white rosette on the radiator.

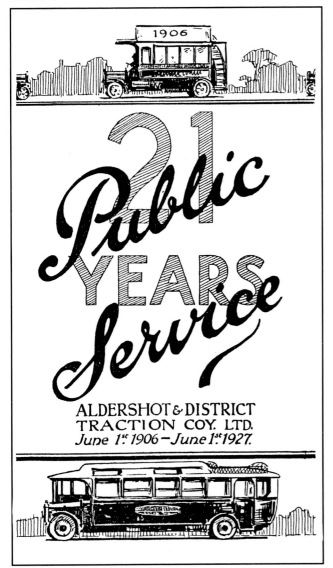

1937 saw the silver jubilee of A&D, and was marked by the issue in September of a booklet giving a short history and a number of photographs, entitled 'Twenty-five Years of Public Service'. The same photographs, with a more extensive text, were used for an Omnibus Society publication by Charles E. Lee, in September 1938, bearing the title 'Aldershot & District Traction Co. Ltd.' price 6d.

In 1951 the 45th anniversary of the formation of the Aldershot & Farnborough Co. occasioned a small leaflet with photographs of 1912 and 1951 double-deckers, and the 47th anniversary in 1953 produced a similar sheet with photographs of a 1919 single-decker and a 1953 coach. However, the golden jubilee of A&D itself was celebrated by a booklet in a glossy coloured cover, with a well-chosen selection of illustrations of buses, garages, steam wagons and personalities, and a text recording a number of historical details. It carried the title 'Fifty Years of Public Service', and was the most comprehensive history published up to that time.

The 80th anniversary, in 1986, was celebrated with self-adhesive stickers attached to letters.

Publicity Material

Illustrated brochures were produced for private hire customers, and regular customers and suppliers of the company received trade calendars. From the beginning of the 'fifties the latter carried coloured illustrations of the type used for timetable covers of the same era, though a greater variety of picturesque scenes was employed.

Alder Valley has produced a variety of calendars over the years, ranging from large single sheets commissioned from artists to the sepia calendar of 1983, featuring photographs of Thames Valley and A&D buses prior to 1930.

Staff Bulletins

In November 1947, the first issue of the A&D Staff Bulletin appeared. Four issues appeared each year, consisting initially of 12 pages, later growing to 20-24. The contents included messages from the management, notices of senior appointments, staff marriages, retirements and obituaries, accounts of social and sporting events, and 'bouquets' – extracts from complimentary letters received from passengers. Photographs were included in the second issue, and in 1955 the front cover started to carry an illustration. For some years the Christmas issue carried a multi-coloured pasted-on 'Christmas card scene' instead of the black and white photographs used for the other issues.

Under the NBC, there were editions of the nationwide 'Bus News' for each of the major companies, with a page or two devoted to the particular company's staff and social matters, with the bulk of the publication being of wider interest.

Belsize AA 5662 lies in a ditch awaiting rescue. The forlorn expression of the conductress tells it all!

Hampshire Museums Service

Accidents

Inevitably, any bus company has its share of accidents, ranging from minor collisions to serious fatal mishaps. Disasters always make good material for journalists.

The earliest major accident to Aldershot & Farnborough's DY35 has been recorded elsewhere in this book, but even that did not involve loss of life or destruction of the vehicle. A minute-book entry records the destruction of all the A&D's accident files for the early years, which means that very little information survives. The first reference to a total loss of a bus comes from a ledger entry at the end of 1916, for insurance compensation for the burning of AA 5647, but the circumstances, and indeed the type of bus, have not been discovered.

On 4 February 1918, another fire occurred, causing injury to several passengers and seriously damaging a bus. This was due to the rather foolhardy action of refilling the petrol tank of the stranded vehicle on the road by the light of an oil lamp! The operation was undertaken in the presence of the Engineer, Mr George Millard: not surprisingly, he left the company's service on the following day.

Accidents due to mechanical failure were quite common in pioneering days. Loss of control was compounded by the limited power of brakes on early buses. In March 1919 a bus with 36 soldiers on board ran away on Portsmouth Hill in Guildford, and overturned in Park Street, causing minor injuries to many of its occupants.

When the garage at Haslemere was extended in 1925 the addition was provided with an entrance high enough to take double-deck vehicles. Very soon after, when Tom Foster and a party of officials were visiting the garage, a double-decker was negligently driven into the older section, with dire results to the top deck. Thereafter it was ordered that the doors should be kept closed, and opened only on request by an arriving or departing driver.

No passenger was killed until September 1926, when a steering defect on an Aldershot to Haslemere bus (Daimler HO 6174) caused loss of control in Tilford Road, Hindhead. It ran up a bank and overturned on its near side, with thirty passengers trapped inside, mostly injured. There was no emergency door, so the only way for Driver Waybourne to get his passengers out was to make use of the roll-top roof, some panels of which could still be opened. Two of the passengers were detained in hospital and one died a few days later.

Another alarming accident took place less than a year later, in August 1927, when Daimler HO 2326 was climbing Fridays Hill, near Fernhurst, and stopped in the process of changing gear but then started to run backwards. On this occasion, however, although the rear of the bus was demolished when it eventually ran off the road, there were no serious injuries. Three weeks afterwards, on 12 September, a new Dennis F coach (OT 4951) broke down at Milford and fitter George Rapley was called out to attend to it after the passengers had been put aboard another bus.

162

A Daimler CD (from the AA5267-9 batch) on the Aldershot–Leatherhead service suffered a serious collision with a car at Westcott on 29 June 1914. The front axle of the bus was forced backwards under the driver's compartment. Note the roof ladder at the front, unique to this small batch of buses.
Author's collection

While he was underneath making adjustments, a back-fire caused petrol which had dripped on the road to catch fire. By the time the driver had dragged him clear, he had been severely burned, and the rear of the bus, the hedge and a telegraph pole had been destroyed. Nevertheless, the high book value of this four-month-old vehicle justified the expense of total rebuilding.

Since that time, a few other buses have been destroyed by fire while on service. These include Tilling-Stevens OU 7945, after an accident on 7 September 1938, and Dennis Lance CCG 321, which succumbed to an electrical fault in 1946. AEC Reliance coach 466 FCG, once proudly exhibited at the Commercial Motor Show but since demoted to stage services, caught fire in Heath End in May 1976 and was totally gutted, and in August of the previous year a two-year-old Bristol RELH coach, No. 68, was burnt out while on a long-distance tour in the Whinlatter Pass, near Keswick, and was subsequently broken up in a nearby scrapyard.

The driving record of the company's staff was virtually unblemished until July 1929, when the newly-recruited driver of a London–Haslemere coach was convicted and fined £10 for being 'drunk in charge'. His driving had been so erratic that some passengers got out at the earliest opportunity. He continued, striking glancing blows to a car at Kensington and a car and a lamp post at Barnes. Several more alarmed passengers asked to be dropped off at Roehampton: one complained to a policeman, who commandeered a passing car and gave chase, eventually stopping the coach at Thames Ditton.

The chances of a head-on collision of two A&D buses might have been regarded as remote, but in January 1931 it happened in dense fog in Farnham on the stretch of private road alongside the railway goods yard. A double-decker to Shortheath and a single-decker from Rowledge were involved, and two people were injured. Another psv collision occurred on 25 May of the same year, when an A&D coach returning from London collided with an empty

On Sunday 12 September 1927, one of the newest coaches, OT 4951, was badly damaged by fire, following a breakdown at Milford. The remains were photographed in the garage afterwards. Despite the extensive damage, the vehicle was rebuilt and returned to service within a few months.
Author's collection

A sad end to a Commercial Motor Show exhibit. Coach 466 FCG is dumped at Aldershot after a fire at the junction of Cranmore Lane and Farnborough Road, Heath End in May 1976. It had by then been demoted to local services. It appears that an unexplained delay in calling the fire brigade turned a minor incident into a total disaster.

N. Hamshere

Thames Valley single decker late at night in Portsmouth Road, Camberley. Both left the road, and the A&D vehicle finished with a broken front axle in a front garden.

The new year started badly in 1932, when Tilling-Stevens OU 7952 had its picture in the 'Evening Standard'. It was severely damaged en route to Bognor, when it met a London-bound coach at Lavant. The A&D driver and four passengers were detained in hospital.

Another January mishap occurred in 1936, on the day of King George V's funeral. A coach taking people to see the procession left the road on the Jolly Farmer Hill, Bagshot, plunged into a deep ditch and overturned. Two passengers received slight injuries.

Shops often suffered damage to their sun blinds from buses on heavily-cambered roads in early years, but on rare occasions they suffered more severely when vehicles left the road. Brown's chemists shop at Windlesham recorded its third such event in February 1947!

During the 'fifties, no fewer than three Dennis Lancets suffered premature withdrawal as a result of damage sustained in head-on collisions. The veteran driver of EOU 440, Mr S.H. Cockerton, was fatally injured in a collision with an army lorry in the spring of 1954. In January 1958, HOU 906 met its fate at Broadbridge Heath, near Horsham and a few weeks later GAA 582 was in violent collision with a road roller at Shalford.

Snow and ice always present a special hazard to bus services, particularly in hilly areas. In 1927, a bus was abandoned near Puttenham Cross Roads for several days when snowdrifts up to 21 feet high were encountered: it received a mention in the BBC news bulletins. Occasionally, overturned double-deckers have had to lie in the snow for days until the weather improved sufficiently for breakdown teams to get to work. Dennis Lance CCG 311 suffered this fate in Alma Lane, Hale in January 1954, and in the early sixties, Lance K4 LOU 56 was extensively damaged when it went into a deep ditch en route for Guildford from Aldershot.

Two conductors died on duty under rather similar circumstances in 1941 and 1950. The first was leaning out of his bus as it entered Godalming Station approach, and was struck by a lamp post, while the second was leaning from the platform of his double-decker changing the near-side indicator blind as it reversed into its bay at Aldershot bus station. He was crushed against the neighbouring bus, and died a few days later.

Another tragedy caused by a reversing vehicle occurred in August 1968 when a garage employee was killed by a bus in Aldershot depot: the serious injury to a conductress in the same month caused considerable anxiety over the adequacy of safety rules for reversing, and new codes of practice were drawn up.

Mishaps with double-deckers under low bridges often achieve notoriety in national newspapers, perhaps because of the element of comedy implied. Aldershot's buses have been remarkable free from such accidents: the only one to be reported in the press was in 1981. A driver making an unauthorised detour in Farnborough, to oblige an elderly passenger, took his vehicle (Bristol VR 930) under a 10ft 9in bridge, with results which merited a photograph in the Daily Telegraph!

Dennis Lance CCG 311 lay for a few days beside Alma Lane, Upper Hale, after the driver lost control on an icy road in January 1954. The photograph was taken by a member of the recovery team. The damage was repaired, and the bus returned to service for another four years.

J.T. King

Lists of Officers

Chairmen of Aldershot & District Traction Co.

1906-1908	J. May
1908-1910	Dr D. Donald
1910-1921	W.E. (later Sir William) Foster
1921-1922	C.S.B. Hilton
1922-1930	L.M. Myers
1930-1931	T. Wolsey
1931-1946	S.E. Garcke
1946-1953	W.T. James
1953-1965	T.R. Williams
1966-1968	F.K. Pointon
1968-1971	D.S. Deacon

Directors

1906-1908	J. May
1906	Capt Batchelor
1906-1907	R.H. Lloyd
1906-1909	R.J. Stirling
1906-1932	T.M. Foster
1906-1910	Dr D. Donald
1907-1912	C.J. Harland
1908-1921	W.E. Foster
1910-1912	J. McLaren
1910-1912	W.J. Stiff
1912-1948	S.E. Garcke
1912-1919 and 1922-1924	W.S. Wreathall
1919-1922	C.S.B. Hilton
1921-1933	L.M. Myers
1922-1952	E.S. Shrapnell-Smith
1925-1928	Lt Col H.E. Howley
1928-1931	T. Wolsey
1930-1946	R.G. Davidson
1930-1937	Lt Col G.S. Szlumper
1933-1942	S. Kennedy
1937-1939 and 1944-1949	J.C. Chambers
1939-1944	C.W.G. Eliff
1942-1946	A.W.A. Chivers
1946-1954	W.T. James
1946-1949	H.A. Short
1946-1965	T.R. Williams
1949-1960	W.H.F. Mepsted
1949-1954	H.E. Osborn
1952-1959	W.P. Allen
1952-1962	Marquess of Linlithgow
1953-1956	A.G. Evershed
1954-1965	A.F.R. Carling
1956-1957	J.W.J. Webb
1957-1964	F.W.B. Burton
1959-1969	Sir Harold Emmerson
1960	S.A. Fitch
1960-1964	P.A. White
1962-1969	Sir Richard Snedden
1964	S.D. Ward
1965-1969	E.S.H. Eales
1965-1968	W.M. Dravers
1965-1968	F.K. Pointon
1968-1970	S.J.B. Skyrme
1968-1971	D.S. Deacon
1970-1976	P. Scully
1970	C.A. Rose
1970-1971	Sir John Gutch
1971-1972	T.G. Pruett
1971	D.W. Glassborow
1971	L.S. Edwards

Chairmen of Thames Valley & Aldershot Omnibus Co.

1972	D.S. Deacon (NBC Regional Chairman)
1972-1977	F.K. Pointon (NBC Regional Director)
1977-1981	I. Dalton (NBC Regional Director)
1981-1983	D.L. Fytche (NBC Regional Director)
1984-1986	J.B. Hargreaves (NBC Regional Chairman)
1987-1988	R. Beattie (Frontsource)
1988-	L. Wright (Q Drive)

Senior Officers

Managing Director	1907-1908	C.J. Harland and T.M. Foster (joint)
	1908-1921	T.M. Foster
Deputy Chairman	1921-1932	T.M. Foster
General Manager	1921-1928	Major H. Darby
	1929-1948	J.B. Parker
	1948-1967	P.N. Gray
	1967-1976	P. Scully
	1976-1980	B. Rootham
	1980-1984	D. Adie
	1984-1988	B. Hirst
	1989-	R. Soper
Traffic Manager (Traffic Superintendent until 1942)	1914-1926	E.G. Hawkins
	1926-1948	P.N. Gray
	1948-1969	A.I. Evans
	1970-1971	D.N. Flower
	1975-1981	T.A. Harrison
	1981-1984	T.C. Archer
	1984-1985	A.J. Braddock
	1986-1988	R. Soper
Chief Engineer	1919	Col Hellawell
	1919-1921	E.A. Eager
	1921-1943	P.L. Rivitt
	1943-1965	N.G. Brookes
	1965-1968	C.E. Clubb
	1969-1978	D.T. Searle
	1978-1980	R.J. Hawkins
	1980-1985	D. Allison
	1985-1988	J. Bryant (Fleet Engineer)
	1988-	D. James
Company Secretary	1906-1908	B.C.K. Snagg
	1908-1916	A.E. Webster
	1916-1925	J. Robart
	1925-1931	G.F.W. George
	1931-1952	P.W. Nancarrow
	1952-1971	S.N. Wilson
	1972-1976	N.A.L. Keeping
	1976-1978	B. Francis
	1978-1985	C. Miller
	1985-1989	J. Winstanley

Mr Wilfred Lunn, Superintendent of Docks and Running Shed at Aldershot for over 30 years, was awarded the British Empire Medal in the New Year Honours in 1954. He had by that time been an employee of the company for nearly 41 years, during which time he had never been absent or late for duty.

Mr A.I. Evans, the retiring Traffic Manager, appeared in the New Year Honours List for 1970 as a Member of the Order of the British Empire; Mr A.A. Brake, the Assistant Secretary, had received the same award in the Birthday Honours of 1957.

Driver Charles Hodson, whose charitable work included fund-raising for buses for the disabled, and advice on their adaptation, was awarded the BEM in the 1982 Birthday Honours.

Aldershot & District Traction Co. Ltd. Statistics

Year to 31 May	Share Capital Issued £	Total Revenue £	Profit Gross £	Profit Net £	Dividend	Cars Owned
1913	9,742	7,083		469	10%	
1914	14,317	17,218		1,677	10%	30
1915	30,000	78,714		12,635	15% + 25% bonus	31
1916	50,000	85,456		5,280	10%	32
1917	50,000	62,903		−9,605	–	37
1918	50,000	81,835		18,230	10%	48
1919	50,000	88,149		4,370	10%	50
1920	60,000	107,944		5,298	10%	53
1921	62,231	111,713		−2,662	–	56
1922	62,231	106,334		10,714	10%	59
1923	62,231	112,023		12,983	10%	73
1924	75,000	133,926		14,368	10%	93
1925	75,000	159,192		13,299	10%	109
1926	100,000	187,131		8,167	10%	136
1927	100,000	217,320		11,762	10%	143
1928	150,000	241,797		12,225	10%	210
1929	200,000	287,219		−2,779	–	234
1930	200,000	328,639		2,156	–	250
1931	200,000	336,760		24,887	7½%	215
1932	200,000	325,206		19,237	7½%	210
1933	200,000	310,947		16,061	7½%	217
1934	200,000	302,626		20,624	7½%	216
1935	200,000	314,907		33,077	8%	239
1936	200,000	330,414		26,341	8%	246
1937	200,000	347,367		28,750	8%	236
1938	200,000	337,897		26,985	8%	227
1939	250,000	345,287		35,780	8% + scrip 1 for 4 bonus	243
1940	250,000	457,527		51,741	10%	248
1941	250,000	556,914		39,345	10%	269
1942	250,000	667,194	281,201	26,668	10%	286
1943	250,000	714,233	313,925	30,008	10%	291
1944	250,000	765,445	329,363	23,277	10%	291
1945	250,000	831,272	323,325	28,985	10%	280
1946	250,000	746,283	183,729	41,515	10% + 5% bonus	254
1947	250,000	787,337	178,870	91,204	15% + 7½% bonus	276
1948	250,000	910,673	220,834	160,898	20% + 7½% bonus	317
1949	250,000	929,149	124,065	102,348	20% + 7½% bonus	333
1950	250,000	917,148	78,623	74,304	20% + 7½% bonus	372
1951	250,000	907,531	40,717	37,808	20%	372
1952	250,000 Stock	1,014,793	57,791	48,649	20%	345
1953	500,000	1,050,575	57,777	25,993	5% Interim on 250,000 7½% Final on 500,000	330
1954	500,000	1,070,660	63,555	52,810	10%	337
1955	625,000	1,108,167	71,292	46,462	8%	325
1956	625,000	1,223,953	109,435	52,656	10%	324
1957	625,000	1,263,310	107,734	72,002	10%	326
1958	625,000	1,186,423	67,551	59,541	10%	340
1959	625,000	1,273,359	128,390	84,914	10%	317
1960	625,000	1,309,438	146,070	81,770	7½% Free of Tax	304

Year to 31 March	Share Capital Issued £	Total Revenue £	Profit		Dividend	Cars Owned
			Gross £	Net £		
1961*	625,000	1,182,755	150,637	77,983	7½% Free of Tax	310
1962	625,000	1,476,128	161,422	120,938	9% Free of Tax	304
1963	625,000	1,527,693	144,237	124,213	9% Free of Tax	309
1964	1,250,000	1,556,449	135,105	93,665	2½% Free of Tax on £625,000 3¾% Free of Tax on £1,250,000	304
1965	1,250,000	1,551,222	111,597	109,997	5¼% Free of Tax	305
1966	1,250,000	1,627,401	150,277	88,577	5¼% Free of Tax	298
1967	1,250,000	1,794,458	150,697	108,997	5¼% Free of Tax	285
1968x	1,250,000	1,769,954	194,110	99,695	1½% Interim Free of Tax	285

* 10 months only
x 11 months to 29th February 1968 (the end of BET ownership)

The Head Office block, built in 1924, is shown decorated for the Coronation in 1953. The curtained windows above the door belonged to the Board Room, while on the right the forthcoming excursions are advertised by boards inserted into a display panel. *Alder Valley*

Bibliography

Books

C.E. Lee, *Aldershot & District Traction Co. Ltd.*, The Omnibus Society, 1938.

A.A. Townsin, *75 Years of Aldershot & District*, Transport Publishing Co., 1981.

Fifty Years of Public Service, 1912-62, Aldershot & District Traction Co., 1962.

J.A. Birks, *National Bus Company, 1968-1989*, Transport Publishing Co., 1990.

Fleet Lists

Fleet History of the Aldershot & District Traction Co. Ltd., PSV Circle publication PK3, 1959. New edition to be published in 1993.

Fleet History of Alder Valley, PSV Circle publication PK12, 1977. With supplement issued in 1986.

Alder Valley Fleet List, Aldershot and Guildford Group of the Omnibus Society. Editions produced in 1974 and 1975.

Alder Valley Fleet List. Alder Valley South Ltd., 1987. Compiled by P. Gascoine.

Collections of Photographs

Pictures from the Past (c.1975). *In the Fifties* (c.1978). Aldershot and Guildford Group of the Omnibus Society.

M. John. *Aldershot & District Traction Co. Ltd. Anniversary Souvenir Book, 1906-1981*. John Hallewell Publications, 1981.

Publications on companies absorbed by, or interfacing with, A&D and Alder Valley

N. Hamshere and J. Sutton, *Happy Family (the story of Yellow Bus Services)*, 1978.

B. King, *Tillingbourne 1924-1974*, 1974.

G. Burnett and L. James, *Tillingbourne (The Tillingbourne Bus Story)*, Middleton Press, 1990.

N. Hamshere and J. Sutton, *Safeguard of Guildford, 1924-1984 Diamond Jubilee*, 1984.

P.J. Holmes, *Thames Valley*, Transport Publishing Co., 1984.

A.A. McCall, *Green Line*, New Cavendish Books, 1980.

"Bell Street" (R.J. Durrant, J.T. King and G.J. Robbins), *East Surrey*, H.J. Publications, 1974.

P.J. Holmes, *Odiham Motor Services – The Nancy Bus*, 1990.

J. Cummings, *Railway Motor Buses and Bus Services in the British Isles, 1902-1933, Vol. 2*, Oxford Publishing Co., 1980.

Acknowledgements

Material for this book has been accumulated over a period of fifty years, so where does one begin? My earliest attempts to compile an Aldershot & District fleet list were pooled with those of my schoolmate, Jeffrey Bunting, so that by the end of World War II, the current scene of 'The Tracco' was well documented. Our 'mole' within the company was Irene Longbottom, who ran the enquiry office at Farnham, and whose husband George passed on news from the workshops at Aldershot. She arranged one evening for A&D's Farnham area regulator, Harry Hunt, to spend some time telling us of earlier years, and from that day, the 'numbers game' matured into historical research.

The idea of a book about A&D was initiated in the mid-seventies by Eric Nixon's newspaper appeal for photographs. His collection now covers virtually every vehicle type in the company's history, and provided most of the material for the book published by the Transport Publishing Company in 1981. We have made a conscious effort to ensure that as far as possible, the pictures in the present book avoid duplication with those previously used.

Past and present staff of the company have been generous with their help: successive occupants of the General Manager's office – Douglas Adie, Brian Hirst and Richard Soper – have kindly allowed me to have access to the official archives. (These have subsequently, in November 1990, been removed to the safe keeping of the Kithead Trust). Assistance with locating material and information has been given by John Bryant, Ian Hewitt, Michael Lustig, Jim Peet, Brian Randall and Prim Vickery, and other useful discussions have been held with Percy Morgan, Phil Perkins and Jim Stenner.

A special category of acknowledgement must be the bus people who are also enthusiasts – Peter Trevaskis, photographer, owner of two preserved A&D buses and rescuer of irreplaceable timetable paperwork; Malcolm Chase, ticket expert and observer of commercial developments; Les Smith, photographer of virtually every vehicle which has passed through the Halimote Road premises over the past 25 years, as well as a keen collector of tickets, and Bill Tutty, expert on the Guildford area.

Many other enthusiasts have given valuable assistance. The PSV Circle's fleet histories of Aldershot & District, published in 1959, and of Alder Valley, have been the basis of much vehicle information, and I have corresponded with the PSVC's President, Peter Jaques, and its Editor, David Gray, over several years, sorting out numerous matters of vehicle history, especially for the ill-documented early period of A&D. My thanks are due to the PSVC Editors for allowing me to use both published and unpublished material. The Omnibus Society's timetable library has been consulted, and Mike Stephens, the OS Route Recorder for the area, has been an invaluable source of details of route changes and dates, while Reg Durrant has provided excerpts from the OS ticket collection.

Other helpful individuals have included Lady Foster and her family, who provided information on the company's founders; Roger Atkinson of the Transport Ticket Society; Tim Childerhouse and Peter Smith of the Aldershot Historical and Archaeological Society; Patrick Foulds of the Aldershot Society; John Cummings, expert on railway bus services; Tony Holt, Paul Lacey, Alan Lambert, Richard Peskett and David Sharwood. The original A&D manuscript was vetted by Jack Parker, son of the former General Manager, and by Doug Jack.

Thanks are due to the library staffs who have enabled me to study files of local newspapers and local history collections. Aldershot, Alton, Basingstoke, Farnham, Fleet, Guildford, Winchester and Woking public libraries have all been used, as well as the Hampshire Record Office at Winchester, the National Motor Museum at Beaulieu, the Newspaper Library at Colindale, the Guildford Muniments Room and Farnham Museum.

Photographs are credited wherever possible, though we must ask forgiveness of those photographers whose pictures have reached us without any indication of their true origins. (Where photographs are known to have been copied from originals in the once-extensive A&D archive, they are credited to Alder Valley.) Not least among providers of photographs are my helpful local dealers in old postcards – Graham Barson, David Brown and Tim and Jackie Winter – who have kept a lookout for any scenes and ephemera relating to buses in the area. I know of well over 100 postcards which include an A&D bus!

After all that, I am left wondering why mine is the only name on the cover!